AF574967

The IMPRINT *of* PLACE

MAINE PRINTMAKING
1800-2005

Design by Jean Wilcox, Wilcox Design

Published by the Center for Maine Contemporary Art
with Down East Books

Printed in China

Library of Congress Cataloging-in-Publication Data

Becker, David P.
The imprint of place : Maine printmaking 1800-2005 / by David P. Becker.
p. cm.
Includes bibliographical references.
ISBN-13: 978-0-89272-718-6 (trade hardcover : alk. paper)
ISBN-10: 0-89272-718-7
1. Prints, American--Maine. I. Title.
NE535.M27B43 2006
769.9741--dc22
2006010467

Distributed to the trade by National Book Network, Inc.
Book Orders: 800-685-7962
www.downeastbooks.com

Center for Maine Contemporary Art
Rockport ME 04856
www.artsmaine.org

Major funding for *The Maine Print Project: Celebrating 200 Years of Printmaking in Maine* and for *The Imprint of Place: Maine Printmaking 1800-2005* is provided by the Maine Arts Commission, an independent state agency, in partnership with the National Endowment for the Arts American Masterpieces Program; and by a major grant from the Maine Community Foundation. Generous funding is also provided by the Davis Family Foundation, with additional support from June Fitzpatrick Gallery.

Cover: Will Barnet, *Dawn* (detail), 1975, Plate 49
Title page: Stevan Dohanos, *West Quoddy Lighthouse* (detail), ca. 1930, Plate 28

Note about illustrations: Measurements are height before width. Unless otherwise specified, measures for etchings and woodcuts refer to the plate or block area, for lithographs, the image area. If no publisher or printer is indicated, it is assumed to be the artist, or the information is unknown.

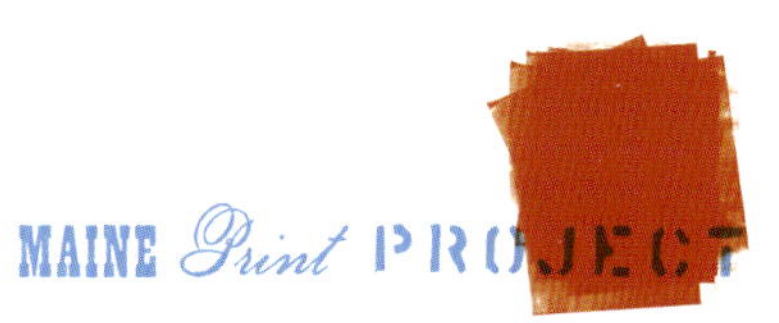

The Maine Print Project: Celebrating 200 Years of Printmaking in Maine
A statewide collaboration in 2006 of exhibitions, educational programs, and this publication, devoted to the 200-year history and variety of printmaking in Maine.
For further information, see *www.maineprintproject.org*

Participating Institutions
Bates College Museum of Art, Lewiston
Bowdoin College Museum of Art, Brunswick
Center for Maine Contemporary Art, Rockport
Chocolate Church Arts Center, Bath
Colby College Museum of Art, Waterville
College of the Atlantic, Blum Gallery, Bar Harbor
Farnsworth Art Museum, Rockland
Institute of Contemporary Art at Maine College of Art, Portland
L.C. Bates Museum, Hinckley
Maine Art Gallery, Wiscasset
Maine Historical Society, Portland
Ogunquit Museum of American Art, Ogunquit
Old York Historical Society, George Marshall Store Gallery, York
Portland Museum of Art, Portland
River Tree Center for the Arts, Kennebunk
Round Top Center for the Arts, Damariscotta
SPACE Gallery, Portland
The Tides Institute & Museum of Art, Eastport
University of Maine, Augusta—Art Gallery
University of Maine, Machias—Art Gallery
University of Maine Museum of Art, Bangor
University of Maine, Orono, Department of Art
University of Maine, Presque Isle
University of New England—Art Gallery, Portland
University of Southern Maine, Gorham

The IMPRINT *of* PLACE

MAINE PRINTMAKING
1800-2005

DAVID P. BECKER

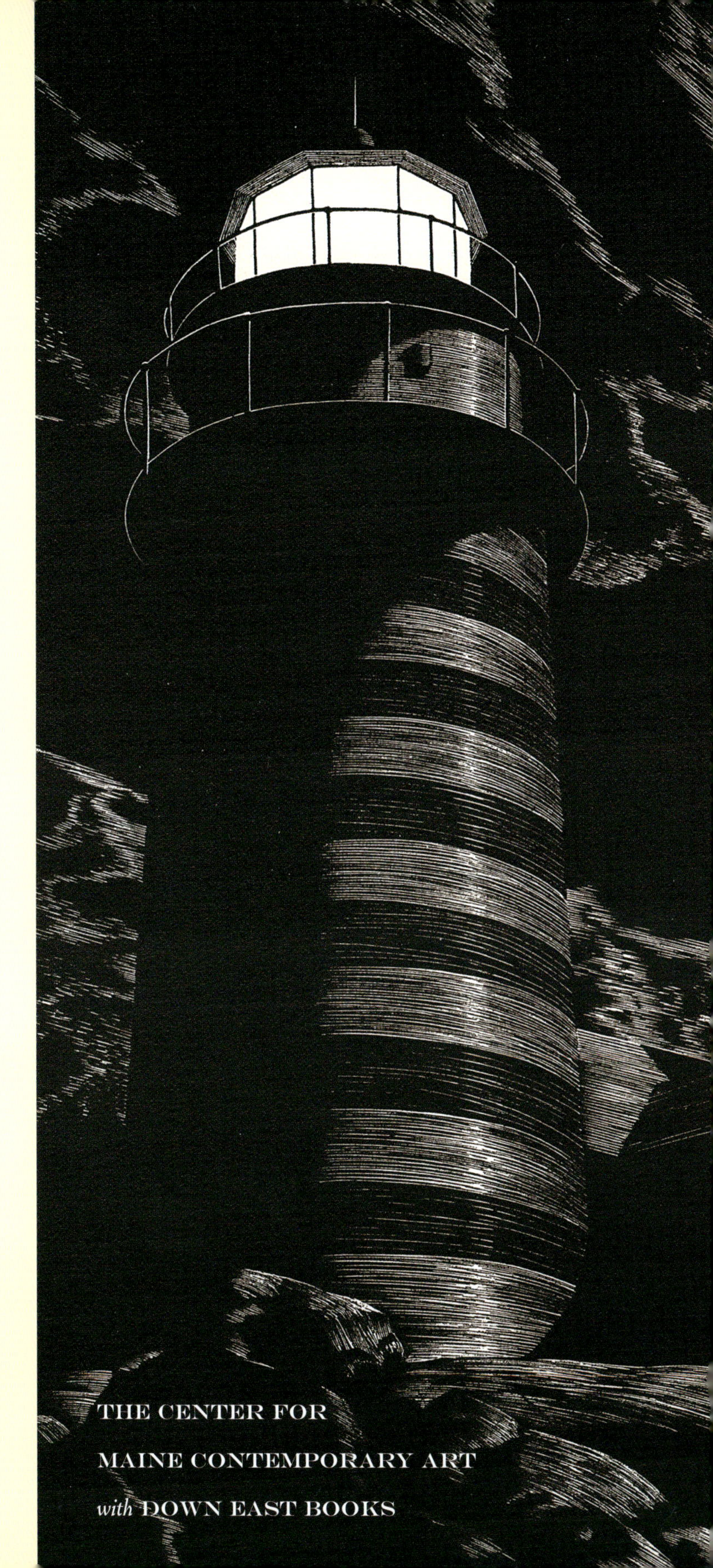

THE CENTER FOR
MAINE CONTEMPORARY ART
with DOWN EAST BOOKS

FOREWORD

The Genesis of "The Maine Print Project: Celebrating 200 Years of Printmaking in Maine"

BRUCE BROWN

"The Maine Print Project: Celebrating 200 Years of Printmaking in Maine" sprang to life at a spirited gathering of nine Maine curators held at the Center for Maine Contemporary Art on September 23, 2003. The curators chose to gather, in part, to discuss how Maine museums and nonprofit galleries might share exhibitions that otherwise might not be economically feasible.

The group's response to the notion of offering several concurrent exhibitions devoted to Maine printmaking — an art form seldom highlighted by galleries and museums through the years — was both surprisingly positive and immediate. Tabling the idea for a future meeting was not considered. Instead, we embraced the project on faith, and turned to our calendars to determine when possibly ten or even a dozen Maine print exhibitions might be presented more or less concurrently. Early fall 2006 to March 2007 fit the bill. We all agreed that each institution would determine the focus of its own print exhibition.

The enthusiasm that electrified that fall meeting has never flagged. Indeed, "The Maine Print Project: Celebrating 200 Years of Printmaking in Maine" now includes 25 museums and nonprofit institutions, and the project now stands as the largest collaboration among art institutions in Maine history. Moreover, the collaboration, extending from Ogunquit and York in Southern Maine to Presque Isle, Machias, and Eastport in the North and East, has been complemented further and made richer by additional concurrent exhibitions of Maine printmakers organized by commercial galleries and other nonprofit institutions.

Why such a sudden interest in exhibiting Maine prints? My best hunch is that it stems from a need: A need to discover the story, both historical and contemporary, of printmaking by Maine artists who live and work here either year round or seasonally. A need to open the files of museum collections to see what's there. A need for current printmakers, several of whom quietly pull prints on small presses at home, often with little thought of sharing their efforts with the public, to identify themselves and meet colleagues who share their passionate interests.

ACKNOWLEDGMENTS

As chair of the Maine Print Project, I profoundly appreciate the extraordinary talents of so many remarkable people who define the Maine visual arts community. Each person's contribution, willingly given, has made my position as chair a joy. First and foremost, I applaud all the printmakers whose works grace our respective walls throughout Maine from late August 2006 through mid-March 2007. Their accomplishments are the foundation upon which the rest of us enthusiastically offered our support.

David Becker deserves highest accolades for *The Imprint of Place: Maine Printmaking, 1800–2005*. Well known for his passion for prints, awakened during his undergraduate days at Bowdoin College, David has devoted his professional life to studying, collecting, curating, and writing about the history of the graphic arts. His willingness to research and to write the first illustrated historical overview of Maine printmaking within the impossibly short period of nine months is astonishing. David traveled the length and breadth of the state examining Maine prints in museum and private collections and interviewed artists, curators, and historians to prepare himself for the task at hand. His book is a gift to all who care about the cultural life of Maine.

David Becker's efforts might have come to little had it not been for Alison Ferris, curator at the Bowdoin College Museum of Art, who saw to it that a book would be published as a permanent record to complement the Maine Print Project. She found an ideal publisher in Michael Steere at Down East Books and an exceptional book designer in Jean Wilcox. Alison Ferris along with Kate Westley worked diligently to obtain images and their copyrights for the book illustrations, and to coordinate the book's preparation. Her work was supported by a Book Committee: David Becker, Sharon Corwin, Bill Low, and Oliver Wilder.

Warmest appreciation to Sarah Gallagher, who early on gave us the confidence we needed to design an efficient and successful fundraising strategy. Her enthusiastic commitment to the project, and her extensive knowledge of both the arts community and potential funding partners, enabled us to secure the financial support we needed for the project to grow and flourish.

Anne Zill chaired the Publicity Committee, whose members included Jeannie Fine, Kristen Levesque, Liz K. Sheehan, David Stucky, and Oliver Wilder. Special thanks to Kristen Levesque, the director of marketing and public relations at the Portland Museum of Art, a seasoned arts professional, who applied her acumen to maximize public awareness of the Maine Print Project and to see that the programs and exhibitions received the local, regional, and national visibility they deserved. Invaluable, too, were the efforts of Liz K. Sheehan, assistant curator at the Bates College Museum of Art, who designed and maintained the project Web site, www.maineprintproject.org, and worked with Maine College of Art faculty advisor Miek Bertus and students Jon Doyle and Jessica Huddy, designers of the project's logo.

Susan Danly ably chaired the Education Committee, whose membership included Todd Bernard, Cathy Melio, Pat Nick, and Vanessa Nesvig. The Committee determined that four diverse seminars touching upon issues both historical and contemporary would be held at Bowdoin College in Brunswick, the Center for Maine Contemporary Art in Rockport, the Portland Museum of Art, and the SPACE Gallery in Portland.

A very capable Project Team provided the essential link between the original curators' group and each participating venue. Their ongoing efforts were invaluable in maintaining lines of communication among us for three years. My heartiest thanks are extended to Claire Adams, Karen Adrienne, Nancy Ault, Todd Bernard, Beverly Broyles, Sharon Corwin, Michael Culver, Susan Danly, Carolyn Eyler, Alison Ferris, Jeannie Fine, Helen Fisher, Cindy Foley, Hugh French, Mary Harding, Sukey Heard, Sandra Huck, Philip Heckscher, Toby Kamps, Robert Katz, Susan Lerner, James Linehan, William Low, Wally Mason, Jon Mayer, Suzette McAvoy, Genetta McLean, Kristin McKinlay, Donna McNeil, Cathy Melio, Vanessa Nesvig, Jessica Routhier, Gail Scott, Liz Sheehan, Owen Smith, David Staber, Deborah Staber, David Stucky, Jean T. Sylvia, Bernard Vinzani, Candace Vlcek, Oliver Wilder, Greg Williams, and Anne Zill.

I offer warmest thanks to my colleagues at CMCA, who, by dint of their professional association with me, devotedly carried out all manner of projects, both large and small, in conjunction with this initiative. Thank you Michelle Davis, Lori Dierckes, Kelly Jackson, Cathy Melio, and Oliver Wilder, who offered wise counsel in countless public and private meetings and oversaw project finances.

The Maine Print Project was as readily and enthusiastically supported by our funding partners as it has been by all of us. We are deeply grateful for the generous support provided by the Maine Community Foundation, and convey our appreciation to its Board of Directors for their interest in funding David Becker's excellent work; to the Maine Arts Commission and to the National Endowment for the Arts, who supported the project as part of their American Masterpieces Program; to the Davis Family Foundation, a longtime benefactor of Maine arts institutions and imaginative arts programs; and to June Fitzpatrick, a much-loved presence in the Maine art world, who provided support and arranged a book signing to herald the arrival of *The Imprint of Place: Maine Printmaking, 1800–2005*. On behalf of all the participating institutions, I extend our warmest appreciation to all our generous funders who helped us bring to fruition our vision set forth in September 2003.

BRUCE BROWN
Project Chair and Curator, Center for Maine Contemporary Art
Rockport, Maine
February 22, 2006

The invitation to undertake this project came from Bruce Brown, print fan and organizer extraordinaire, and I owe him a great debt of gratitude indeed. His enthusiasm and constant support throughout have been inspirational. The support of the Maine Print Project's Book Committee has been equally crucial and appreciated. A huge thank-you to Alison Ferris, chair, and members Sharon Corwin, Bill Low, and Oliver Wilder; they have been an enormous support to me.

Several individuals helped guide my general approach and supplied many avenues of fruitful research. Chief among these is Earle G. Shettleworth, Jr. The first chapter on the nineteenth century would have been far, far thinner without Earle's almost daily photocopies and e-mails. I am a very grateful recipient of his legendary generosity to researchers of Maine history. William D. Barry was very helpful, especially for printmakers in Portland. I also benefited greatly from conversations with Donna Cassidy, Carl Little, and Donna McNeil. Andrew Stevens, author of Wisconsin's printmaking history, shared early encouragement and helpful hints for undertaking such a project.

One of the most rewarding aspects of this project was traveling through the state, surveying print collections and meeting curators, private collectors, artists, and printers—all of whom were unfailingly generous and enthusiastic. Thank you all:

William Low (Bates College Museum of Art); Deborah Staber (L. C. Bates Museum); Richard Lindemann (George J. Mitchell Department of Special Collections & Archives, Bowdoin College Library); Katy Kline, Suzanne Bergeron, José Ribas, and Laura Latman (Bowdoin College Museum of Art); George and Dadée Burk; Sharon Corwin, Patricia King (Colby College Museum of Art); John Day; Helen Fisher, Angela Waldron, Betsey Jewell (Farnsworth Art Museum); Lauren Fensterstock; Susan Groce;

Philip Heckscher; Adriane Herman; Frances Hodsdon; Neil Jensen; Robert and Jackie Laskoff; Christopher Livesay; John Mayer (Maine Historical Society); Deanna Bonner-Ganter (Maine State Museum); Julie L. McGee; the Muench family; Michael Culver (Ogunquit Museum of American Art); Susan Danly (Portland Museum of Art); Hugh French and Kristin McKinlay (Tides Institute & Museum of Art); Wally Mason, Steven Ringle (University of Maine Museum of Art); Anne Zill (Art Gallery at the University of New England); Carolyn Eyler (University of Southern Maine Art Gallery); Susie Bock (Special Collections, University of Southern Maine Libraries); Andres Verzosa; Patricia Nick (Vinalhaven Press); Richard Wilson; Peggy Zorach—and many other individual artists who shared information about technique and imagery with me.

In addition, many colleagues "from away" were equally supportive and helpful, including Phil Alexandre (Alexandre Gallery); Georgia B. Barnhill (American Antiquarian Society); Karen Shafts (Boston Public Library); Roger Howlett (Childs Gallery); Susan Dackerman (Harvard University Art Museums); Eric Gleason (Marlborough Galleries); Clifford S. Ackley, Sue W. Reed (Museum of Fine Arts, Boston); Ruth Fine (National Gallery of Art); Helena Wright (National Museum of American History, Smithsonian Institution); Shelley Langdale (Philadelphia Museum of Art); Susan Hover Oehme (Riverhouse Editions); Robert Volz (Chapin Library, Williams College); Peter Pettengill (Wingate Studio); David G. Wright.

A number of people have worked on the actual production of this book and made the process a pleasure for me. It is always terrific to work with Lucie Teegarden, my editor, on any project, and her sharp eye and great judgment have been invaluable as I have tried to make my text as sensible as possible. I owe a great debt of gratitude to the artists, museums, and collectors who granted permission to reproduce their prints here. The fearsome task of securing those images and permissions was accomplished by Alison Ferris and Kate Westley of the Bowdoin College Museum of Art with care and good spirit; I am very grateful for their efforts. Michael Steere of Down East Books has been very supportive of this book from the start, and I am especially grateful for the truly handsome design by Jean Wilcox.

I have felt of Maine as home ever since arriving as a first-year college student forty years ago, and I offer this book in at least partial gratitude for the welcome the state has given me.

DAVID BECKER

INTRODUCTION

The **IMPRINT** *of* **PLACE**

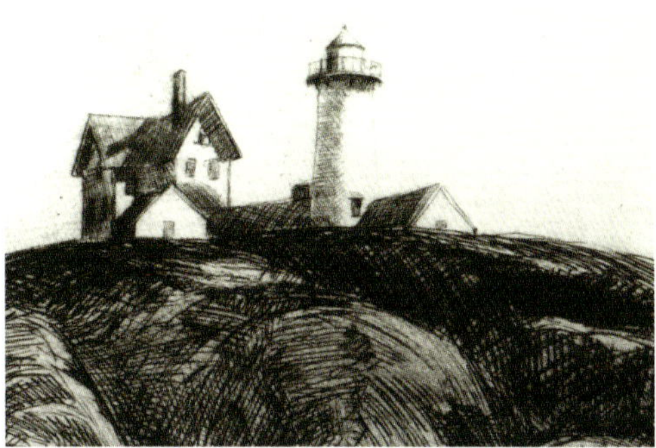

Writing in the landmark catalogue of the 1963 Colby College Museum of Art exhibition, *Maine and Its Role in American Art*, art historian James Carpenter wrote that "artists who have worked in Maine have felt the impress of a place." It is in homage to this sentiment that the title of this survey was chosen, changing a word to render it more appropriate to printmaking. Any survey of the art from a single region is an exploration and test of that thesis, and Maine has been one of the most explored and tested areas in the country, if only based on the sheer number of artists who have worked here. To be sure, its dramatic and spare landscapes have been a predominant component of Maine's "imprint." The artist and teacher John Muench once memorably stated that the "Maine landscape is impossible to ignore."[1] Other elements often cited when reflecting on the Maine influence are its rough climate, rural character, and individuality, to name only a few. Yet these characterizations may also be seen as presenting a classic "image" of Maine preserved in amber without acknowledging the variety of experiences—and artists—to be found here throughout its history. Its art encompasses not only the expected lighthouses and lobster pots (which will be found in this survey), but also many frontiers of experimentation.

Edward Hopper, *The Lighthouse, Maine Coast* (detail), 1923, Plate 19

A history of printmaking in Maine has never been written, and the medium has never been featured in previous surveys of the arts in the state. *Maine and Its Role in American Art* gives brief mentions to only three printmakers: Stow Wengenroth, Karl Schrag, and John Muench. However, the wealth of printmaking's history within the arts is no surprise to people familiar with its ubiquitous role within any culture. The task of gathering the prints themselves and records of their makers is, therefore, daunting, to say the least. The present survey is just that, a preliminary overview of the presence of prints and printmakers in Maine, from the end of the eighteenth century to the beginning of the twenty-first.

It is hoped that the richness of the tradition of printmaking in the state will be readily apparent in the selection illustrated in this book—a hint of the infinite variety of styles, subject matter, and technical approaches that may provoke viewers to look further for themselves. The extraordinary wealth of print collections in Maine may be gleaned from the wide range of repositories from which the illustrations have been gathered, and they are supplemented by several outside the state.

Prints are in many ways the most democratic visual medium—at least before television and computers—and they are found not only in museums, but also within historical societies, libraries, corporate archives, antique shops, bookstores, and of course private homes—not to forget newspapers, magazines, compact disc covers, and street posters. The classic definition of a print, by the influential print curator William Ivins, as an "exactly repeatable pictorial statement" continues to be stretched all the time, both by technology and by the restlessness of artists' materials and imaginations. These explorations happily ignore any categories imposed by a curator.

This survey will ideally provide an impetus for further research, and it may not be inappropriate to suggest further areas that the author did not have the time or resources to pursue. The nineteenth century is a huge landscape of emerging print culture in both the commercial and domestic spheres. Much remains to be discovered of individual printmakers, printers, and publishing houses. The extent of printmaking by artists who came to Maine's summer art colonies in the late nineteenth and early twentieth centuries remains to be accurately examined. The decade of the 1930s is a potentially lively field of study, and comparatively little is known of printmakers working outside of Portland. The growth of interest in the teaching of printmaking in the 1960s and 1970s could be better understood, as could the ensuing "renaissance" of appreciation in the following decades. Finally, as will be clear, the last twenty-five years of printmaking in the state deserve a far fuller picture than has been "imprinted" here.

With the historically strong influence of artists in the state who do not live here year-round, the question of what constitutes "Maine" printmaking inevitably arises—as it does in all discussions, exhibitions, and publications about "Maine" art. Understanding the fact that each printmaker at some point spent some time in the state, the bottom line for this survey was that no print would be included that was executed before the artist had first arrived here. Otherwise, the definition of a "Maine artist" was relatively flexible, and the compiler strove to achieve a strong variety of experience, technique, and subject matter. Because of various factors, including the lack of printing facilities in the state or an artist developing an image later from sketches done earlier, a number of prints in this survey were not actually "produced" in the state. Not every image reproduced in this survey depicts a Maine scene or motif, though many do. Reflecting both the geography and history of the state and its artistic history, there is a strong sense of landscape here, and much of that reflects the coast.

"Maine printmaking" does not exist in a vacuum or isolated retreat. While of course exhibiting its own character, printmaking in Maine also strongly reflects national trends, not only because a historically significant number of "movers and shakers" in American art have chosen to work in Maine at various times, but also because "instate" Maine artists have studied or experienced the world outside the state—and some have had considerable influence outside its boundaries. Intriguingly, the critic Edgar Allen Beem, writing in 1989, ventured that by participating in "the national and international art dialogue, [artists] may be losing their regional identity," arguing that this is not necessarily a bad thing.[2] Whatever the finer points of influence and imprint, it is hoped that this survey may provide a testimony to the richness and vitality of printed art that has recorded the life and landscape of the state, reflecting the experience of the artists themselves.

NOTES

1. Judith Sobol and Martin Dibner, *John Muench—Paintings and Prints 1950-1990* (Freeport, Me.: Maquoit Press, 1991), p. 3.
2. Beem, Edgar Allen, *Maine Art Now* (Gardiner: Dog Ear Press, 1990), p. xviii.

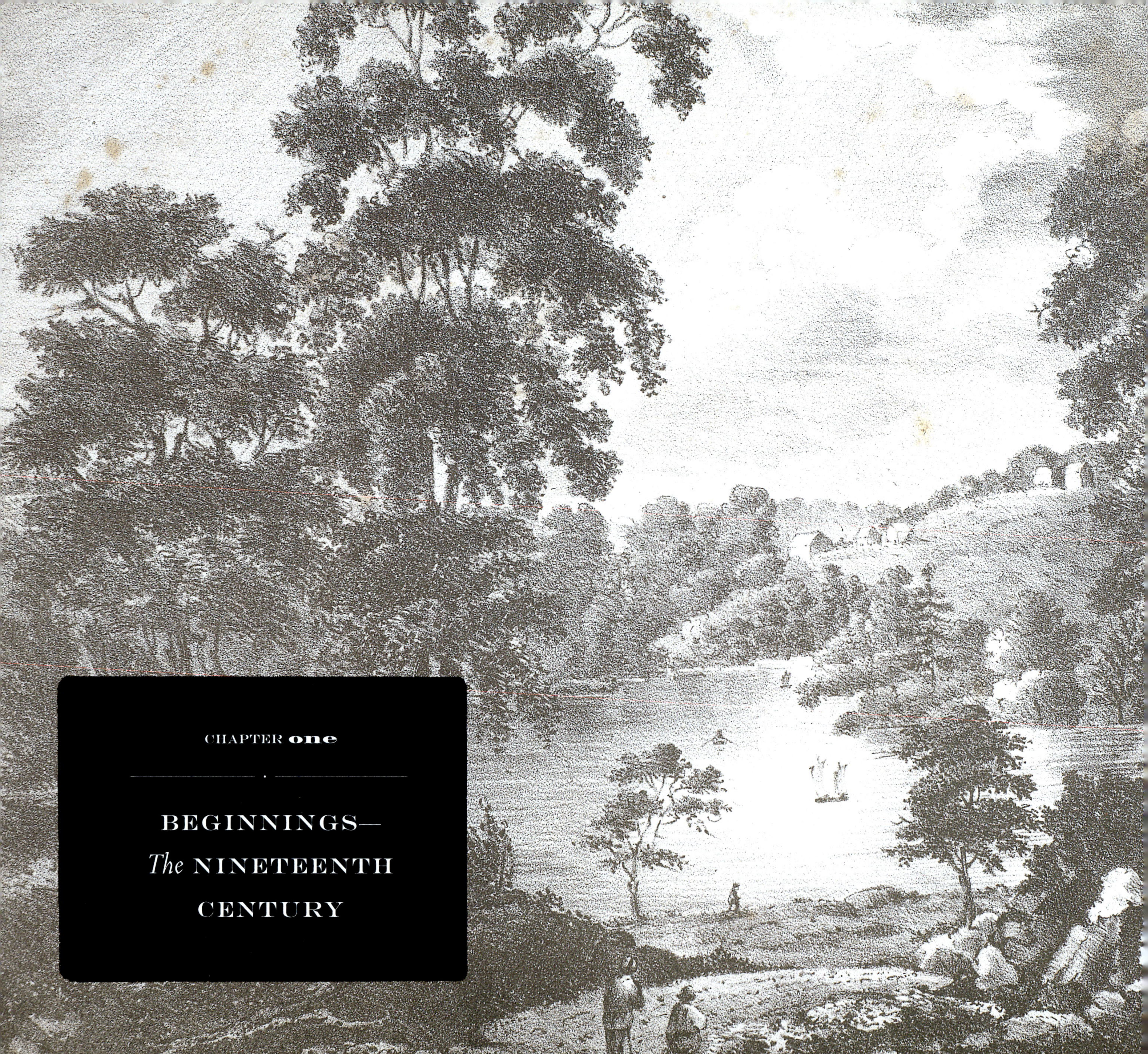

CHAPTER **one**

BEGINNINGS— *The* NINETEENTH CENTURY

The history of printmaking during the nineteenth century primarily concerns the establishment of commercial and advertising viability for the medium. Even the production of decorative and inspirational prints for domestic interiors and the illustration of books and newspapers were largely commercial enterprises. In this model, there was traditionally a separation between the actual engraver or lithographer who produced the print and the artist who had originally drawn or painted the image. So-called "original" printmaking by individual artists from their own designs developed slowly, at first through isolated amateur efforts (often in the new technique of lithography, which began to be available in the 1820s). After the Civil War, however, printmaking and print culture in Maine saw a flood of technically sophisticated (but not always artistically inspired) commercial printed images, especially in the techniques of color lithography and steel engraving. This in its turn inspired a reaction beginning in the 1880s by a growing number of artist/printmakers to work on their own, primarily in the more private medium of etching. The end of the nineteenth century also saw the establishment of summer artists' retreats and "colonies" in the state, bringing increasing numbers of both established and amateur artists, and hence establishing artistic printmaking as a distinct practice by the turn of the twentieth century.

Perhaps the earliest printed images of Maine, with the important exception of maps, are several simple woodcuts of plants in a book published in London in 1672 by John Josselyn, *New-Englands Rarities Discovered: in Birds, Beasts, Fishes, Serpents, and Plants of that Country*. The author had just returned from an eight-year sojourn in New England, largely spent with his brother in Prouts Neck, Maine. The unsigned cuts were based presumably on drawings Josselyn made from direct observation of plants native to the region, such as the "Humming Bird Tree" (Fig. 1), easily recognizable as jewelweed, a flowering plant indeed attractive to hummingbirds.

The first printing press in Maine itself was not set up until 1785, in Portland; others were established in Hallowell, Wiscasset, and Castine by the end of the century. While newspapers and books printed in the state occasionally had woodcut mastheads or decorative motifs (some broadsides commemorating natural disasters include an appropriate number of caskets), the introduction of more elaborate printed illustrations developed relatively slowly. Many early illustrations actually were produced

Fig. 1
A Branch of the Humming Bird Tree, ca. 1672 from John Josselyn, *New-England's Rarities Discovered* (London: 1672 [Bedford (Mass.): Applewood Books, 1992]), p. 73
woodcut, 4 3/8 x 2 3/8 in.
Courtesy of the Collections of the Maine Historical Society

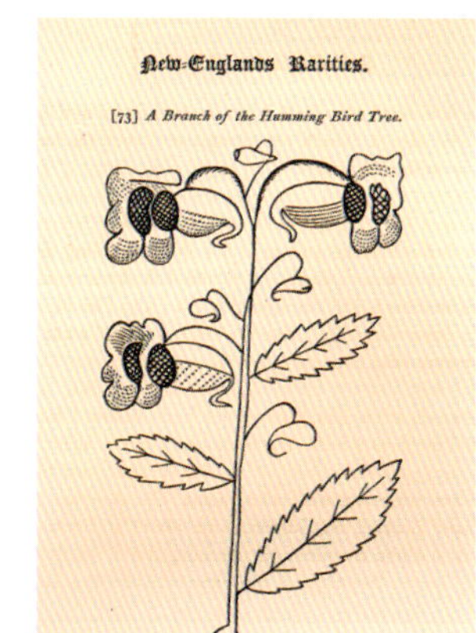

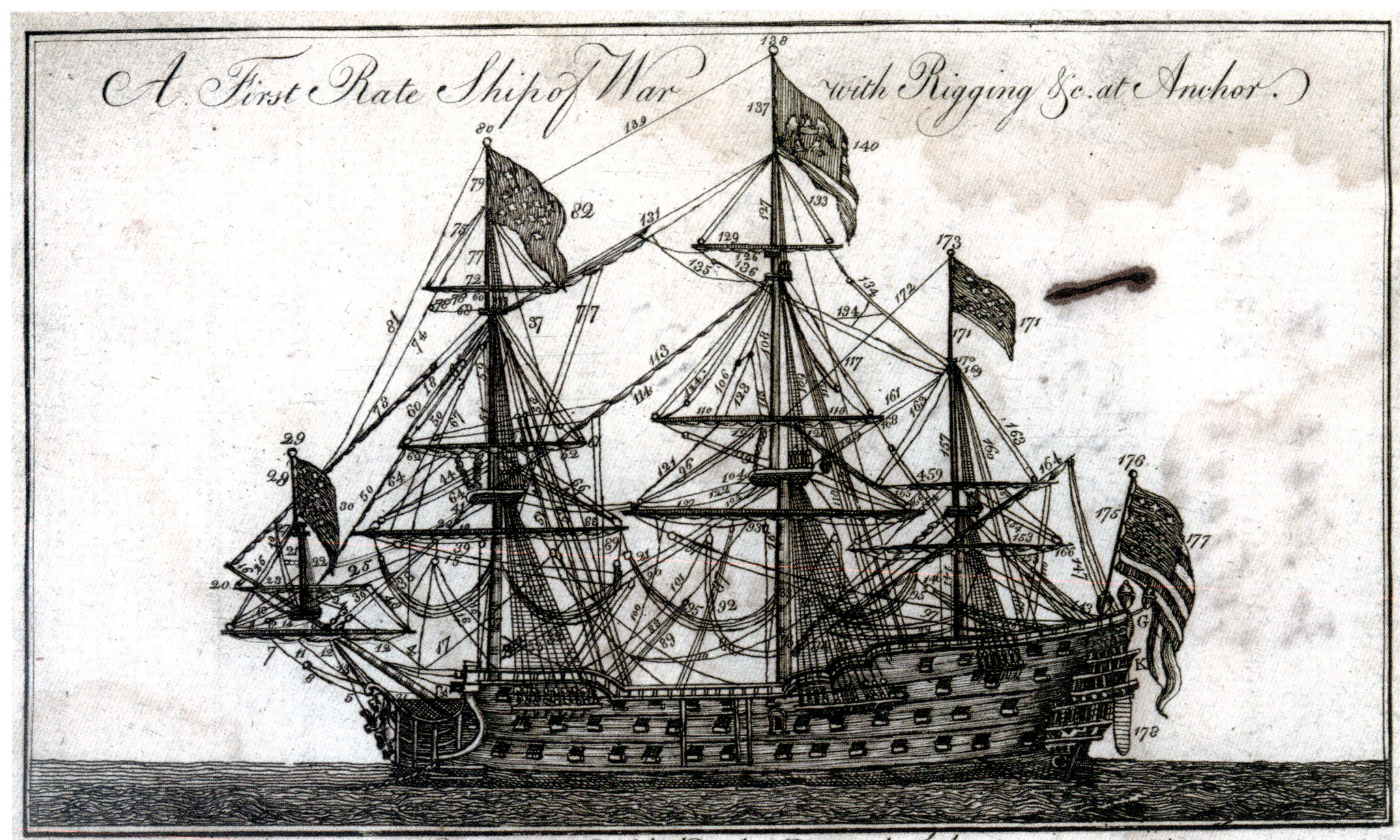

Plate 1

A First Rate Ship of War with Rigging &c. at Anchor

from *The American Ship Master's Daily Assistant*

(Portland: Daniel Johnson, 1807), frontispiece

engraving, 4 1/2 x 6 3/4 in.

Courtesy of Christopher Livesay

in Boston and other large cities, as were Samuel Hill's woodcuts for *A Discourse to Children* (Portland: 1792), or John Norman's view of the burning of Portland by the British in 1775, published in *An Impartial History of the War in America* (Boston: 1782). The practice of outsourcing illustrations continued for decades, presumably made feasible by convenient transportation access to larger commercial and artistic centers. It is not known if the impressive ship's diagram in *The American Ship Master's Daily Assistant* published in Portland by Daniel Johnson in 1807 (Plate 1) was actually engraved in Maine or not, but its practical importance ensured its wide circulation among the state's mariners and merchants.

Statehood in 1820 seemed to offer the first incentive for professional engravers to actually move to Maine, with the hope of taking advantage of the area's potential economic and cultural growth. With Portland serving as state capital until 1832, several engravers did set up shop there, but, as Maine historian Earle Shettleworth has documented, they were usually not able to attract enough business to last more than a year or so, after which most of them moved on to other cities.[1] The first was Danforth Newcomb (ca. 1800–1821), who set up business in July of 1820, but died a year later. His premises on Middle Street were purchased in 1822 by Abel Bowen (1790–1850), a Boston artist and entrepreneur, who installed his brother Sidney as branch manager of the Portland shop. Bowen had already supplied illustrations from 1820 for the *Maine Farmer's Almanac* (Hallowell: 1819ff.); in 1823 he engraved *A New and Correct Plan of Portland Maine*, which was the first known printed map of the city. Bowen seems to have closed his Portland operation soon thereafter.

The brothers Orramel Hinckley Throop (b. 1798) and Daniel Scrope Throop (b. 1800) came to the city in late 1823, but they, too, stayed only briefly. Orramel's 1823 advertisement in a Portland newspaper is typical of many engravers of this period, emphasizing the practical over the picturesque. He listed his abilities for "the engraving of bank notes, maps, charts, portraits, bookplates, heads of bills, bills of exchange, diplomas, merchants and manufacturers cards [see his own in Fig. 2], cards of address, all kinds of seals, and Masonic engraving . . . also engraving on wood." Other engravers, such as David G. Johnson (active 1824–45), who worked in Portland from 1824 to 1827, specified further skills in die stamps, doorplates, and seals. During his residency, Johnson engraved a chart of Portland harbor, a certificate for the Portland Nautical Society, a view of the Portland First Parish Meeting-House, and a portrait of the Marquis de Lafayette (Fig. 3), printed on silk ribbons worn during the French

Fig. 2
ORRAMEL HINCKLEY THROOP
(B. 1798)
Business Card, ca. 1823
engraving, 2 9/16 x 3 11/16 in.
Courtesy of the Collections of the Maine Historical Society

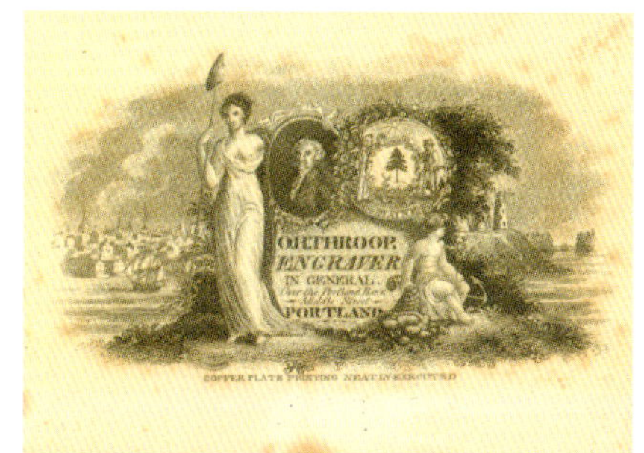

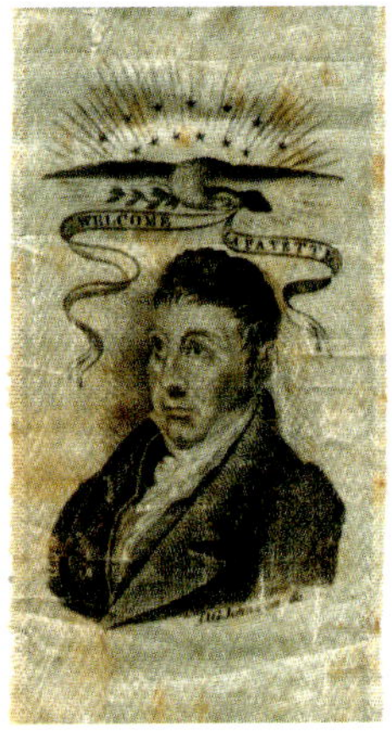

Fig. 3
DAVID G. JOHNSON
(ACTIVE 1824–25)
Lafayette Ribbon (detail), ca. 1825
engraving on blue silk ribbon
9 1/4 x 1 5/8 in.
Courtesy of the Collections of the Maine Historical Society

Fig. 4
JOHN F. RICHARDSON
(ACTIVE 1856–1866)
Advertisement, ca. 1863
from S. B. Beckett, *The Portland Directory and Reference Book for 1863-64* (Portland: 1863), title page verso
wood engraving, 1 1/2 x 2 5/8 in.
Collections of the Maine Historical Society

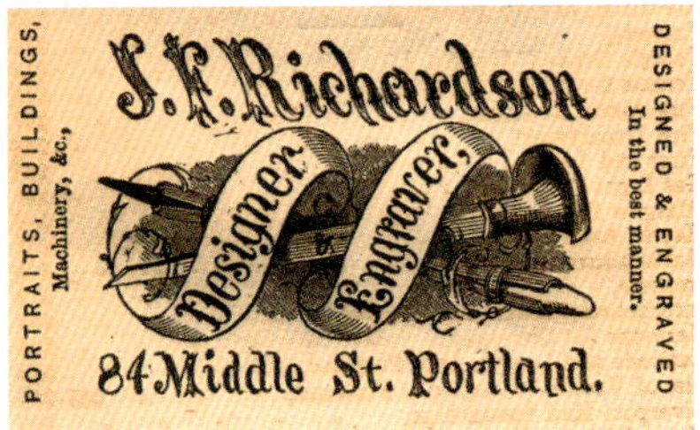

hero's visit to the city in 1825. The last engraver known to have visited Portland in the 1820s was George W. Appleton (d. 1831), who executed a portrait of the English philosopher Jeremy Bentham for the local author and critic John Neal.

Following these early efforts, a growing number of "engravers" are listed in city and state business directories through the end of the nineteenth century. In the 1830s, for instance, David Buxton and John Cullum were listed in Portland directories, the latter offering "the lowest Boston prices" and the advantage of acquiring work "directly from the artist rather than through the hands of others." Elsewhere in the state during the second half of the century, business directories list "designers and engravers" in Augusta, Bangor, Bucksport, and Damariscotta—though some turn out on closer examination to be employed by jewelry stores as decorative metal engravers for silverware and watches. Most printed work by Maine engravers in mid-century was still "job printing"; only gradually did separate, illustrative prints come to be produced as home decoration or for private collecting. However, such material was exhibited and offered for sale in the state at least as early as 1831, judging from bookseller Samuel Colman's advertisement in the Portland Directory of that year of "A Collection of engravings, among which are those from the first Artists." In the 1860s and 1870s, wood engravings of buildings and manufactured products signed by Portland engravers John F. Richardson (Fig. 4), Gardner B. Merrill, and Charles F. Plaisted can be found in local advertisements.

While professional engravers were trying to establish footholds in the state, a number of amateur printmakers recorded scenic views of city life and rural landscapes. The rapid spread of the new art of lithography is demonstrated by the remarkable *View on the Kennebeck at Gardiner* (Plate 2) by Louisa Davis Minot (1788–1858), who drew her sketch on a lithographic stone while on a visit from Boston to her friend Mrs. Robert Hallowell Gardiner and had it printed in Boston at Pendleton's shop, which had been established only the year before. In a letter to Mrs. Gardiner of April 8, 1826, sending along her "first attempts at Lithographic drawing," the artist wrote that "It is very easy to learn to draw on the stone, but it takes more time and requires more nicety than drawing in pencil."[2] She then offered to have stones shipped to Gardiner for her friend's daughter to draw upon and then send back to Boston to be printed. Minot's comments reflect the encouragement of women's artistic endeavors by lithographic printers of the time; an obvious attraction was the ability to share these "snapshots" with others through the multiplication of the print medium.

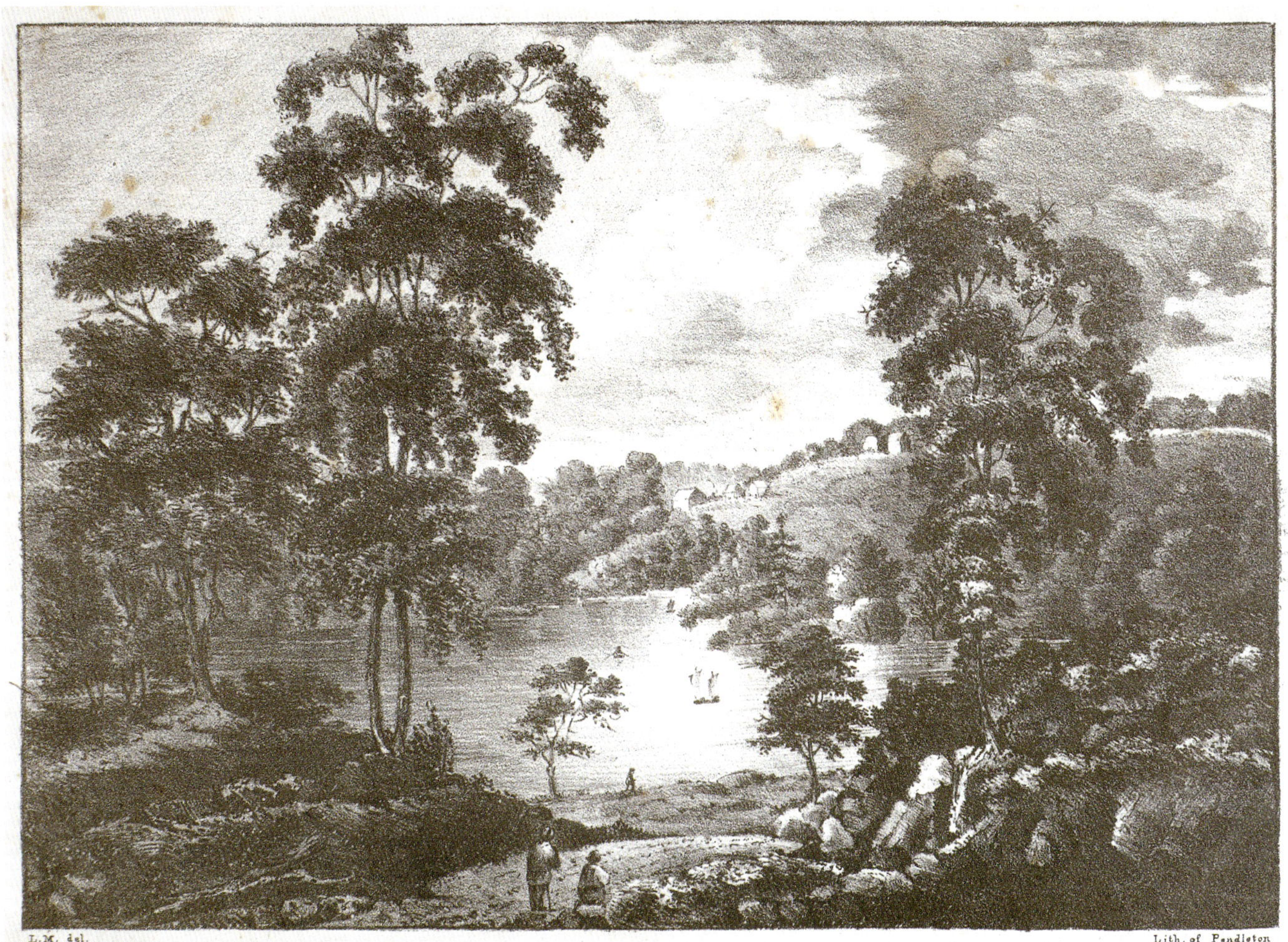

Plate 2

Louisa Davis Minot (1788–1858)

View on the Kennebeck at Gardiner, ca. 1826

lithograph, printed by Pendleton, Boston, 7 3/8 x 10 1/2 in.

Collection of the American Antiquarian Society

A more home-grown effort is the *View of the Whig Pavilion—Mount Joy Sept. 17th 1837* (Plate 3), an etching and engraving by Samuel H. Colesworthy (1808–1899), a Portland bookseller, publisher, and binder, who signed it also as publisher. It shows a view of the Portland Observatory and a political gathering on the land below, the composition owing a debt to an 1830 painting by the Portland artist Charles Codman, *The Entertainment of the Boston Rifle Rangers by the Portland Rifle Club in Portland Harbor, August 12, 1829* (Brooklyn Museum of Art). Colesworthy's depiction is strikingly minimal for the time, especially in black and white; one known impression has been hand-colored.

Jonathan Fisher (1768–1847) of Blue Hill was one of Maine's most remarkable polymaths and artists. A graduate of Harvard College and a learned pastor, he was also an inventor of a very high order, as demonstrated by the many artifacts still in his Blue Hill home, now a museum. The 140 wood engravings he cut for his book *Scripture Animals, or Natural History of the Living Creatures Named in the Bible, Written Especially for Youth*, published in Portland in 1834, were partly based on earlier prototypes, especially images by the English engraver Thomas Bewick. However, a number of Fisher's cuts were his own depictions of neighborhood creatures, such as the "little brown Owl, of the State of Maine, drawn from nature, Feb. 3, 1832," shown in Plate 4. He also engraved several bookplates and at least two illustrated broadsides of public executions in 1811 and 1824.

Twenty-four lithographic views of remote areas of the state appeared in the *Atlas of Plates Illustrating the Geology of the State of Maine*, by Charles T. Jackson, published in Augusta in 1837. The plates depict geologic features in areas such as the Upper Saint John River, West Quoddy Head, and *Mount Ktaadn from W. Butterfield's near the Grand Schoodic Lake* (Plate 5), showing the scientific party studying the distant mountain and diligently gathering samples. They are based on drawings by Francis Graeter (active 1827–1842), and were printed by Moore's Lithography in Boston. A number of copies, as here, were hand-colored. The German-born artist and illustrator Graeter was a drawing teacher at several progressive academies in the Boston area during the 1830s, including at Bronson Alcott's Temple School.

Beginning in the 1830s, many topographic views of cities, towns, and scenic places began to be recorded in both lithography and engraving, and these images rapidly became required artifacts of state and municipal pride. Before the Civil War, Boston lithographic workshops supplied a large number of such views. The Pendleton firm printed both the *S. E. View of Portland in 1832 taken from Fort Preble*, drawn

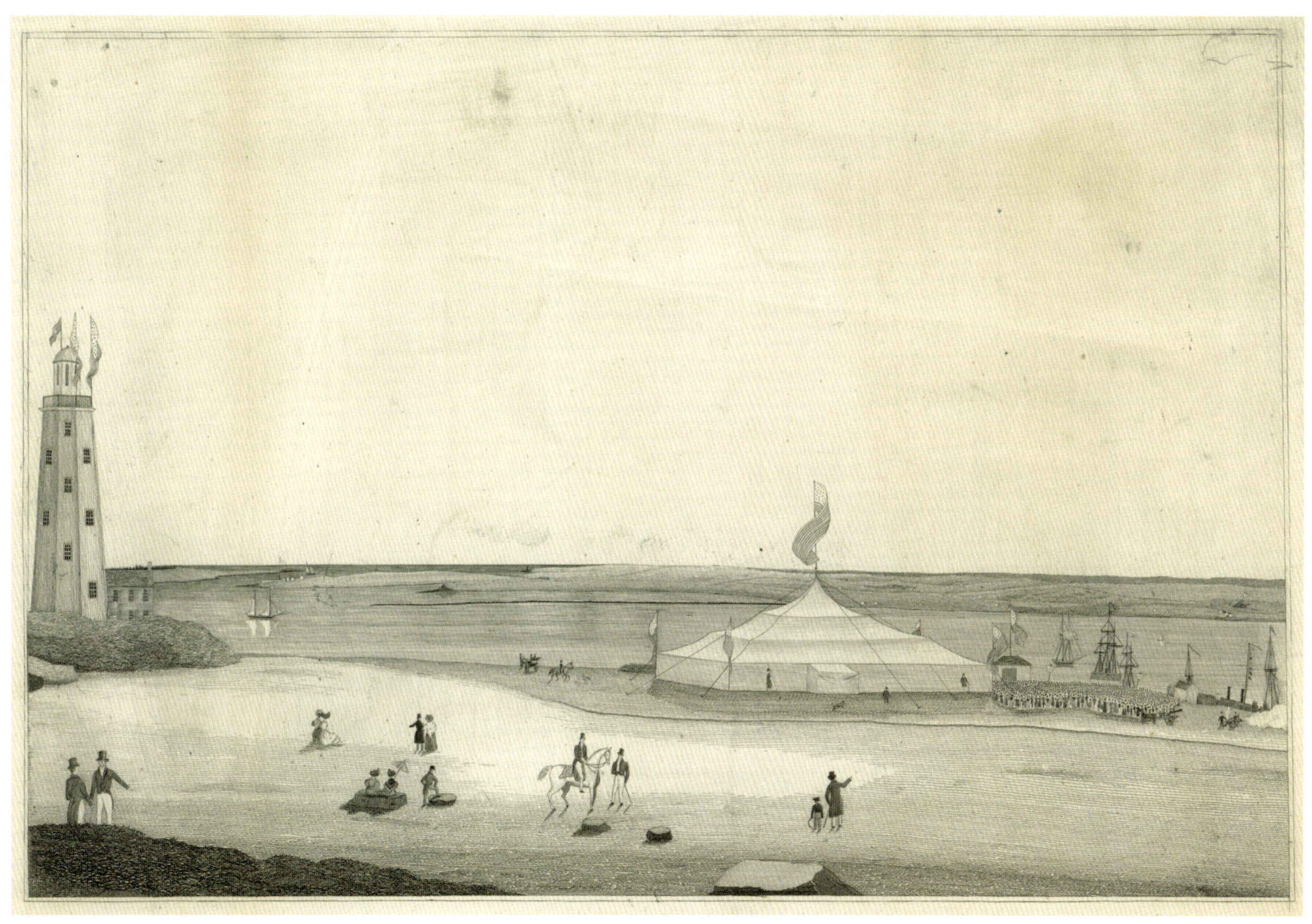

Plate 3

Samuel H. Colesworthy (1808–1899)

View of the Whig Pavilion — Mount Joy Sept. 17th 1837, ca. 1837

etching and engraving, 9 3/4 x 13 3/4 in.

Collections of the Maine Historical Society

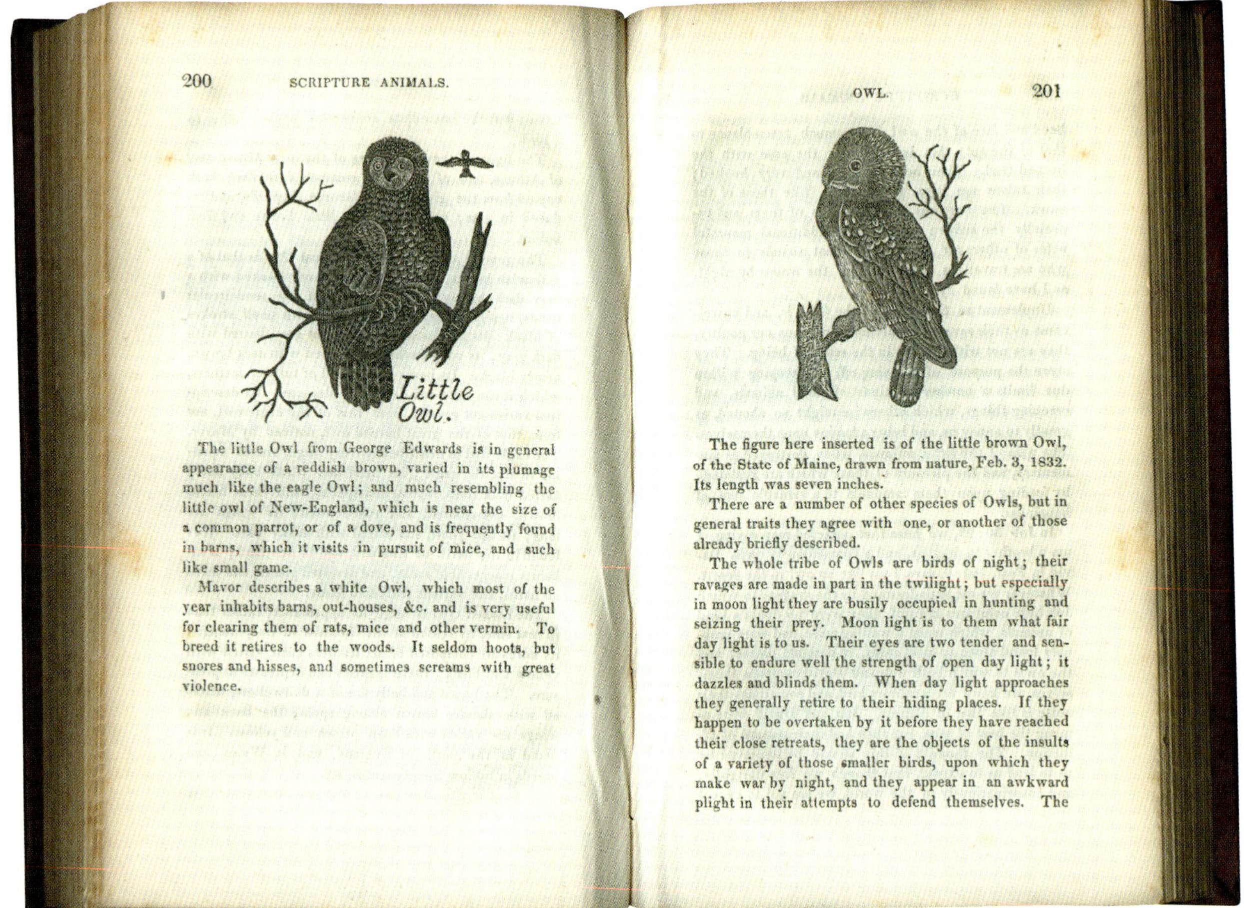

200 SCRIPTURE ANIMALS.

Little Owl.

The little Owl from George Edwards is in general appearance of a reddish brown, varied in its plumage much like the eagle Owl; and much resembling the little owl of New-England, which is near the size of a common parrot, or of a dove, and is frequently found in barns, which it visits in pursuit of mice, and such like small game.

Mavor describes a white Owl, which most of the year inhabits barns, out-houses, &c. and is very useful for clearing them of rats, mice and other vermin. To breed it retires to the woods. It seldom hoots, but snores and hisses, and sometimes screams with great violence.

OWL. 201

The figure here inserted is of the little brown Owl, of the State of Maine, drawn from nature, Feb. 3, 1832. Its length was seven inches.

There are a number of other species of Owls, but in general traits they agree with one, or another of those already briefly described.

The whole tribe of Owls are birds of night; their ravages are made in part in the twilight; but especially in moon light they are busily occupied in hunting and seizing their prey. Moon light is to them what fair day light is to us. Their eyes are too tender and sensible to endure well the strength of open day light; it dazzles and blinds them. When day light approaches they generally retire to their hiding places. If they happen to be overtaken by it before they have reached their close retreats, they are the objects of the insults of a variety of those smaller birds, upon which they make war by night, and they appear in an awkward plight in their attempts to defend themselves. The

Plate 4

Jonathan Fisher (1768–1847), *Little Owl and Little Brown Owl*,

ca. 1834, from *Scripture Animals*

(Portland: William Hyde, 1834), pp. 200–201

wood engravings, 7 1/2 x 4 1/2 in. (page size)

George J. Mitchell Department of Special Collections & Archives,

Bowdoin College Library

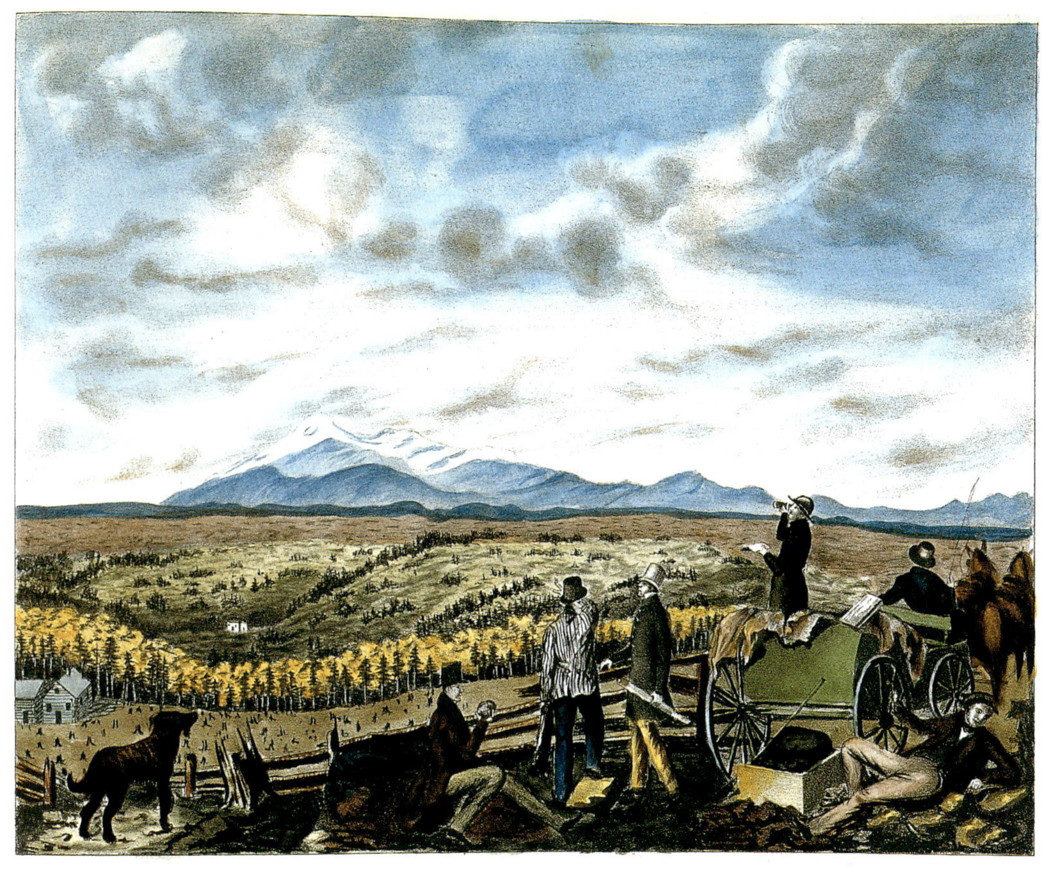

Plate 5

Moore's Lithography, after Francis Graeter (active 1827–1842),
Mount Ktaadn from W. Butterfield's, ca. 1837
from Charles T. Jackson, *Atlas of Plates Illustrating the Geology of the State of Maine* (Augusta: Legislature of Maine, 1837)
hand-colored lithograph, 7 3/8 x 9 1/4 in. (image)
Collection of the Maine State Museum

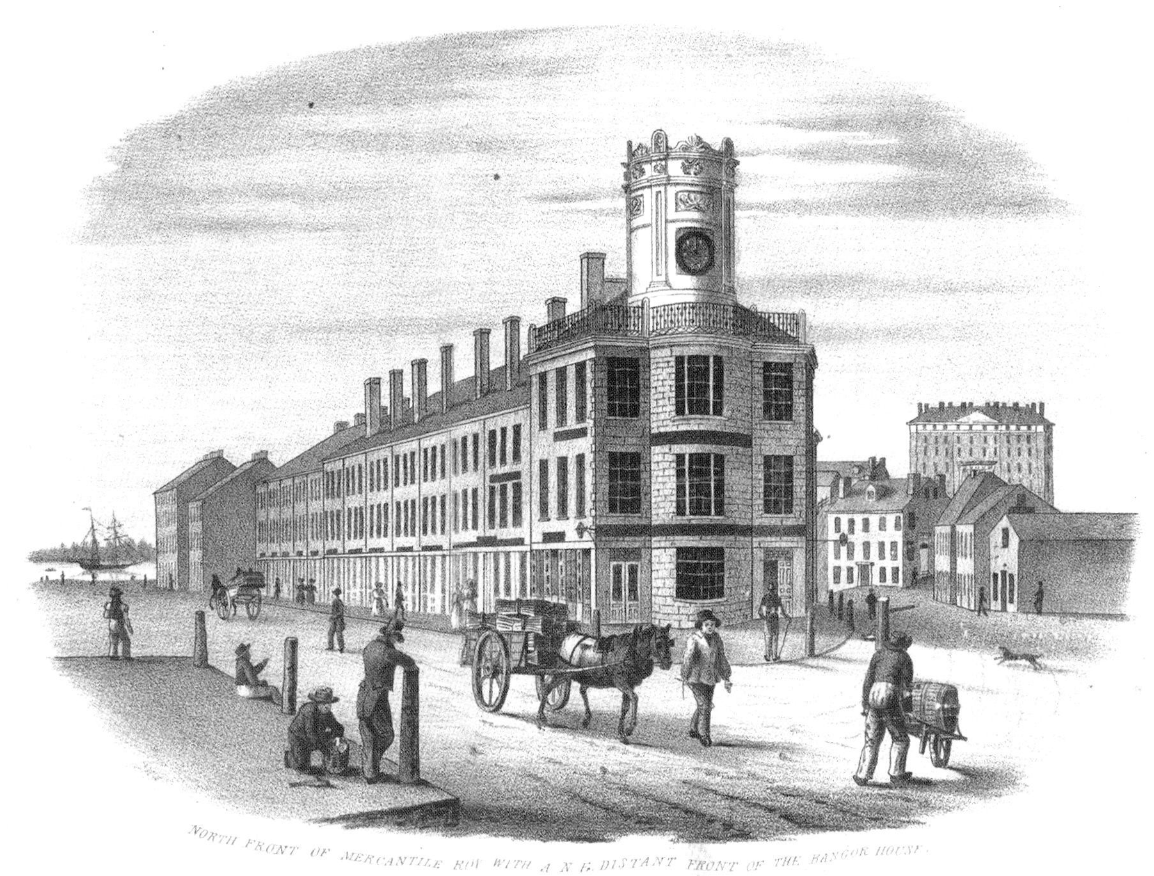

Plate 6

North Front of Mercantile Row with a N. E. Distant Front of the Bangor House, ca. 1835, from Oliver J. Shaw, *Bangor March* (Boston: Pendleton's Lithography [ca. 1835])

lithograph, $5\frac{5}{8}$ x 8 in. (image)

Courtesy of Earle G. Shettleworth, Jr.

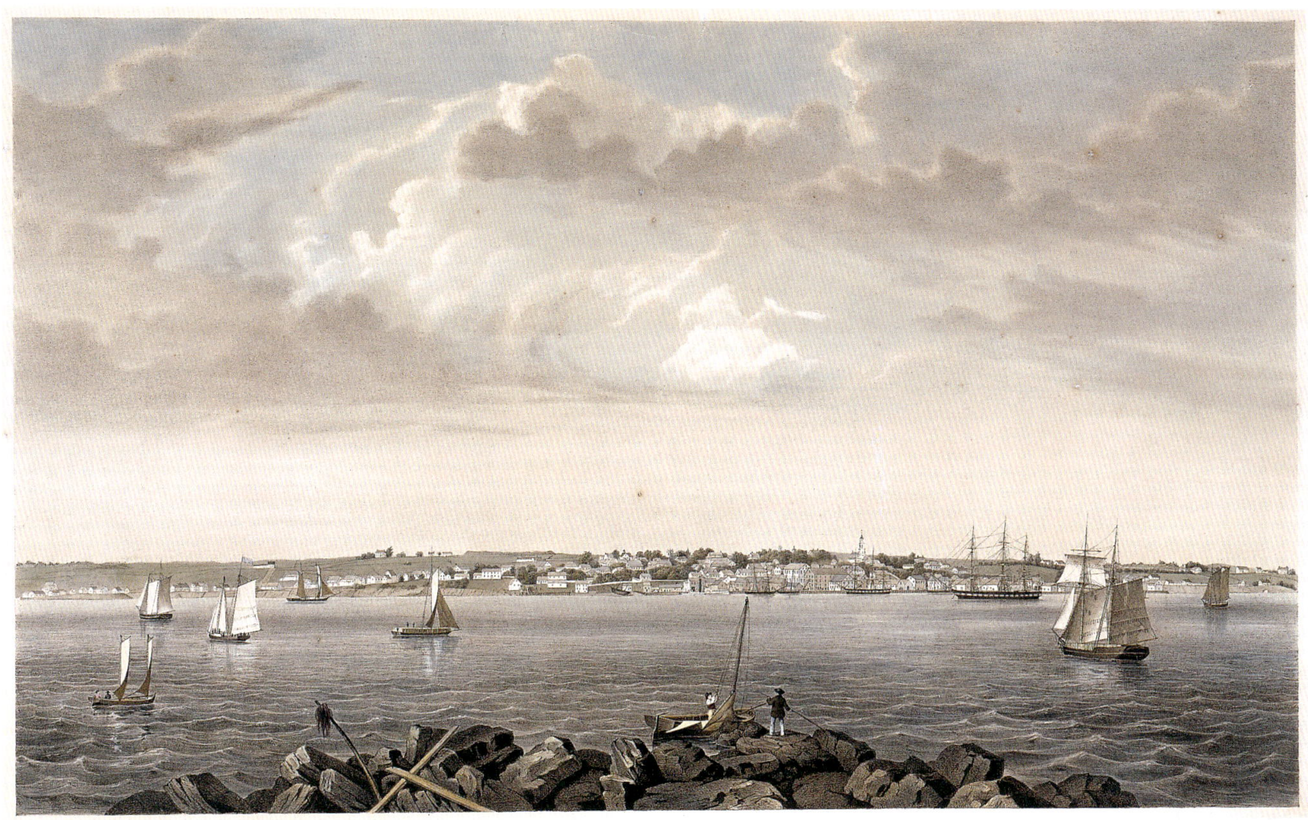

Plate 7

L. H. Bradford & Co., after Fitz Henry Lane (1805–1864)

Castine from Hospital Island, 1855

hand-colored lithograph, 19 3/4 x 32 3/4 in.

Collection of the Farnsworth Art Museum

Museum Purchase, 1944. 44.327

by J. H. Bufford after J. R. Vinton, and the *North Front of Mercantile Row with a N. E. Distant Front of the Bangor House* (Plate 6) of about 1835, after an anonymous artist. The latter forms the cover illustration for sheet music for Oliver J. Shaw's *Bangor March*. George Folsom's 1830 *History of Saco and Biddeford* featured a lithograph frontispiece of Saco Falls by Benjamin F. Nutting after William S. Gookin, printed by the Senefelder workshop in Boston. One of the most magnificent of the genre is the 1855 hand-colored lithograph of *Castine from Hospital Island* (Plate 7), executed by L. H. Bradford & Co. of Boston after a drawing by the noted painter Fitz Henry Lane (1805–1864)[3]. The artist Cyrus W. King (b. 1819), son of Maine's first governor, drew a lithographed view of Bath datable to about 1845. During the 1850s, commercial pride was reflected in such images as a view of J. B. Brown's Portland Sugar House and at least two depictions of steam engines for the Portland Company Locomotive Works, all printed by the Bufford lithograph firm in Boston. The great Portland fire of 1866 occasioned a number of striking views, including "before and after" lithographs of *Elms Locust Street* drawn and published by John B. Hudson, Jr. Overall views of the destruction were also reproduced in many contemporary newspaper illustrations of the day, usually in pictorially accurate wood engravings executed after photographs.

After the Civil War, the use of printed images expanded into all aspects of commercial and domestic life. Prints were increasingly seen in newspapers, literary and technical magazines, calendars, children's books, product labels, and all varieties of display posters for advertising products, events, and travel destinations, to name only a fraction of their uses. With the increased affordability of high-quality printed images, their domestic display dramatically broadened and included subjects such as inspirational portraits (Washington, Lincoln), scenic vistas (Niagara Falls, Yosemite Park), and sentimental scenes (Currier & Ives).

As the techniques of printing color lithography, or chromolithography, became more sophisticated, the medium evolved into an enormously popular genre. Remarkable facsimiles of oil paintings and watercolors were produced by layering colors over the entire surface of the paper; at times they were printed on paper embossed to resemble canvas.[4] One Maine-related "chromo" is the winsome portrait of *Dotty Dimple* (Plate 8), the title character in a series of six children's novels by the Norridgewock author Sophie May (pseudonym for Rebecca Sophia Clarke). Published in 1869 by the Boston firm of Williams

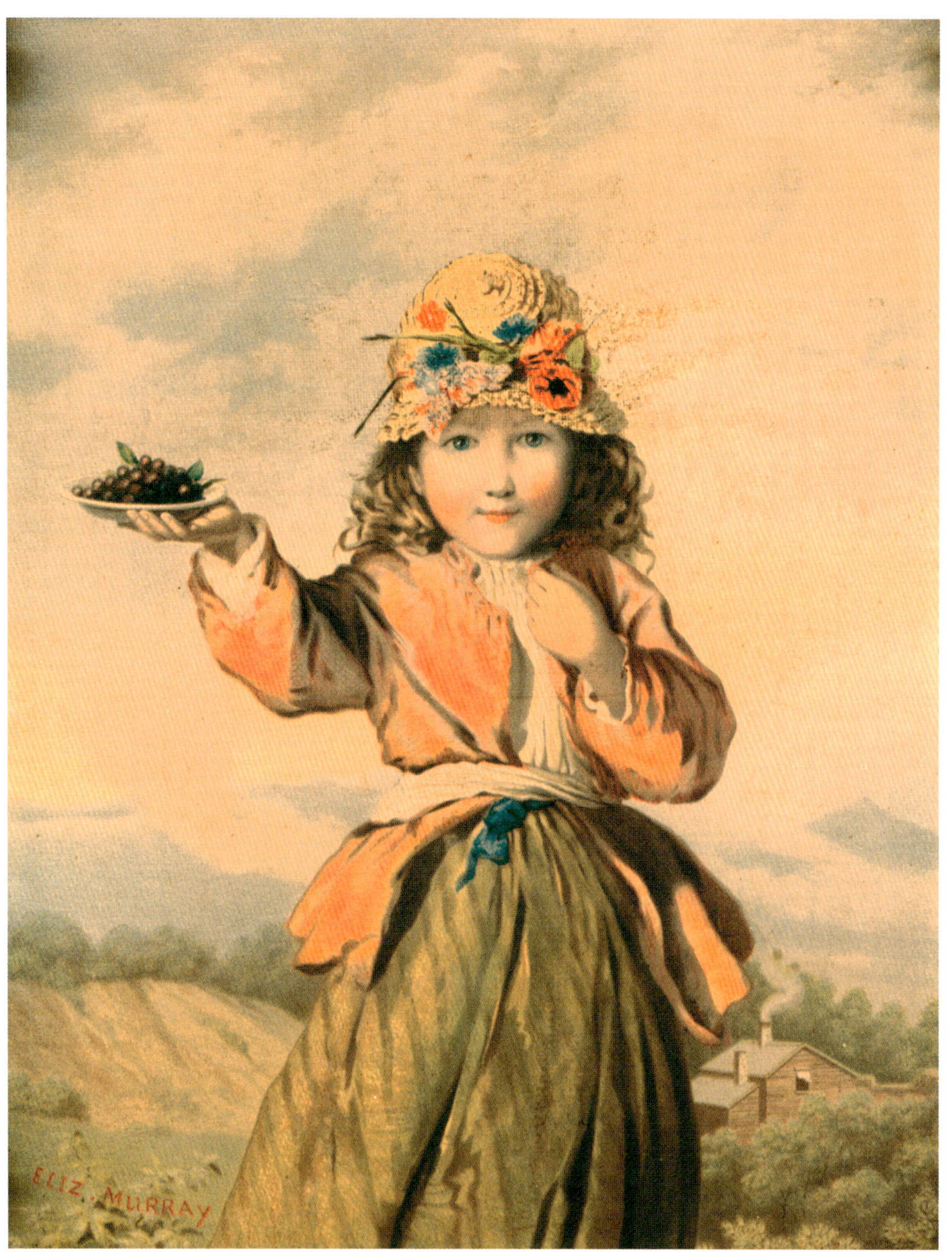

Plate 8

Williams & Everett, after Elizabeth Heaphy Murray, (1815–1882), *Dotty Dimple*, 1869, color lithograph, 12 x 10 in. Courtesy of Earle G. Shettleworth, Jr.

& Everett, the fictionalized portrait reproduces a watercolor by the British-born artist Elizabeth Heaphy Murray (1815–1882), who lived in Portland during the 1860s and 1870s.

The predominant outsourcing of lithographic print production seems to have lasted until 1883, when S. S. Smith's Son of Bangor became the first Maine firm to advertise its ability to print lithographs on site (Fig. 5), as they had imported a pressman from the famous Boston firm of L. Prang & Company. Before then, however, several significant local firms, notably True & Co. and E. C. Allen & Co. of Augusta and George Stinson & Co. and H. Hallett & Co. of Portland, published large numbers of chromolithographs from the 1870s. Subjects published by the Stinson firm (active from 1873 to 1894) were as varied as views of Niagara Falls and the 1876 Centennial Exhibition in Philadelphia, and maudlin religious poems about dying children. Actually printed in Boston or elsewhere, an edition often would be split among publishers in different cities, each firm having its name on a share of the impressions of the same image. According to a newspaper article, the Stinson firm sold over "four million pictures of all descriptions" in 1878, with prices ranging from ten cents to twenty dollars apiece. The article further argued that "American homes should be made beautiful by refined works of art, and prices for really meritorious pictures are now so low that there can be no excuse for the walls to remain gloomy, unadorned and cheerless."[5]

Fig. 5
FRANK K. SMITH
Business Card for S.S. Smith's Son, ca. 1888, $2^1/_2$ x 4 in., reproduced in William Beckford Hale, *Leading Business Men of Bangor, Rockland and Vicinity* (Boston: 1888), p. 121, Bowdoin College Library

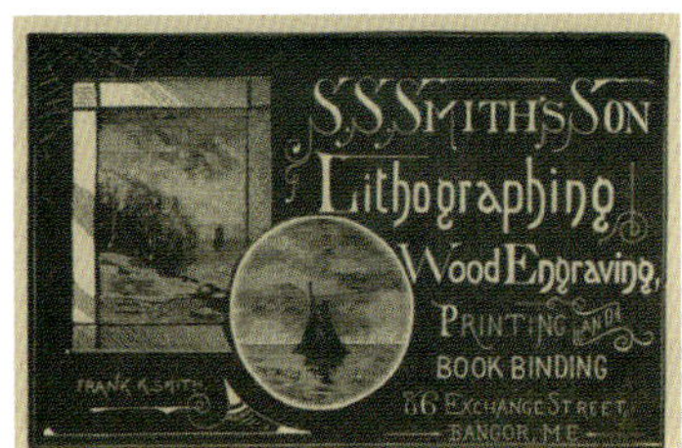

The two print media of lithography and wood engraving dominated popular imagery at this time, leaving the more refined medium of metal engraving for pricier gift books and high-end reproductions after popular paintings, plus the specialized production of currency and corporate stationery. As in other media, much metal engraving (including currency) seems to have been ordered from specialty shops in Boston, New York, or Philadelphia. No record has yet been found of such material produced in Maine (though Stinson and other firms were publishers). However, engraved depictions of scenic Maine views, many based on the work of famous landscape painters, began to be seen in ever greater quantities, collected by bibliophiles in the state and elsewhere. Such images played an important part in attracting visitors, both recreational and artistic, to the coast of Maine in particular.

Well-known artists such as Thomas Doughty, Thomas Cole, Frederic E. Church, and Fitz Henry Lane had been traveling to the state since the 1830s, and the grandeur of Maine paintings by Cole and

Church attracted much attention in exhibitions in the larger cities of the East Coast. This interest was soon reflected in printmaking. As early as 1840, an engraving of *Desert Rock Light House* by W. Radclyffe after a painting by Doughty appeared in Nathaniel Parker Willis's *American Scenery*, published in London. The scenic wonders of Mount Desert Island also formed the first chapter in the lavishly produced *Picturesque America; or The Land We Live In*, edited by William Cullen Bryant and published in New York from 1872 to 1874. The serene 1871 view of *Mount Desert, Coast of Maine* (Plate 9), engraved by Robert Hinshelwood (b. 1812) after Harry Fenn (1845–1911), was followed by eleven wood-engraved vignettes of scenes around the island. Bryant justified his choice of engravings by maintaining that "Photographs, however accurate, lack the spirit and personal quality which the accomplished painter or draughtsman infuses into his work."

Toward the end of the century, art colonies and summer schools were beginning to spring up, especially along the coast. These centers of activity reinforced a break from purely commercial printmaking activity in the state and provided participants with an opportunity to work as "pure" artists. The centers also fostered a growing audience for such art, at first among artistic circles themselves, but soon through public exhibitions and sales. Along with their sketchbooks, watercolors, and oil paints, a number of visiting artists also brought along printmaking materials, or produced prints later in their studios from sketches made in Maine. The dominant artistic print medium in the last two decades of the nineteenth century was etching, spurred by the so-called "Etching Revival" begun in France and England in the 1860s by artists such as Charles Meryon, Francis Seymour Haden, and the American expatriate James McNeill Whistler. The resurgence of etching at this time had much to do with a reaction against the overall dominance of commercial lithography (especially "chromos") and slavishly engraved reproductions of popular paintings. The "revivalists"' saw etching as a means to demonstrate the freedom of artistic originality, especially on a more spontaneous and intimate scale. The genesis of the etching revival in the United States is marked by the foundation of the New York Etching Club in 1877, and similar clubs soon appeared in other cities.

Both visiting and native artists took part in the etching revival in Maine. Among the visitors were Samuel Colman (1832–1920); James Smillie (1833–1909); R. Swain Gifford (1840–1905, whose

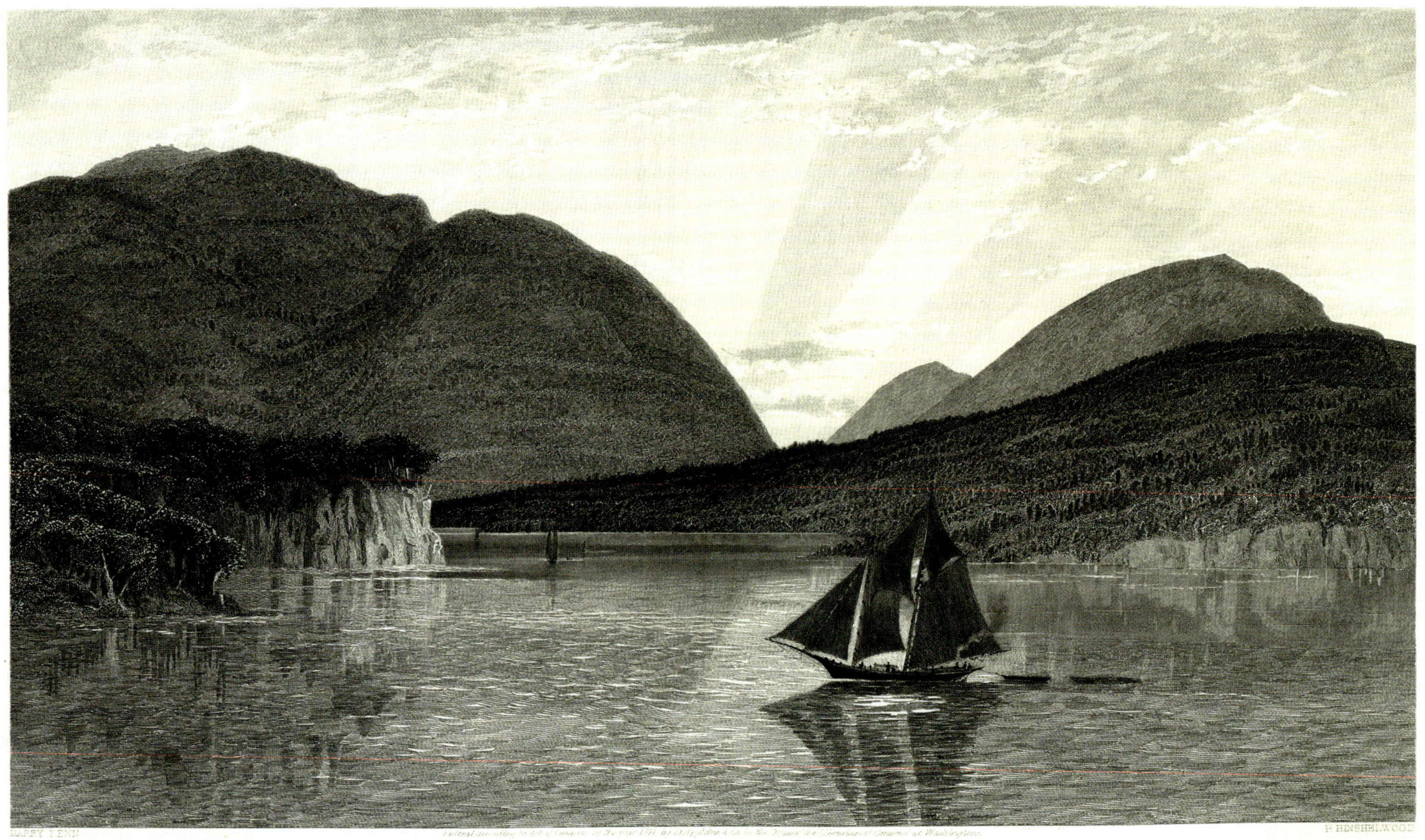

Plate 9

Robert Hinshelwood (b. 1812), after Harry Fenn (1845–1911)

Mount Desert, Coast of Maine, 1871

from William Cullen Bryant, *Picturesque America*

(New York: D. Appleton, 1872–74), facing p. 1

steel engraving, 5 x 9 in.

Special Collections, University of Southern Maine Libraries

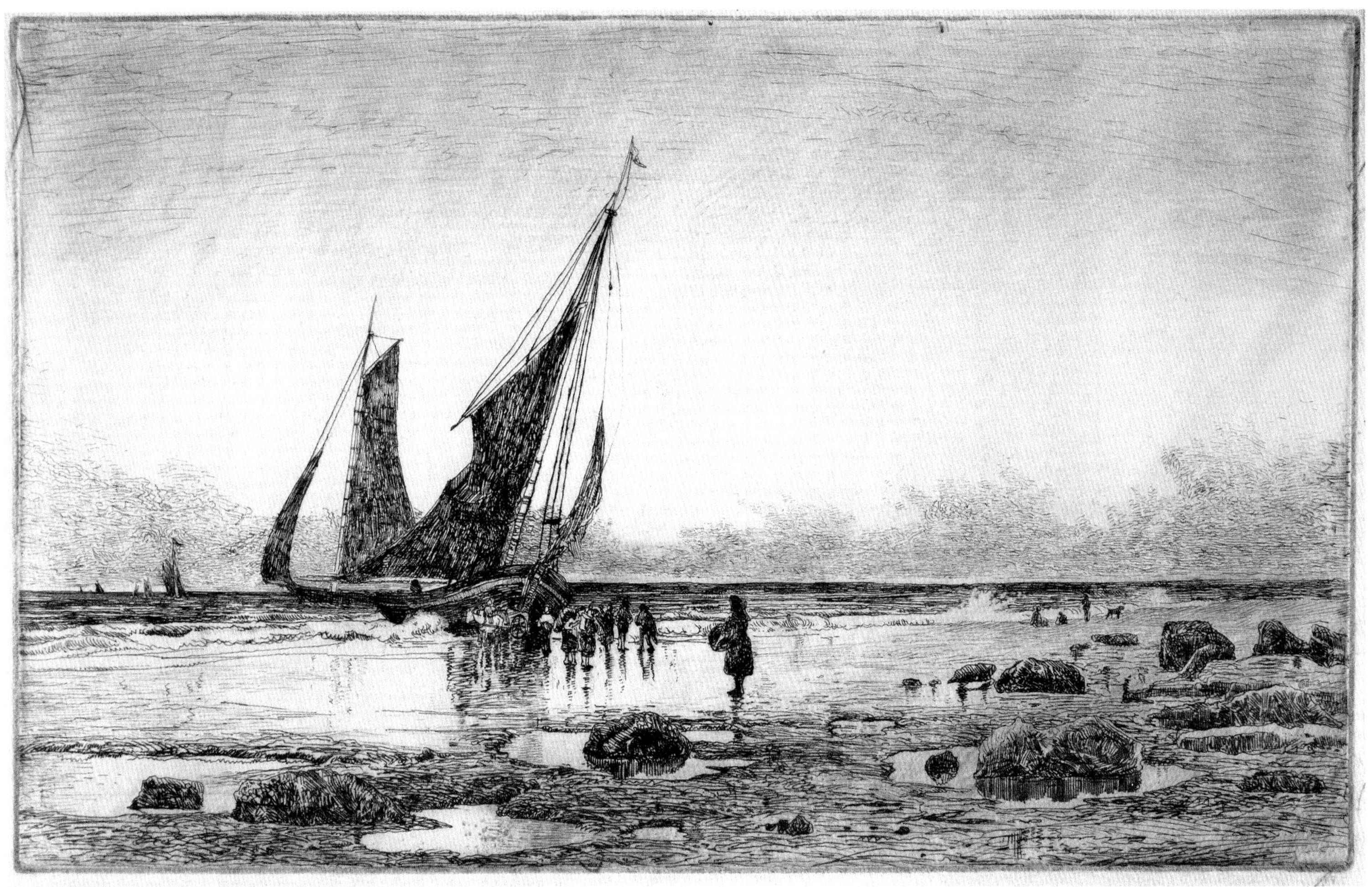

Plate 10

Emily Kelley Moran (ca. 1850–1900), *Long Beach, York Harbor, Maine*, 1883, etching, 7 1/2 x 12 1/8 in. Graphic Arts Collection, National Museum of American History, Smithsonian Institution (Photograph number: 5194-13547)

In the Maine Woods of 1883 was used to illustrate an edition of Hawthorne's works); and Sears Gallagher (1869–1955), an early art visitor to Monhegan in the 1890s. Peter Moran (1841–1905) and Emily Kelley Moran (ca. 1850–1900) explored the York area on the coast of Maine in the summer of 1882. Peter Moran evoked a seventeenth-century Dutch theme with his etching *The Downs at York Harbor*, featuring a group of cows wandering the dunes. Emily Moran's etching of *Long Beach, York Harbor, Maine*, dated 1883 (Plate 10) is a grander composition, perhaps evoking a homecoming at the end of the day.[6] Her print was included in the influential 1887 Museum of Fine Arts, Boston, *Exhibition of the Work of the Women Etchers of America*, which comprised 388 works by 23 artists. Also included were two 1884 views of the Kennebec River by Louise Prescott Canby (active 1874–1903).

The organizer of the Boston exhibition was Sylvester Rosa Koehler, the museum's first curator of prints and a tireless crusader for the art of etching, who sponsored numerous exhibitions and published many articles and monographs. One of his articles featured the work of the Portland artist Charles Frederick Kimball (1831–1903), who attracted Koehler's admiration, and seeming surprise, at his "genius without development, springing up suddenly before us fully equipped." Kimball was a gifted landscape painter, a founder of the group of area artists known as the Brush'uns, and a forceful advocate for the arts, being a founder in 1882 of the Portland Society of Art (the forerunner of the Portland Museum of Art and Maine College of Art). There are a total of nine etchings known by him, most derived from his painted compositions, including *Coal Sheds at Topsham*, 1889 (Plate 11). Another Portland artist and teacher, Horace G. Hewes (b. 1849), supplied two etched illustrations for a limited edition book by James Phinney Baxter, *Idyls of the Year* (Portland: 1884). The Portland Society of Art's first exhibition in 1882 included both national and local etchers, such as Colman, Peter Moran, Stephen Parrish, Charles A. Platt (an architect and etcher who did several works in Maine), "S. Hayden" (probably Seymour Haden), and Kimball himself.

One notable omission, however, was in fact the dominant artist in Maine at this time, Winslow Homer (1836–1910), who prior to his fame as a painter and watercolorist had been a prolific designer of wood-engraved illustrations for the popular press in Boston and New York. During the 1880s, having settled permanently in Prouts Neck, he became intrigued by the possibility of increasing the audience for his work and capitalizing on its fame by producing large-scale printed interpretations of his most

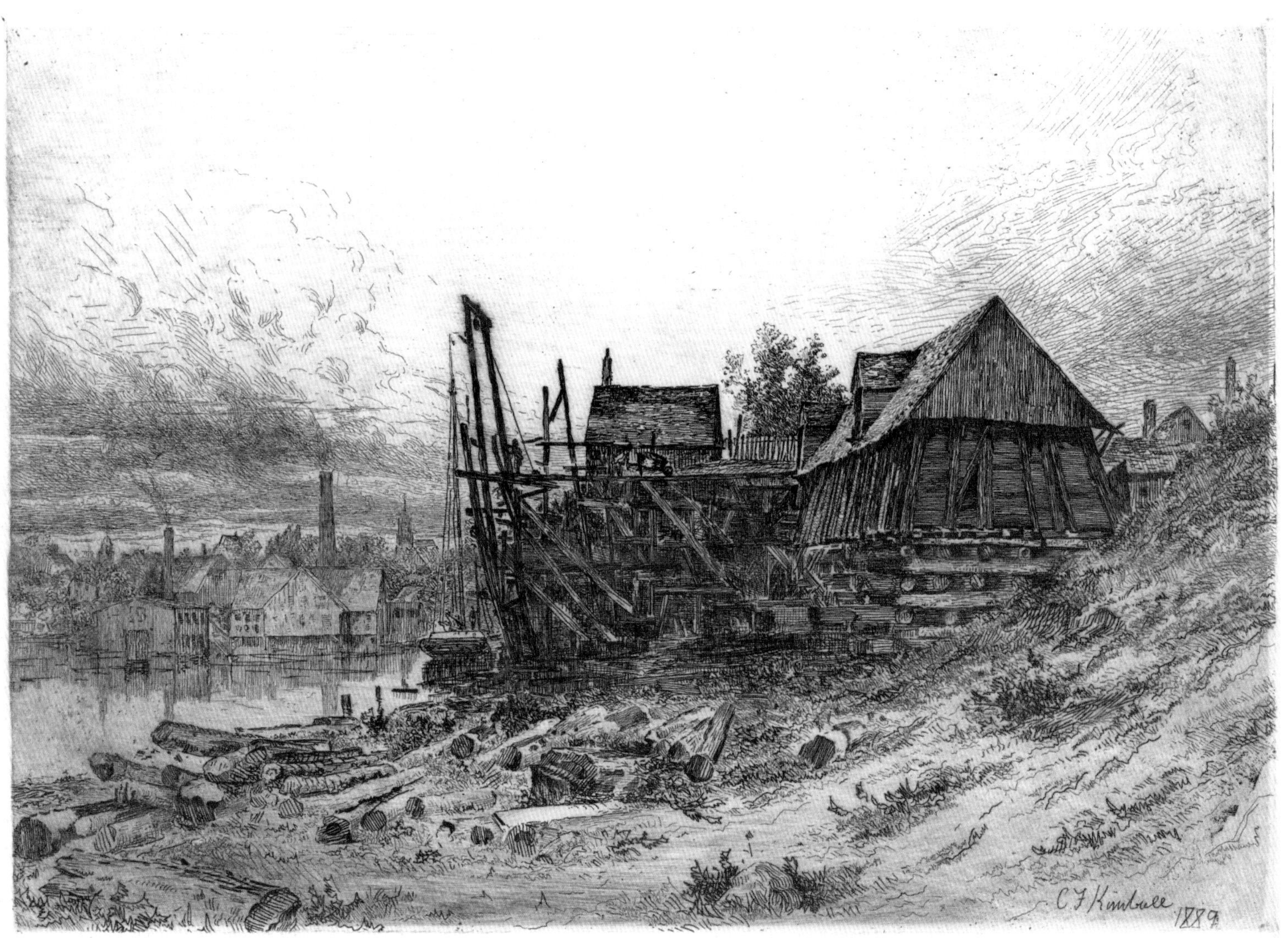

Plate 11

Charles Frederick Kimball (1831–1903), *Coal Sheds at Topsham*, 1889, etching, 6 9/16 x 9 11/16 in.
Courtesy of Earle G. Shettleworth, Jr.

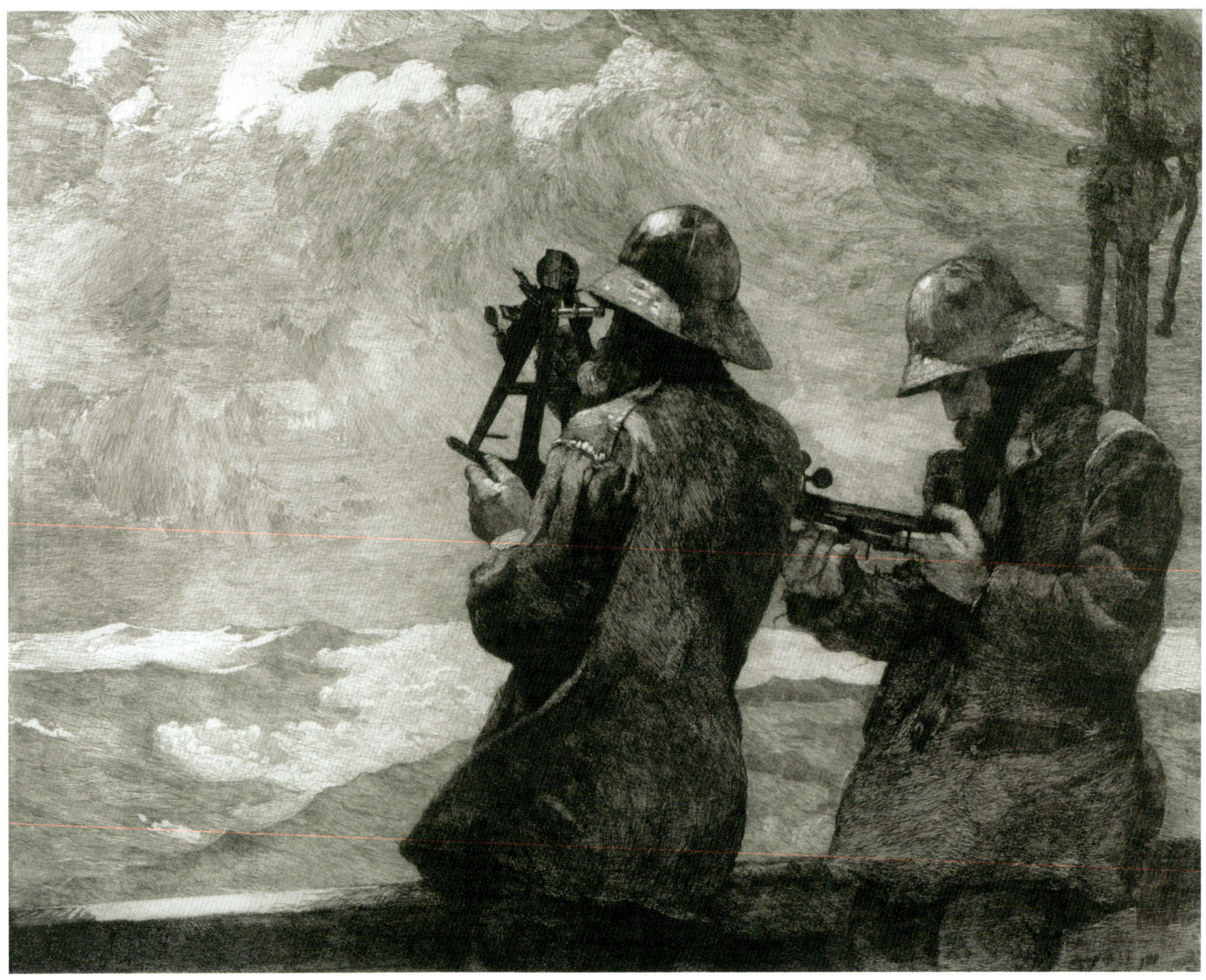

Plate 12

Winslow Homer (1836–1910), *Eight Bells*, 1887

etching, 18 3/4 x 24 1/4 in.

Collection of the Farnsworth Art Museum

Museum Purchase, 1943. 43.101

famous compositions. He uniquely chose to produce these works himself and to execute them in etching; he finished a total of seven compositions. However, his concept of the medium did not at all resemble that of the etching revivalists. While they concentrated on the intimate and personal, Homer utilized an uninflected, fluid draftsmanship for his large-format plates, undoubtedly drawing on his earlier training as an illustrator. *Eight Bells* of 1887 (Plate 12), for instance, is based on an 1886 painting now in the Addison Gallery of American Art, but he has cropped it more tightly around the two figures, creating a bolder structure that is reinforced by the rich tonalities of the monochrome etched lines. Drawing and etching the plates in his Prouts Neck studio, Homer would then send them to George W. H. Ritchie in New York to be professionally printed. Unfortunately, his etchings sold very poorly, and his commercial hopes for the project were unfulfilled.

In many ways the end of the nineteenth century marks the definitive close of the largely commercial emphasis on artisanal printmaking in the state. From the beginning of the twentieth century, there is an increasing separation between artists who worked primarily in advertising, illustration, and the growing field of graphic design, and those who pursued printmaking within the context of an artistic career in itself. While again acknowledging the ubiquitous presence of printed imagery in modern culture, this survey from this point highlights the independent status of artistic printmaking.

NOTES

1. See Earle G. Shettleworth, Jr., "Portland, Maine, Engravers of the 1820s," *Old-Time New England — Bulletin of the Society for the Preservation of New England Antiquities*, vol. 61, nos. 3–4 (Winter and Spring, 1971), pp. 59–65, 105–10.

2. Sally Pierce, et al., *Early American Lithography — Images to 1830* [exh. cat.] (Boston: Boston Athenaeum, 1997), p. 59.

3. Formerly known as Fitz Hugh Lane; recent archival research has uncovered the artist's true identity as Fitz Henry [see John Wilmerding, *Fitz Henry Lane* (Gloucester: Cape Ann Historical Museum, 2005)].

4. See Peter C. Marzio, *The Democratic Art — Chromolithography 1840–1900: Pictures for a 19th-Century America* (Boston: David R. Godine, 1979). Interestingly, the Portland author and critic John Neal (1793–1876) virtually predicted the explosion of chromolithography ("colored impressions in oil") as early as 1828, following a visit to Pendleton's shop in Boston and marveling at the already rapid progress of lithographic skills (Marzio, p. 206).

5. *Gardiner Home Journal* (Gardiner, Me.), August 6, 1879. I am grateful to Earle Shettleworth for this reference.

6. I am grateful to David G. Wright for sharing his unpublished research on the Morans.

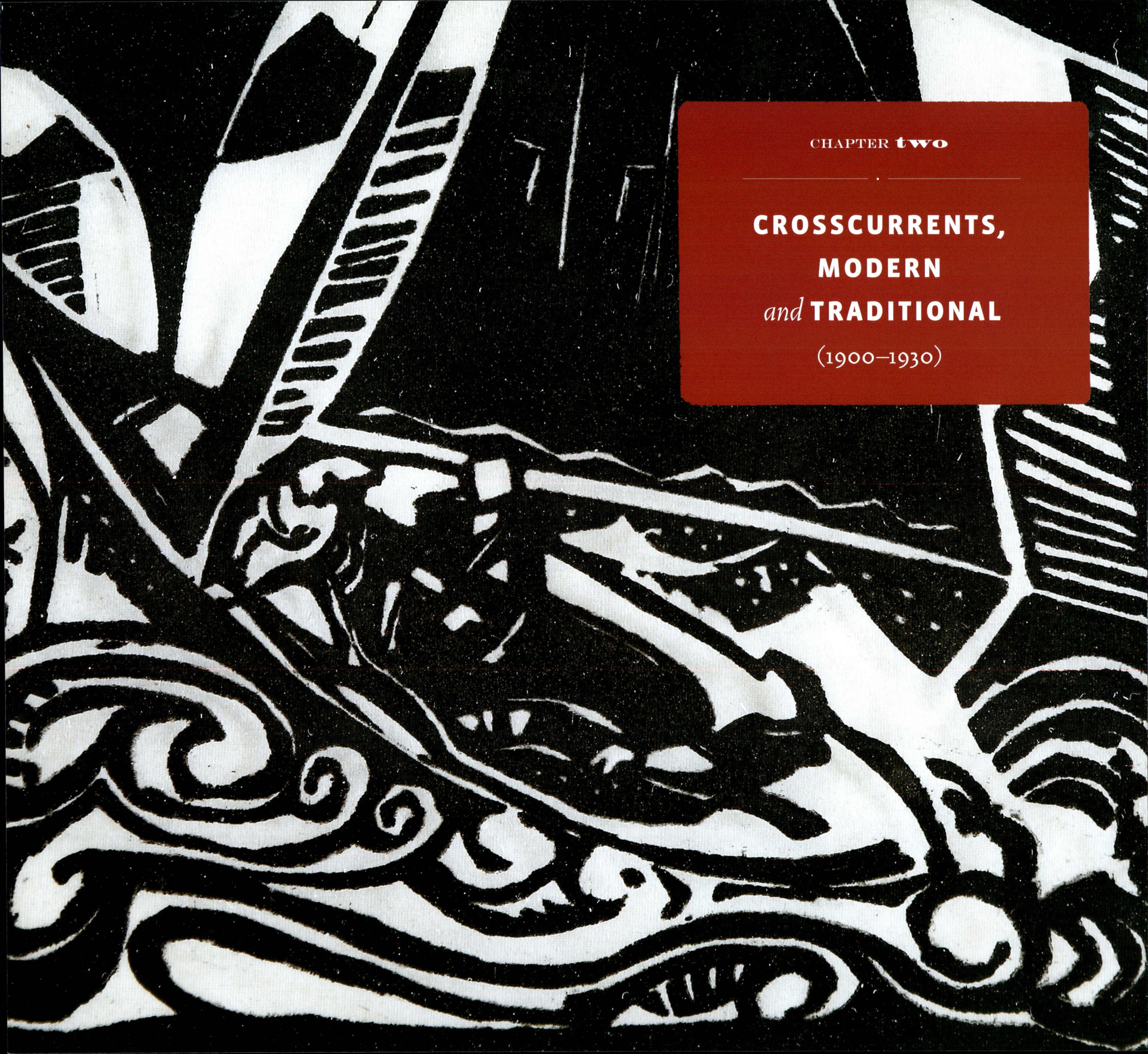

CHAPTER **two**

CROSSCURRENTS, MODERN *and* TRADITIONAL

(1900–1930)

The rapidly evolving artistic changes of the early twentieth century in Europe and the United States were quickly brought to Maine—especially to its summer art colonies—by many of the major players in those changes. In some cases, traditional and modernist ideas coexisted in the same community, as with Hamilton Easter Field's avant-garde circle and Charles Woodbury's academic classes facing each other across Ogunquit's Perkins Cove, or the lively mix of artists of all stripes on Monhegan. Printmaking reflected this artistic ferment, as certain artists continued to work in a classic etching tradition, while many of the most innovative works were created in other media, primarily lithography and woodcut.

A traditional outlook is seen in the work of Cadwallader Washburn (1866–1965). A graduate of Gallaudet University with an architecture degree from MIT, Washburn was an inveterate traveler and prolific painter and printmaker, etching hundreds of architectural views and scenes of life in Europe, Mexico, Japan, and the Pacific Islands, in addition to Maine and New Jersey. He also was a war correspondent during the Russo-Japanese War of 1904–05 and the Mexican revolution in 1910–11. In addition, his skill in oology (the study of birds' eggs) led to a collecting expedition in the Marquesas Islands in 1925. Born in Minnesota, he was descended from an important Maine family whose Livermore homestead, Norlands, was the setting for a series of at least sixty prints that he executed over the course of several summer visits in the early years of the century. Each of the Norlands prints depicts a modest corner of the local landscape, often revealing specific weather conditions, such as a rain shower or a strong breeze. In a 1911 article, Washburn wrote of this series that "it was my desire to record the varying phases under which nature has shown herself to me with such keen appreciation as is possible only to one who has lived in close intimacy with her from childhood."[1] *Ripples (Norlands Series V)* (Plate 13) dates from about 1912 and recalls similar subjects by Seymour Haden in its exploitation of the dark, velvety effects of strong drypoint burr. The impression illustrated here was printed on extremely thin Japanese paper that imparts a warm glow and enhances the soft effects of the drypoint, which wears down very quickly with repeated printings. Washburn spent the last twenty years of his long life in Maine, eventually returning to his family home in Livermore.

After a four-year stint from 1885 to 1889 as the first teacher at the newly-founded Portland School of Art, Frank W. Benson (1862–1951) went on to become an influential teacher at the School of

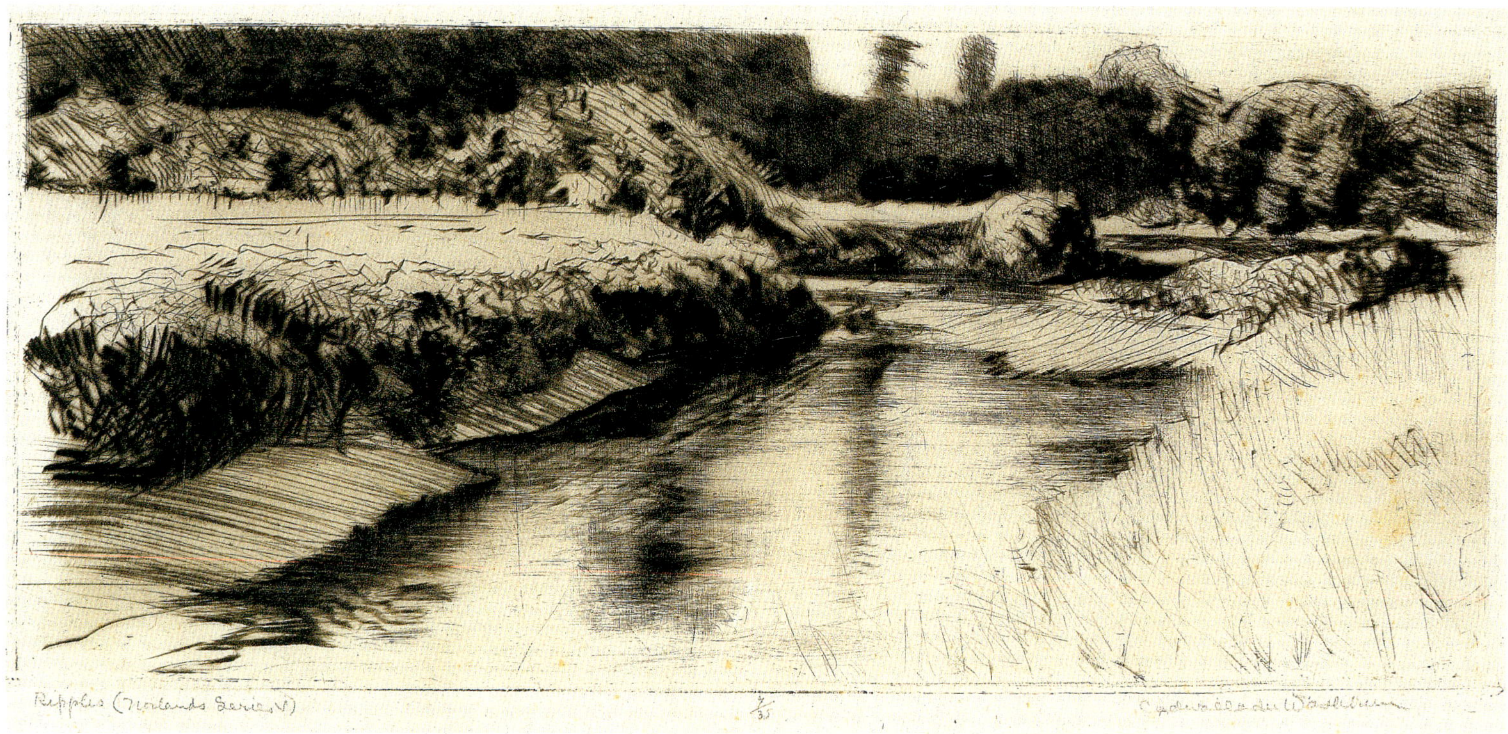

Plate 13

Cadwallader Washburn (1866–1965)

Ripples (Norlands Series V), ca. 1912

drypoint, 5 1/4 x 11 7/8 in.

Collection of the Farnsworth Art Museum

Museum Purchase, 1945. 45.543

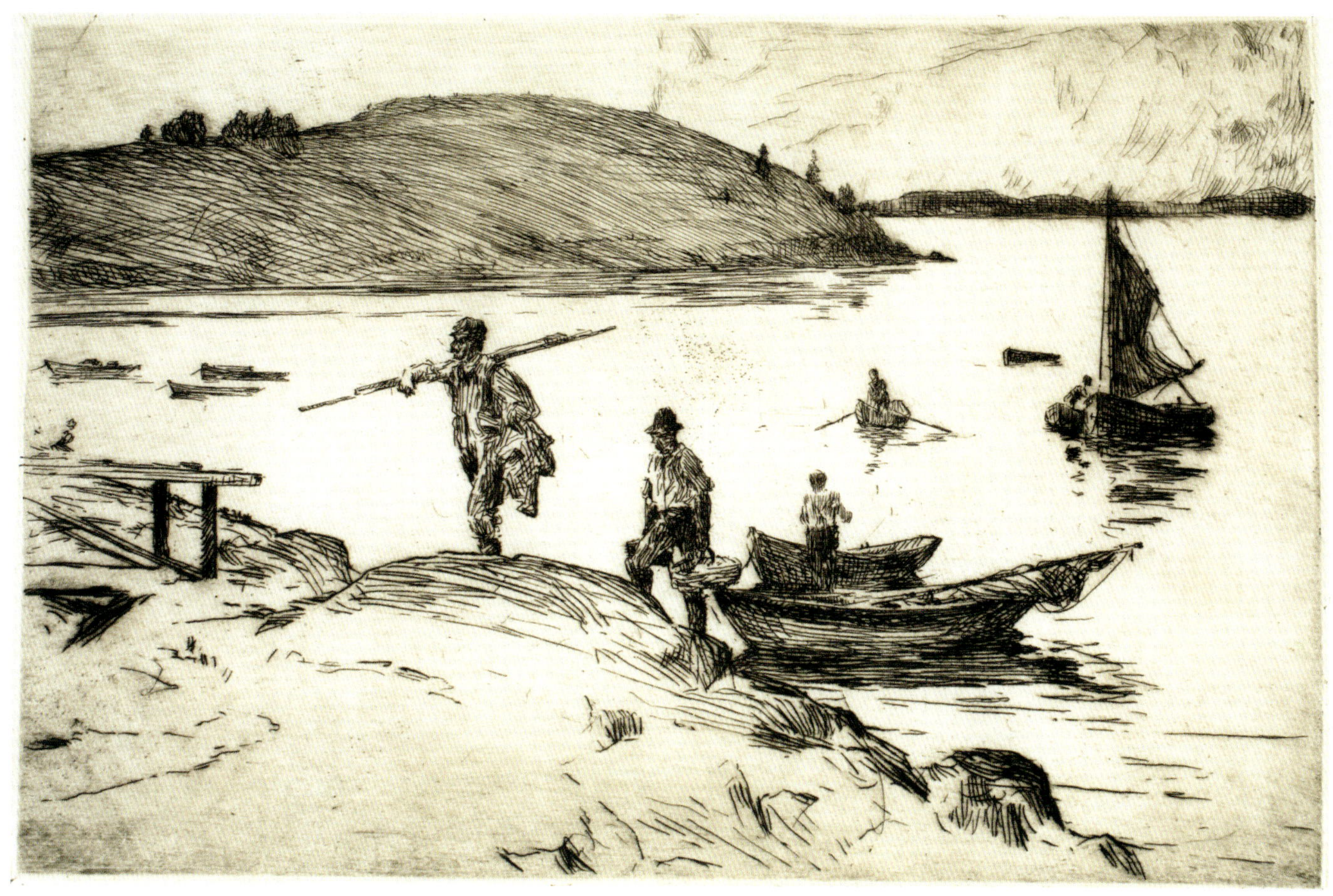

Plate 14

Frank W. Benson (1862–1951), *The Landing*, 1915

etching, 8 x 12 in.

Collection of the Bowdoin College Museum of Art

Gift of Miss Susan Dwight Bliss. 1963.286

the Museum of Fine Arts in Boston. Benson had studied there and in Paris, evolving a nationally recognized impressionist style of painting interiors, portraits, and landscapes, many depicting the coast around his summer home in North Haven. That locale is also the scene of his 1915 etching, *The Landing* (Plate 14), which exhibits his fluid draftsmanship, but still within a traditional mode. Benson executed over 300 etchings in his career and is especially known for his sporting scenes of fishing and bird-hunting. Another well-known American impressionist, Childe Hassam (1859–1935), etched at least one view in Belfast and stayed several summers on Appledore Island in the Isles of Shoals, supplying watercolor illustrations for Celia Thaxter's *An Island Garden* (Boston: 1895).

Another exemplar of a technically and artistically refined etcher is Ernest Haskell (1876–1924), who studied in New York and Paris (where he met Whistler). Haskell achieved his first fame as an illustrator and poster designer, before devoting lifelong study to the traditions and techniques of etching. The majority of his work is devoted to landscape. He purchased a summer home near Bath in 1910, returning every year to depict the pastoral aspects of the local landscape, while also making several trips to California to portray the larger-scale landscapes and trees of the west. The free sketchiness so prominent during the nineteenth-century etching revival is now a refined, quiet draftsmanship seen in *Crystal Morning* (*Kennebec River*) of 1924 (Plate 15). The elongated format, economy of line, and cloudless sky are a clear homage to Rembrandt's etched landscapes. Among other prominent etchers of the period who worked in Maine are John Taylor Arms (1887–1953), who executed a group of 31 prints in 1919–1920 of the Rangeley area; Kerr Eby (1889–1946), who depicted a number of coastal scenes and seascapes during the 1920s and 1930s; and Philip Little (1857–1942), who summered on McMahan Island.

The Boston artist Charles Woodbury (1864–1940) is regarded as the founder of the Ogunquit art colony. He first visited in 1888, built a house and studio on Perkins Cove in 1897, and directed an influential summer art school almost continuously until his death. Originally trained as a mechanical engineer, he studied art in Boston and Europe, achieving early fame for his carefully analyzed and forceful representations of open ocean and shoreline views. He executed several hundred etchings in his career, and his early style soon evolved into evocative, abstracted line studies of landscape and marine motifs. The undated etching *Mid-Ocean* (Plate 16) is one of several portrayals of open ocean, a strong example of

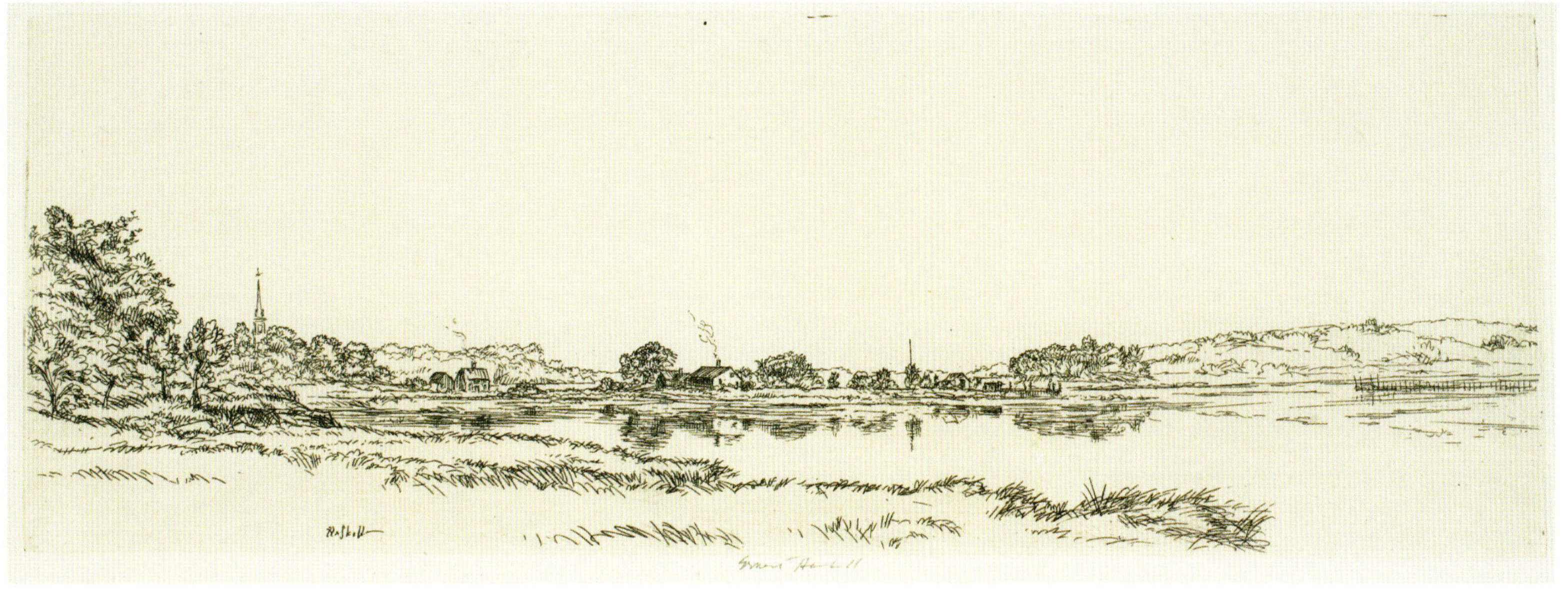

Plate 15

Ernest Haskell (1876–1924), *Crystal Morning (Kennebec River)*, 1924, etching, 3 1/8 x 9 1/4 in.
Collection of the Bowdoin College Museum of Art
Gift of Mrs. Josephine Haskell Aldridge, in memory of Mrs. Ernest (Emma) Haskell, Sr. 1978.32

his belief that "if you accept the characteristics of water to establish the conditions of force and resistance, you can make a wave for yourself that the ocean would be proud to acknowledge."

Another early summer resident of Ogunquit who studied with Woodbury was the painter Gertrude Fiske (1878–1961), whose oils of landscapes, figures, and aspects of modern life show a freedom of subject and color that set her apart from her more conservative compatriots. She studied at the Boston Museum School, was elected to the National Academy of Design, won many prizes, and was a founder of the Ogunquit Art Association in 1930. Her (at least) fifty etchings are stylistically close to Woodbury's,

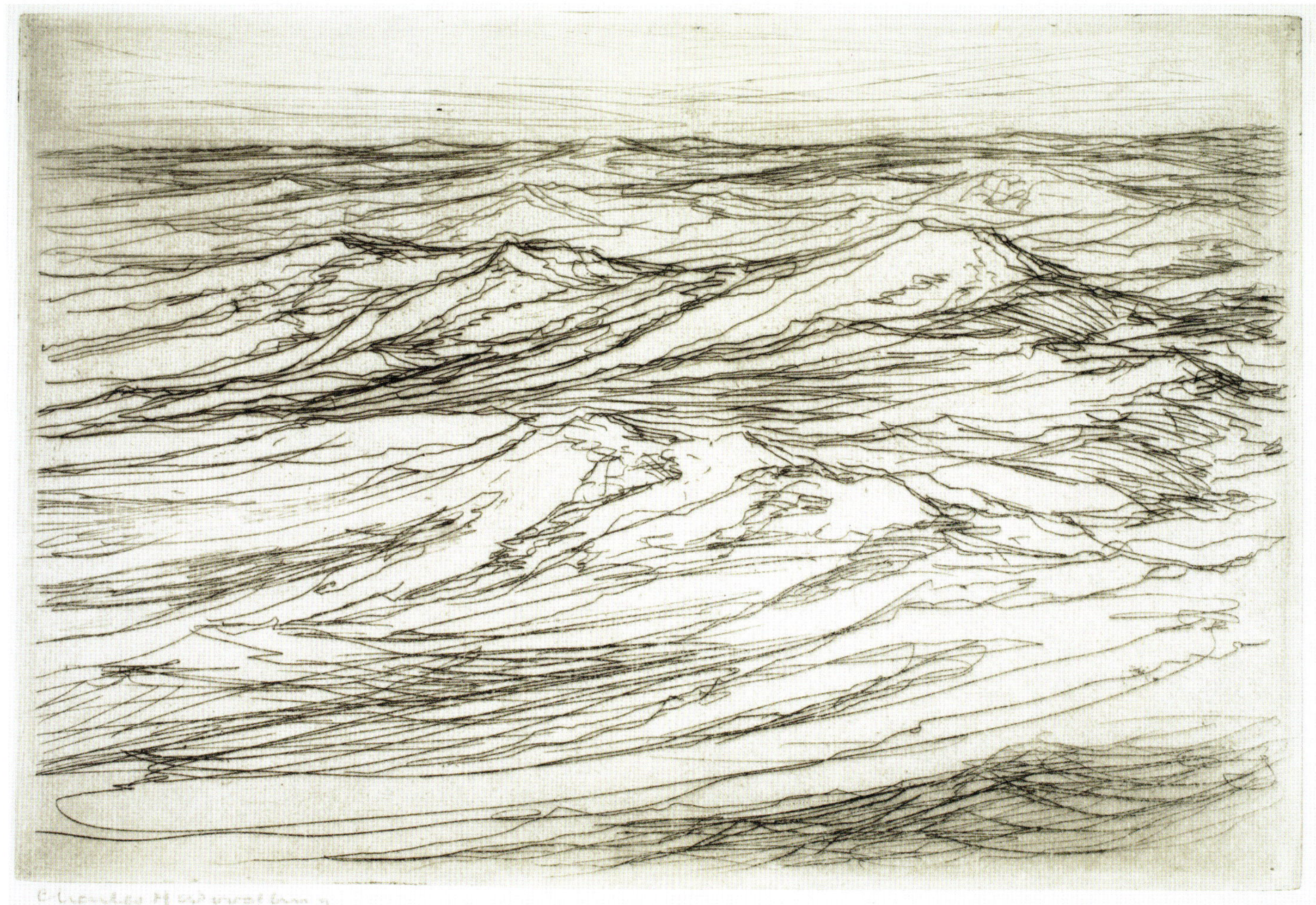

Plate 16

Charles Woodbury (1864–1940), *Mid-Ocean*, n.d.

etching, 7 1/8 x 10 3/4 in.

Collection of the Bowdoin College Museum of Art

Gift of Mrs. Charles Bruen Perkins. 1948.38.5

but their subject matter also reveals her independence, exemplified in *Untitled* (Plate 17, presumed to be a self-portrait), with its proud depiction of a woman artist at her easel in plumed hat. Another presumed self-portrait etching is entitled *A Modern Woman*.

Farther downeast, a number of artists had established themselves on the island of Monhegan by the time that Robert Henri (1865–1929) first visited in 1903. It is difficult to overestimate Henri's influence on the group of artists who gathered around him in these years, forming the core of a new approach to realism in American art. Among many others, they included Rockwell Kent, George Bellows, Edward Hopper, Paul Dougherty, Leon Kroll, Clarence Chatterton, and Randall Davey, all of whom followed their mentor to Monhegan, firmly securing its place in the history of landscape painting. Many members of this group of course also produced prints reflecting their experience on the island.

George Bellows (1883–1925) was one of the most accomplished lithographers of his or any generation, producing almost 200 stones in less than ten years, including his well-known boxing series. He first visited Monhegan in 1911 and soon returned twice (in later years he also summered in Ogunquit). He painted many strong views during his Monhegan stays, and later based two of his earliest lithographs on his experiences there: a small view of wharf shacks on Matinicus Island (closely related to an oil at the Portland Museum of Art) and a nocturnal scene recording a *Prayer Meeting* (Plate 18—the second of two lithographed versions of this composition) at the Monhegan church. Both were done in 1916, soon after he first took up lithography, buying his own press and materials and installing them in his New York studio. Realizing that he needed technical help, he enlisted the help of the lithographic printer George C. Miller, who subsequently specialized in printing artists' lithographs for some forty years. Miller printed *Prayer Meeting* in a dark brown ink, masterfully recording Bellows's bold yet nuanced drawing on the stone. An earlier drawing of this gently satirical subject was reproduced in *Harper's Weekly* of January 2, 1914, with the title "Deponent Testifies that He is no Longer a Sinner."

The power of Bellows's draftsmanship is directly related to a qualification he shared with many of his compatriots, first emphasized by the print scholar Richard Field: they all had had a great deal of experience as magazine illustrators, which forced them to simplify and strengthen their compositions to be easily read.[2] This skill is particularly evident in the prints of such artists as Bellows, John Sloan (1871–1951), Edward Hopper (1882–1967) and Rockwell Kent (1882–1971), among others. All had studied

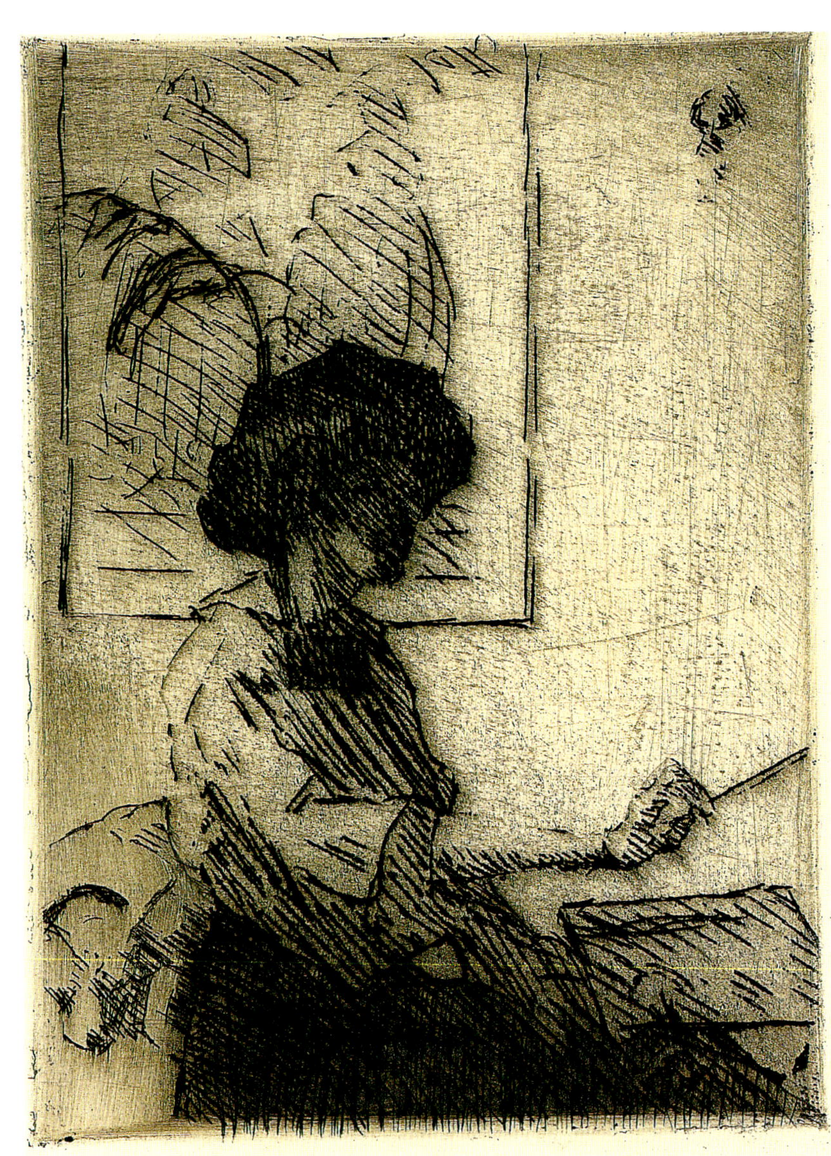

Plate 17

Gertrude Fiske (1878–1961), *Untitled (Self-Portrait)*, n.d.

etching, $5^{7}/_{8}$ x $4^{3}/_{8}$ in.

Collection of the Portland Museum of Art

Gift of William Greenbaum. 1995.51.2

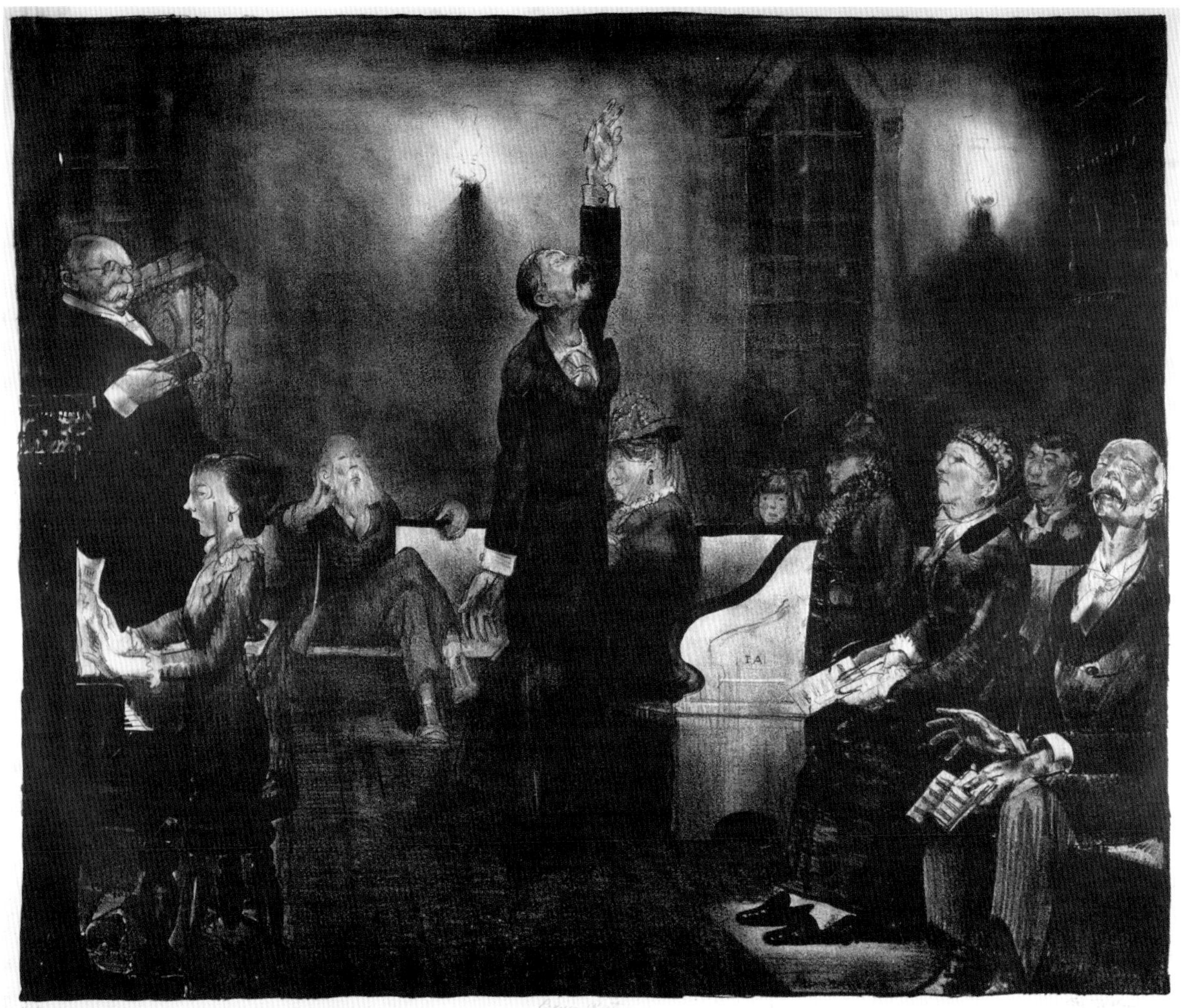

Plate 18

George Bellows (1883–1925), *Prayer Meeting, 2nd Version*,

1916, lithograph, 18 1/4 x 22 1/4 in.

printed by George C. Miller, New York

Courtesy of John M. Day

with Henri and all but Sloan followed him to Monhegan, Kent spending almost five years there from 1905, along with later sojourns. In addition to Monhegan scenes, Hopper depicted several other places along the Maine coast, including Rockland, Portland, and Ogunquit. Among his etchings of the 1920s, Hopper depicted travelers on the Monhegan boat, and *The Lighthouse (Maine Coast)* (Plate 19), an iconic view of the Nubble, off the coast at York, that includes an artist sketching at lower right. Hopper clearly acknowledged the enforced simplicity and strong contrasts of his earlier etchings as a critical influence on his classic painting style.

After first studying law, Paul Dougherty (1877–1947) went on to study with Henri and maintained studios in both New York and Europe until 1930, when he moved to California for the rest of his life. He first visited Monhegan in 1905 and became widely known for his many scenes of the rocky Maine coast, exemplified in his undated monotype *Surf* (Plate 20), almost certainly depicting the rocks of Monhegan. It is a strong reminder of the constant presence for every subsequent artist of Winslow Homer's late paintings of sea meeting rock at Prouts Neck. The hybrid medium of monotype, which mixes painterly freedom with the unpredictable effects of a printing process, seems a suitable choice for the dynamic subject.

A bold use of color is a trademark of the woodcuts of Margaret Jordan Patterson (1867–1950), who was born in Java to Maine parents (her father was a ship captain) and spent her early years in Maine and Boston. She attended Pratt Institute and probably studied with the influential Ipswich artist Arthur Wesley Dow, who was strongly influenced by the aesthetic of Japanese printmaking. Patterson learned the multi-block Japanese woodcut technique from Ethel Mars in 1911, during a period of European study. An art teacher in public and private schools in the Boston area for the rest of her life, Patterson executed a number of paintings and watercolors of the Maine coast, ranging in date from 1903 to 1923. *Monhegan Harbor, Maine* (Plate 21—sometimes called *Old Fish House, Monhegan*) probably dates from the late 1910s, and apparently is the only one of her woodcuts of an identifiable Maine scene. At this time, she began to print her line block in lavender, blue, or gray, as opposed to the normal use of black. At least four other colors seem to have been used (blue, pink, yellow, and purple) to fill in the subject, though the artist's skill in overlaying colors and the transparency of the watercolor inks make a definite count difficult.

The most radical transformations spurred by European innovations are visible in this survey in the cubist- and expressionist-inspired dislocations in the prints of Walt Kuhn, Marguerite and William

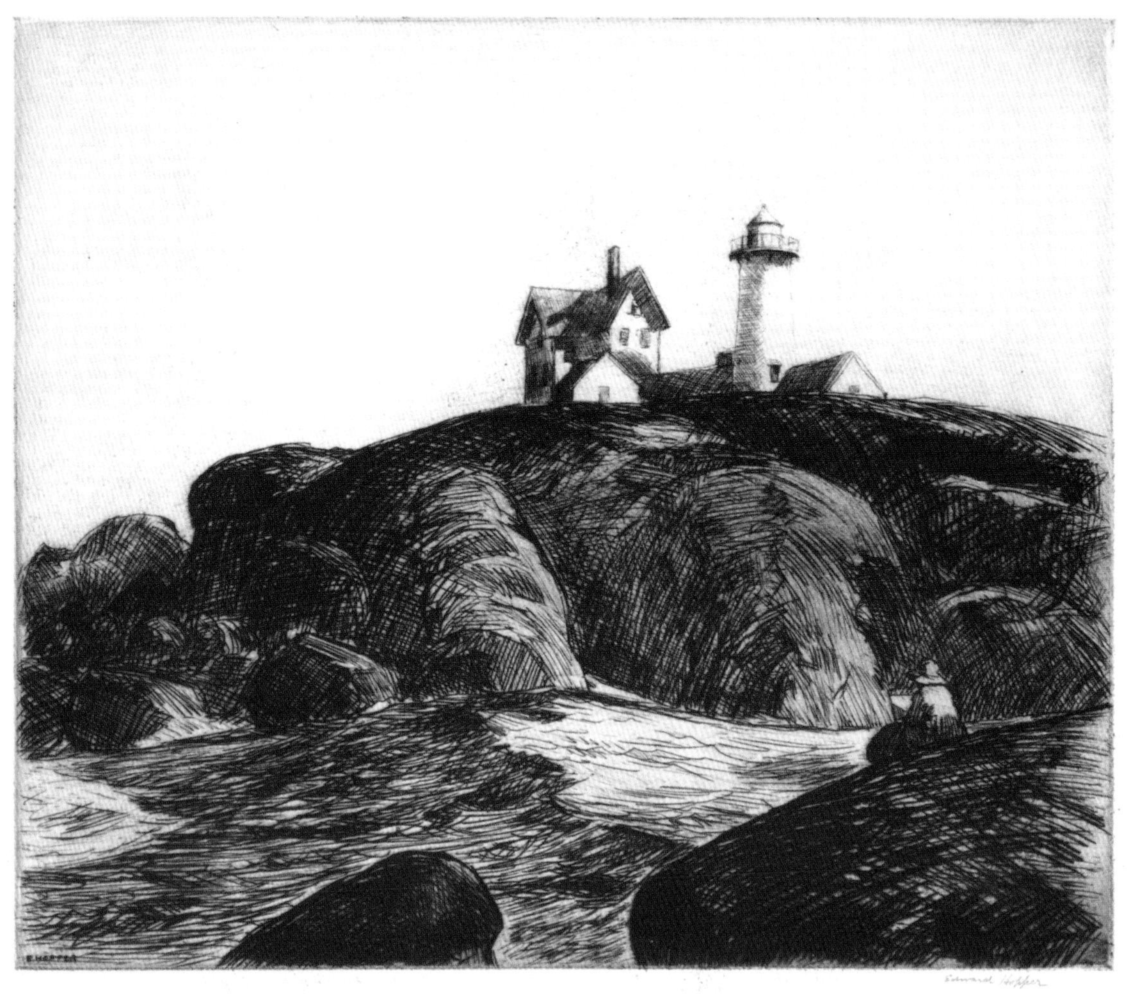

Plate 19

Edward Hopper (1882–1967), *The Lighthouse (Maine Coast),* 1923, etching, 10 x 12 in.
Collection of the Philadelphia Museum of Art
Purchased with the Thomas Skelton Harrison Fund, 1941. 1941-53-498

Zorach, and Marsden Hartley. All of them had spent considerable time studying in Europe and mixing in avant-garde circles there and in New York. They were familiar with Alfred Stieglitz's pioneering exhibitions of such artists as Matisse as early as 1908 and Picasso in 1911 in his 291 Gallery in New York, as well as with the influential Armory Show of 1913, shown in New York, Chicago, and Boston, which was the first large-scale American exhibition of progressive European painting and printmaking and included works by Cézanne, Picasso, Matisse, Kandinsky, and Duchamp, among many others.

Walt Kuhn (1877–1949) was one of the chief organizers of the Armory Show, traveling through Europe in 1911 choosing works for it. From 1915 to 1927 he experimented fairly extensively in etching, drypoint, and lithography, while not editioning a large number of images. Kuhn was part of the community of progressive artists who summered in Ogunquit, many of them in the circle around Hamilton Easter Field. Kuhn's modest but affecting drypoint simply called *Maine* of about 1917 (Plate 22) is a perfect example of an artist using a copper plate as a sketch pad, quickly scratching in the scene with a sharp needle, very different from the careful delineations of the etching "revivalists" of the previous century. Kuhn's flattened depiction of a cabin, fence, and landscape becomes an expressionist composition of line and tone.

William (1889–1966) and Marguerite (1887–1968) Zorach, who had met during their European art studies and then moved to New York after their marriage, first ventured into printmaking during summer stays in New England, especially Provincetown. Both artists executed a number of simple woodcuts and linocuts, few of which were printed in any numbers—some were very informal invitations or birth announcements. Executed during their first visit to Maine in 1919, William Zorach's *Sailing (Stonington, Maine)* (Plate 23) is a dramatic, sharply black-and-white composition in which negative and positive spaces combine in a vibrant pattern. The simplified waves swirling around the boat are both decorative and solidly sculptural. Indeed, it is thought that the practice of cutting his wood and linoleum blocks contributed decisively to his move into sculpture in 1923, the year the family purchased a home in Robinhood. Marguerite Zorach's 1927 lithograph, *Boats at Dock* (Plate 24), one from a group printed by George Miller, seems perhaps to be reminiscent of their Provincetown sojourns, with its more detailed composition incorporating a tower similar to that town's Pilgrim Monument. A cubist vocabulary of shifting planes and ambiguous spaces animates the composition, carefully rendered with a soft lithographic crayon.

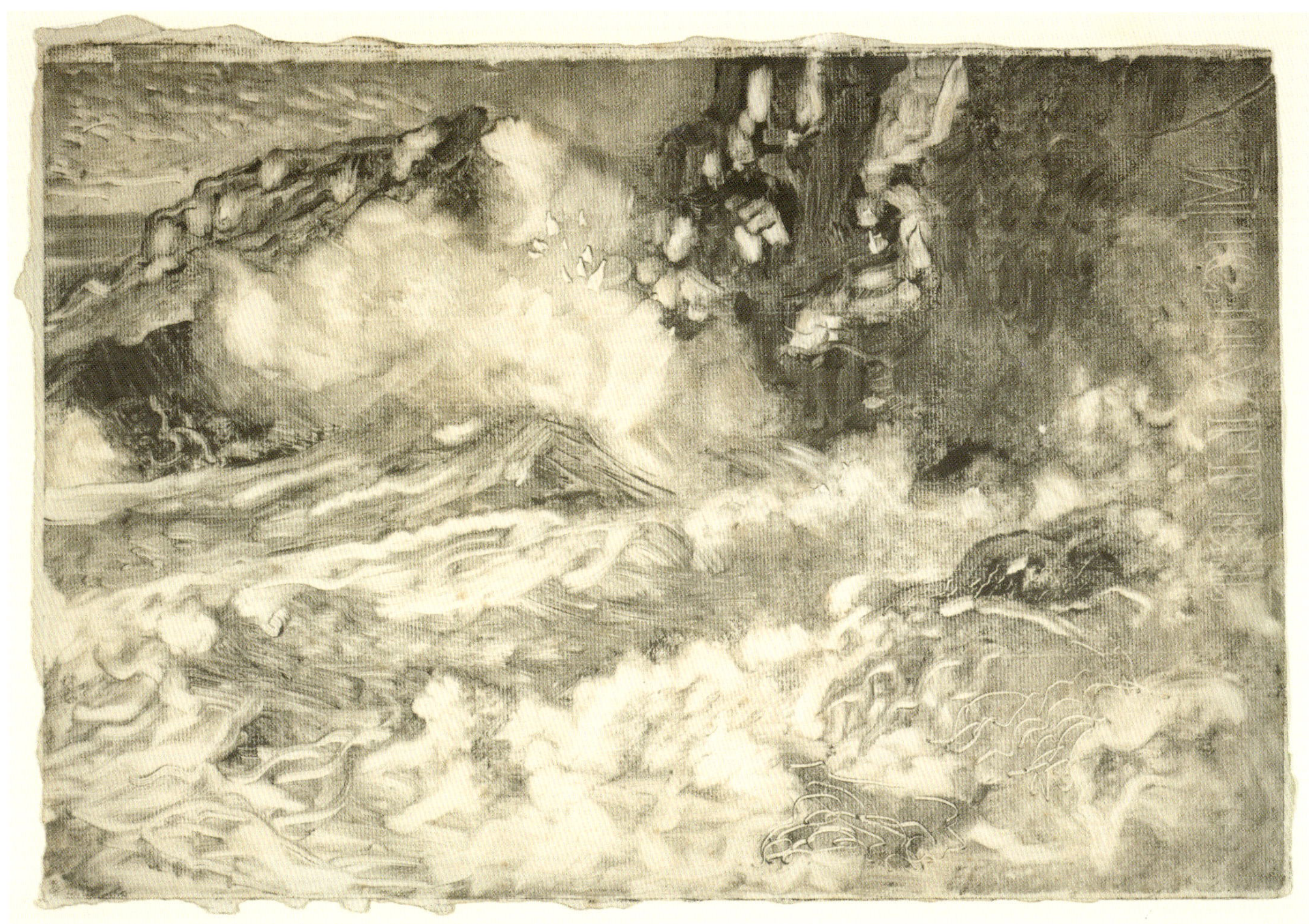

Plate 20

Paul Dougherty (1877–1947), *Surf*, ca. 1920

monotype, 10 3/8 x 15 3/4 in.

Collection of the Fogg Art Museum, Harvard University Art Museums

Anonymous loan in honor of David P. Becker. 9.1991

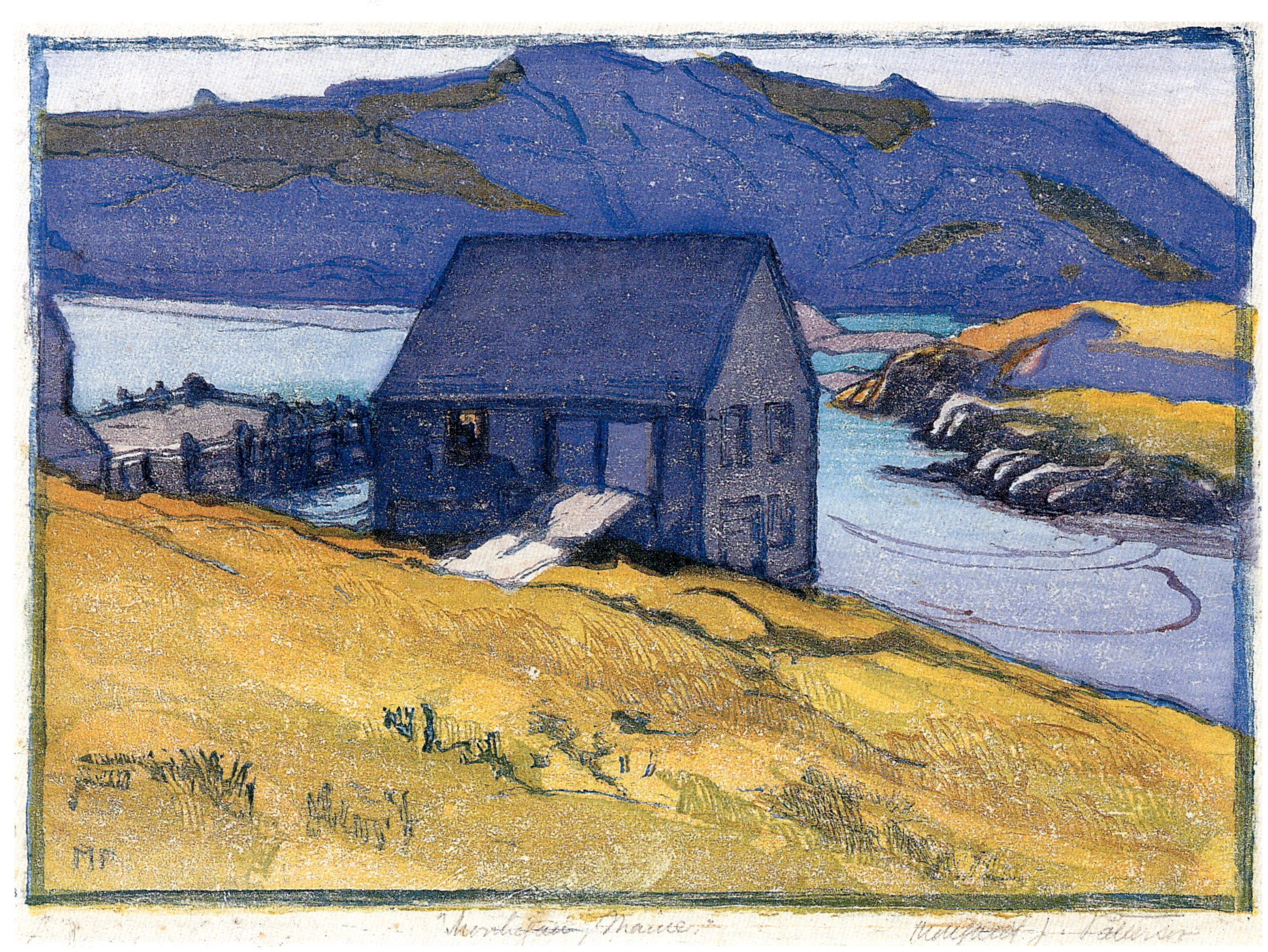

Plate 21

Margaret Jordan Patterson (1867–1950), *Monhegan Harbor, Maine*, n.d., color woodcut, 7 13/16 x 10 7/16 in.
Collection of the Farnsworth Art Museum
Gift of Mr. and Mrs. Leo Meissner,
Cape Elizabeth, Maine, 1971. 71.1795.54

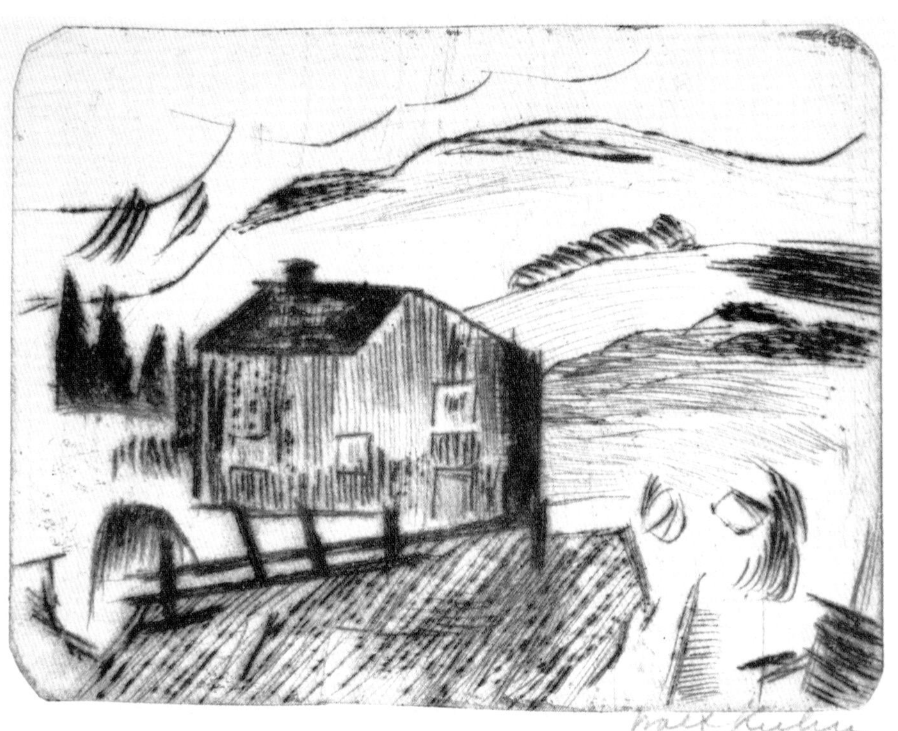

Plate 22

Walt Kuhn (1877–1949), *Maine*, ca. 1917

drypoint, 3 5/8 x 4 7/8 in.

Courtesy of the Burk Collection

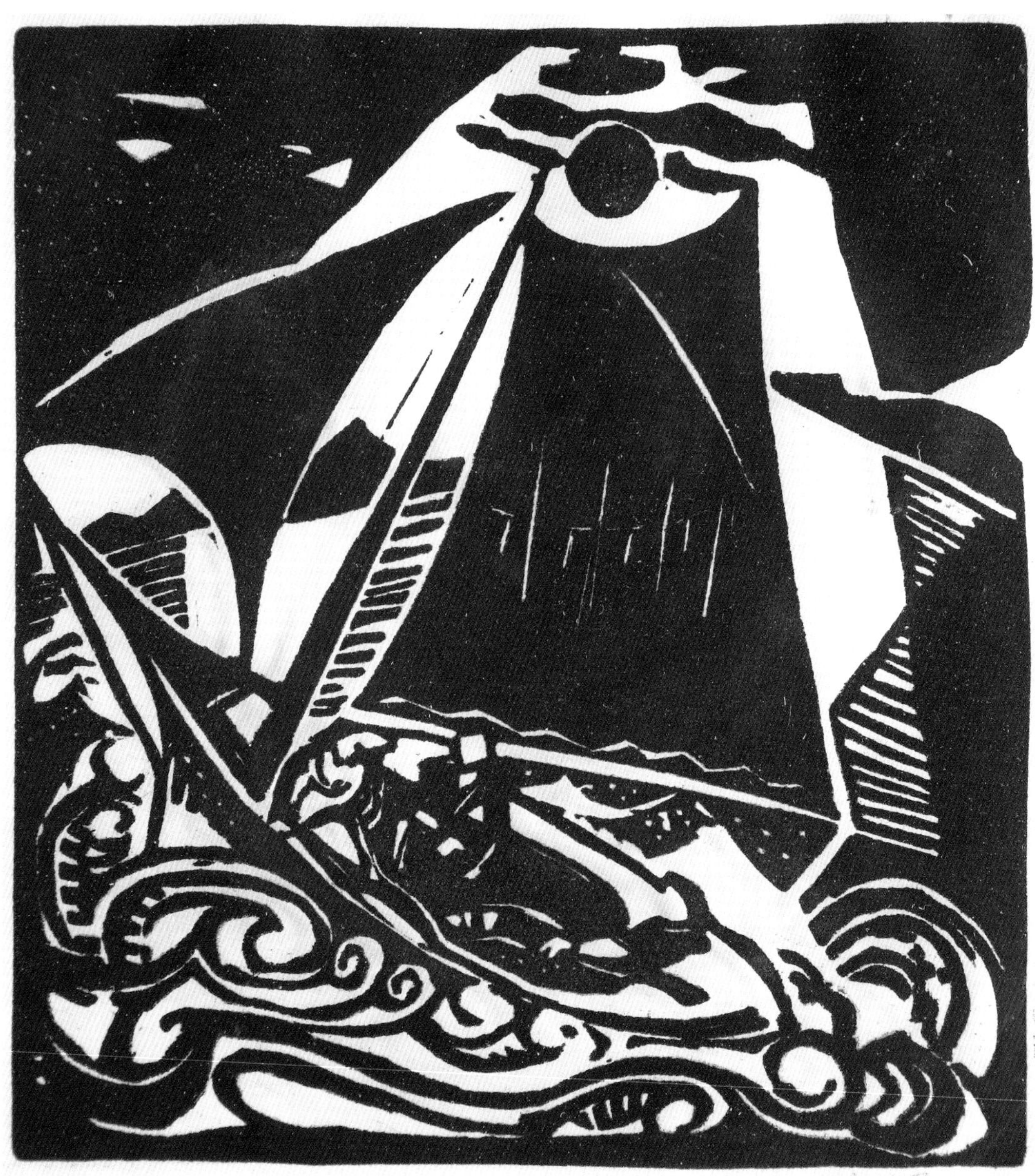

Plate 23

William Zorach (1889–1966)

Sailing (Stonington, Maine), 1919

linocut, $7\,^{1}/_{8}$ x $6\,^{1}/_{2}$ in.

Private Collection

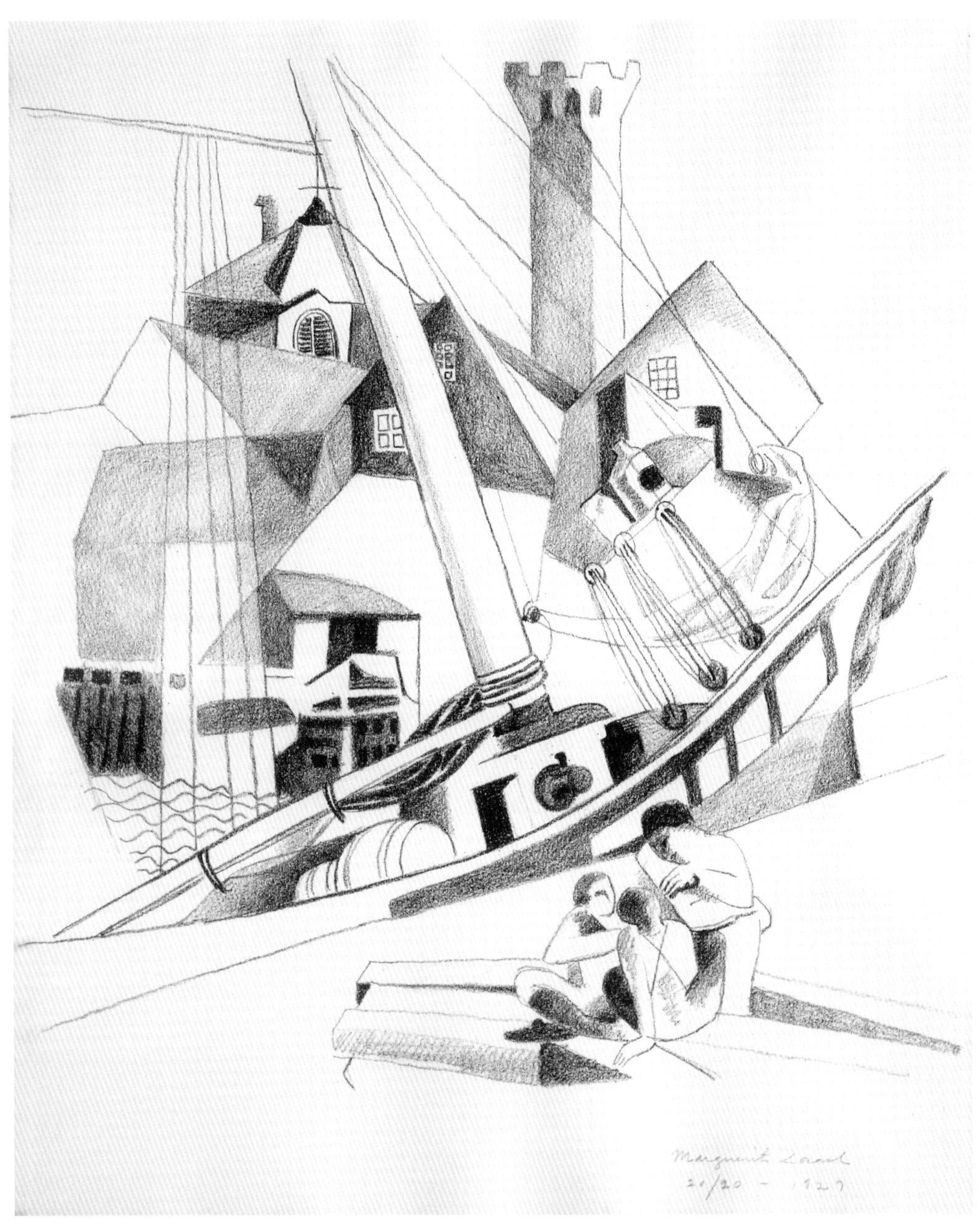

Plate 24

Marguerite Zorach (1887–1968), *Boats at Dock*, 1927
lithograph, 16 1/4 x 13 3/4 in.
printed by George C. Miller, New York
Private Collection

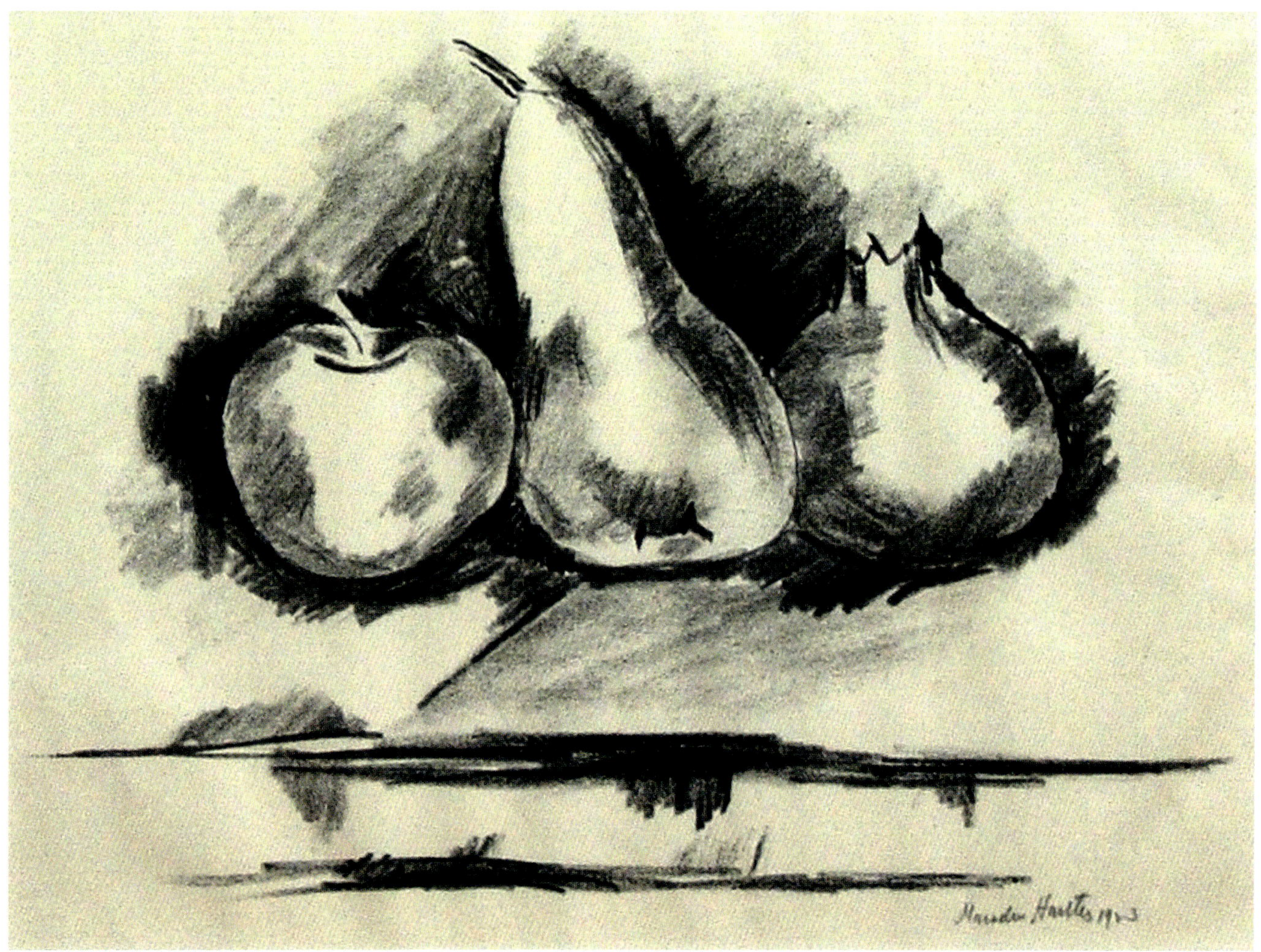

Plate 25

Marsden Hartley (1877–1943), *Pomegranate, Pear, Apple,* 1923

lithograph, 11 x 15 in.

Collection of the University of Maine Museum of Art

Gift of Adeline and Caroline Wing. 53.26.G

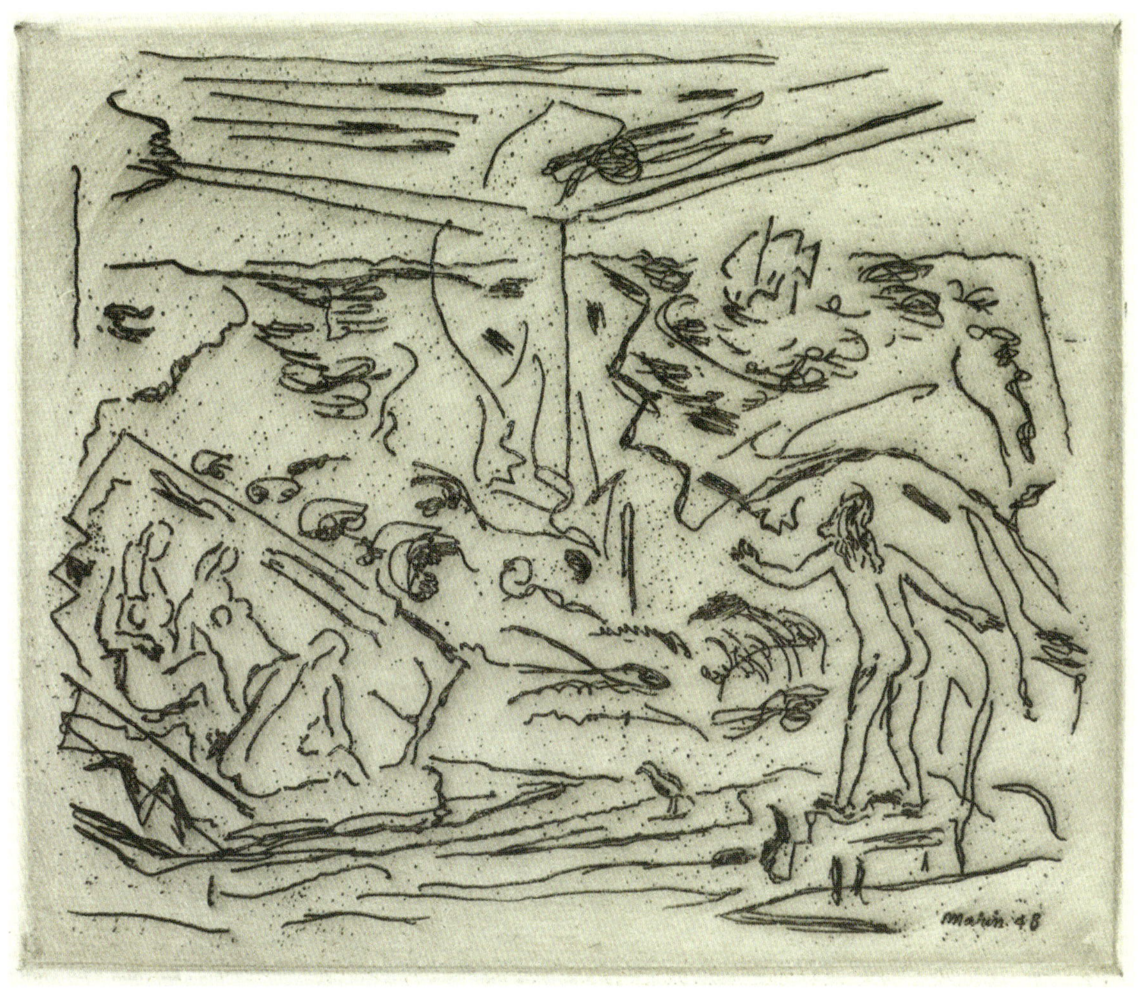

Plate 26

John Marin (1870–1953), *Sea with Figures No. 1*,

1948, etching, 6 5/8 x 8 in.

Collection of the Philadelphia Museum of Art

The J. Wolfe Golden and Celeste Golden Collection

of Marin Etchings, 1969. 1969-81-129.

Born in Lewiston, Marsden Hartley (1877–1943) grew up there and in Cleveland, Ohio, studying in Cleveland and in New York. A restless man and artist, he variously worked in Europe, New Mexico, Nova Scotia, and Gloucester, often interspersed with stays in Maine, and spent much of the last years of his life in Portland, Bangor, and Corea. Through his long and active career (which included art criticism and poetry), Hartley did only two sets of prints, both during European sojourns, and neither of Maine subjects. In 1923, he executed a group in Berlin of 13 floral and fruit still-life lithographs, including *Pomegranate, Pear, Apple* (Plate 25). Clearly influenced by Cézanne, he manages to monumentalize his three fruits, which, though apparently set on a table, actually seem to float over a surreal, barren landscape. In 1933–34 he executed four lithographed mountain views in Bavaria.

The great majority of nearly 200 innovative etchings by John Marin (1870–1953) are of subjects in Europe and New York, but he had a deep commitment to Maine's landscape, having first visited the state in 1914 at the invitation of Ernest Haskell. He spent almost every summer in the state thereafter, exploring the Bath region, Blue Hill and Stonington, and eventually acquiring a second home in Cape Split. Printmaking for him seemed to be a winter activity, however, and his only Maine subjects are *Sailboat* of 1932 and two motifs explored in 1948–49, a lobsterman heading out to sea and *Sea with Figures*, the first version of which is shown in Plate 26. During the 1930s and 1940s, Marin executed a significant number of rather fantastic works of female nudes disporting themselves by the seashore. Evoking Matisse's dancers and Cézanne's bathers (as well as contemporary dancers such as Isadora Duncan), Marin's compositions also take part in an artistic tradition of anti-puritanism and individual freedom.[3]

After studies at the Art Students League in New York, the painter and printmaker Howard Cook (1901–1980) spent much of the 1920s traveling widely in the U.S., Europe, and Asia. He studied etching with Joseph Pennell and later learned woodcut, wood engraving, and lithographic techniques. He developed a particular graphic strength in his wood engravings of urban architecture and dramatic landscapes, such as those around Taos, New Mexico, where he eventually settled. He spent two summers in Maine, the first in 1926 near Augusta, on Maranacook Lake, which inspired a set of five woodcut illustrations titled "South of Augusta" in the February 1927 issue of *The Forum* magazine. Two years later, he summered on Deer Island in Passamaquoddy Bay, executing a number of etchings and wood engravings in the area. Cook has used a striking skein of closely-laid white lines in the water and sky of his 1928 *Fog in Eastport* (Plate 27) to effectively convey the claustrophobic atmosphere of a thick fog.

NOTES

1. Cadwallader Washburn, "Notes of an Etcher in Mexico and Maine," *The Print Collector's Quarterly*, vol. 1, no. 4 (1911), p. 477.
2. See Richard S. Field, "Introduction to a Study of American Prints 1900–1950," in *American Prints 1900–1950* [exh. cat.] (New Haven: Yale University Art Gallery, 1983), pp. 7–29.
3. See Donna M. Cassidy, "John Marin's Dancing Nudes by the Seashore—Images of the New Eve," *Smithsonian Studies in American Art*, vol. 4, no. 1 (Winter 1990), pp. 70–91.

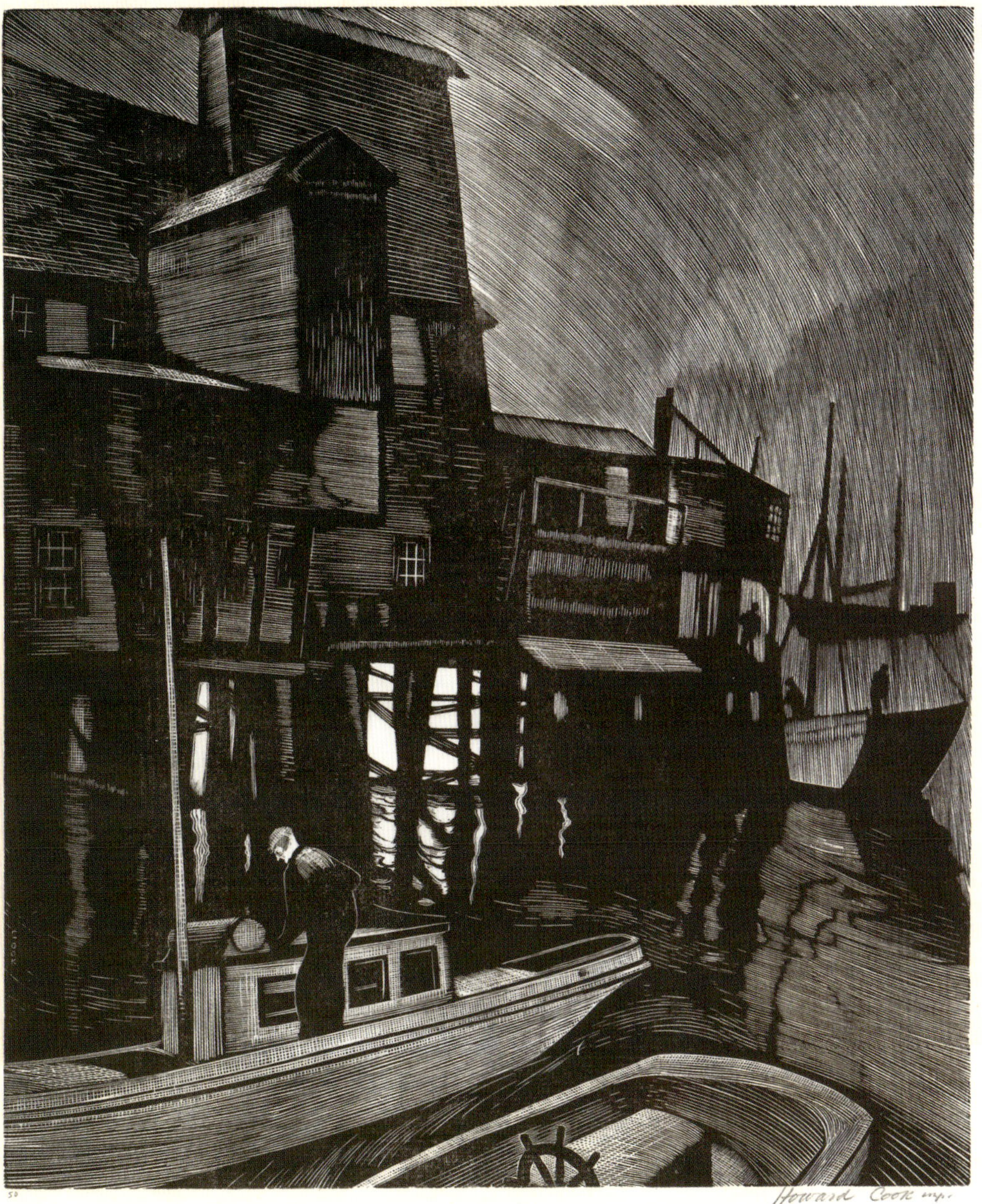

Plate 27

Howard Cook (1901–1980), *Fog in Eastport*, 1928

wood engraving, 12 1/16 x 10 1/8 in.

Collections of the Tides Institute & Museum of Art

Passamaquoddy Fund Acquisition

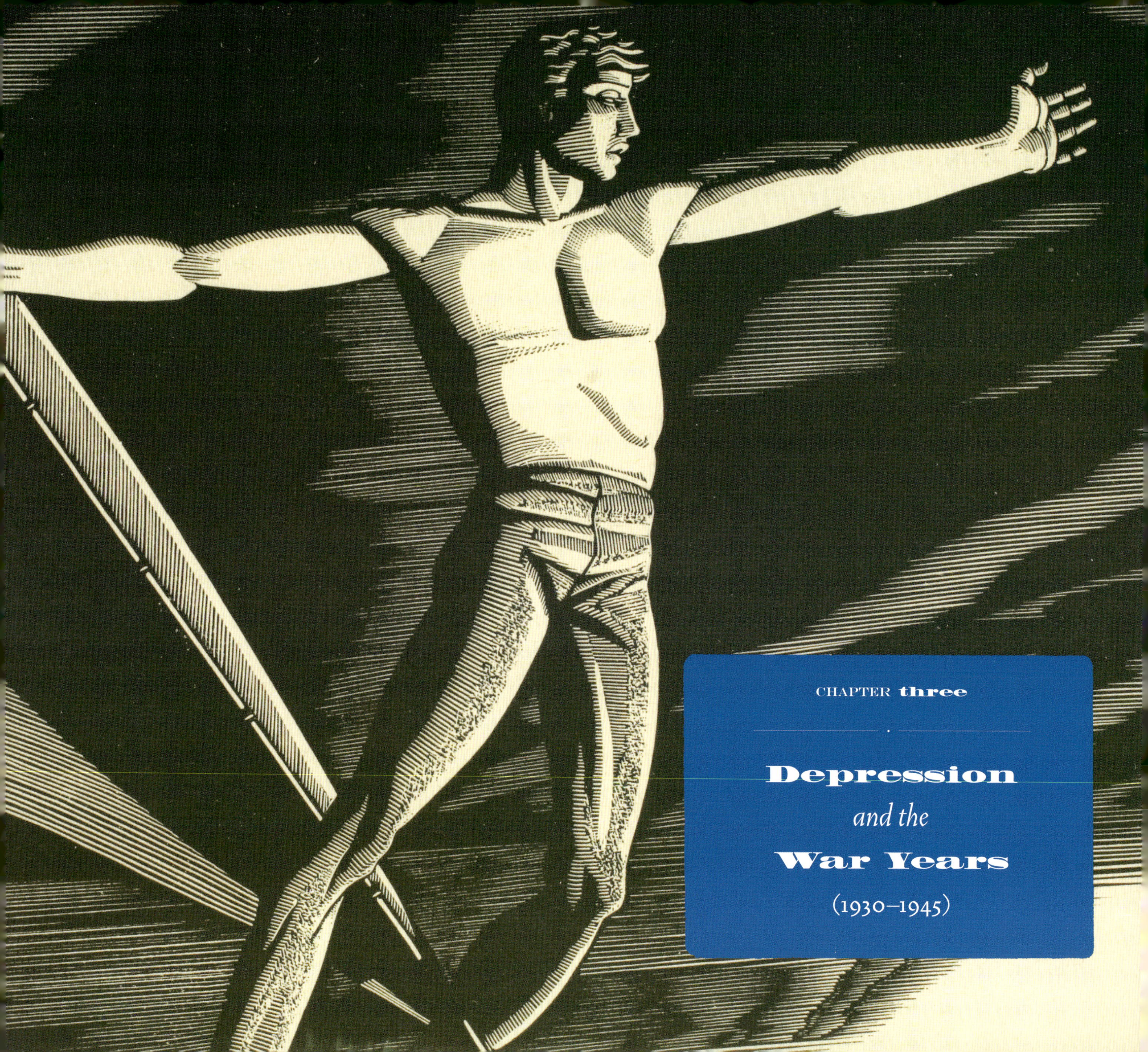

CHAPTER **three**

Depression *and the* War Years

(1930–1945)

The 1930s were years of struggle, both economic and social, throughout the country, with Maine no exception. Printmaking was well poised to reflect the tensions of the period, being at once a very personal (intimate) experience and perhaps the most democratic (public) artistic medium. As artists were struggling to meet their own living needs, there grew up simultaneously a movement of "art for all," for which printmaking was ideally suited. One of the major sources of support for artists was the Federal Arts Project of the Works Progress Administration (WPA), which operated from 1935 to 1943, commissioning thousands of public art works, including murals in post offices and schools, and documenting distinctive forms of local vernacular arts. The Graphic Arts Division of the WPA established a number of printmaking workshops in larger cities, in which hundreds of printmakers created thousands of images. Several associations, most notably Associated American Artists in New York, were formed to supply what reduced art market there was with inexpensive original prints in large quantities. This institutional and economic support also fostered new directions in printmaking media (such as silkscreen) and began to loosen the influence of the traditional aesthetic standards and expand the marketing structures for print artists.[1]

The subject matter of prints reflected two dominant, contrasting motifs at this time: social realism (especially urban and industrial) and a nostalgic preoccupation with idealized themes of traditional American (especially rural) values. The latter trend was strongly reflected in printmaking in Maine, with its primarily rural character and long-established landscape tradition. However, the tensions of the time are sometimes reflected in even the most stereotypical Maine subjects. Without knowing the artist's explicit intentions, it seems possible to interpret *West Quoddy Lighthouse* (Plate 28) by Stevan Dohanos (1907–1994) as a reflection of the national mood of uneasiness. The lighthouse's white beacon of light, the eternal reassurance for mariners, is the only highlight in the markedly dark scene, in which even the bold red and white stripes of the structure are obscured. An Ohio native, Dohanos studied with Stow Wengenroth in Eastport, Maine, at the summer Grand Central School of Art, which had been founded by George Pearse Ennis in the late 1920s. Dohanos also executed a number of wood engravings and lithographs of county fairs, laborers, firehouses, and gritty industrial landscapes around the country, in addition to painting a WPA mural in Florida. He is noted for illustrating over 125 covers for the *Saturday Evening Post*. Other printmakers working in the Eastport area at this time were Ennis himself, Hilton Leech, Nellie Knopf, and Robert Craig.

A non-traditional city view by Dorothy Hay Jensen (1910–1999) portrays *The Million Dollar Bridge* (Plate 29) between Portland and South Portland. (The bridge was replaced by the Casco Bay Bridge in 1997.) In the depths of the Depression, the bridge's nickname (from its supposed original cost) assumes an ironic note, reinforced by the lonely figure camouflaged below the strongly highlighted arches. Born in Cape Elizabeth, Jensen studied printmaking at Smith College, returned to Portland, and enrolled at the School of Art. From 1935 to 1942, she was the director of the WPA Federal Arts Project in Maine, overseeing the work of some forty artists and commissioning a number of public murals and a large series of watercolors for the Index of American Design, a national archive recording vernacular decorative motifs (for Maine, ship carvings, shop figures, and weathervanes). During the 1930s, Jensen executed almost 30 prints, primarily linocuts, including a lively 1937 view of the outdoor farmer's market in Portland. She illustrated at least two children's books, and also wrote the section on the arts for the WPA-sponsored *Portland City Guide* of 1940, which was illustrated by her bridge print and the work of several other local printmakers, including Linwood Easton (1892–1939), Ralph Frizzell (d. 1942), and Josiah Tubby (1875–1958). There was no printmaking division of the WPA in Maine, although a silkscreen poster exists of the Portland Observatory stamped "WPA Maine Arts Project." Two Maine artists who worked in WPA print workshops in New York and Boston respectively were Raymond Skolfield (1909–1996) and Julius Weiss (1912–1978).

Linwood Easton's *White Head-Monhegan* (Plate 30) depicts one of the most classic "monuments" of the Maine coast, portrayed by innumerable artists. His forthright view betrays his participation in the conservative printmaking tradition that continued to appeal to a loyal audience for such fine workmanship. Easton established a considerable national reputation, exhibiting in New York galleries and national juried exhibitions; his view of a shipyard was featured in *Fine Prints of the Year* for 1937. He executed many views of coastal scenes from Scarborough to Lincolnville; several prints also record Portland buildings no longer standing, such as Longfellow's birthplace on Fore Street, and Gerber's Junk Store, an intimate Whistlerian scene reproduced in the *Portland City Guide*.

A 1936 exhibition at the Portland Museum of Art entitled "Portland Printmakers" included several of these local artists, featuring etchings, drypoints, lithographs, and block prints by Jensen, Easton, Tubby, Alice Harmon Shaw, Elsa Libby, Seldom Fox, Rupert Lovejoy, Francis Libby, and Claude Montgomery.

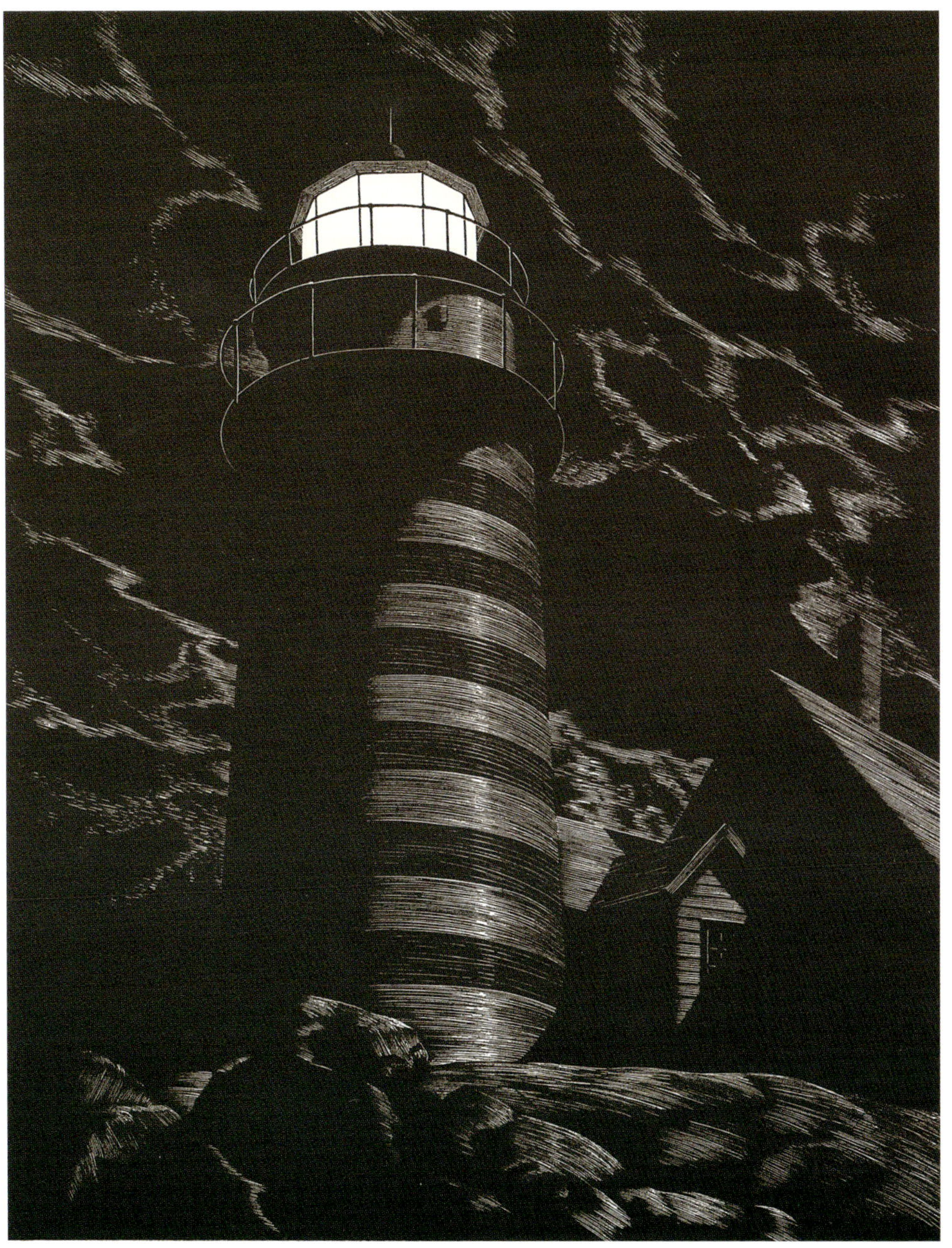

Plate 28

Stevan Dohanos (1907–1994), *West Quoddy Lighthouse*,

ca. 1930, wood engraving, 10 x 7 15/16 in.

Collections of the Tides Institute & Museum of Art

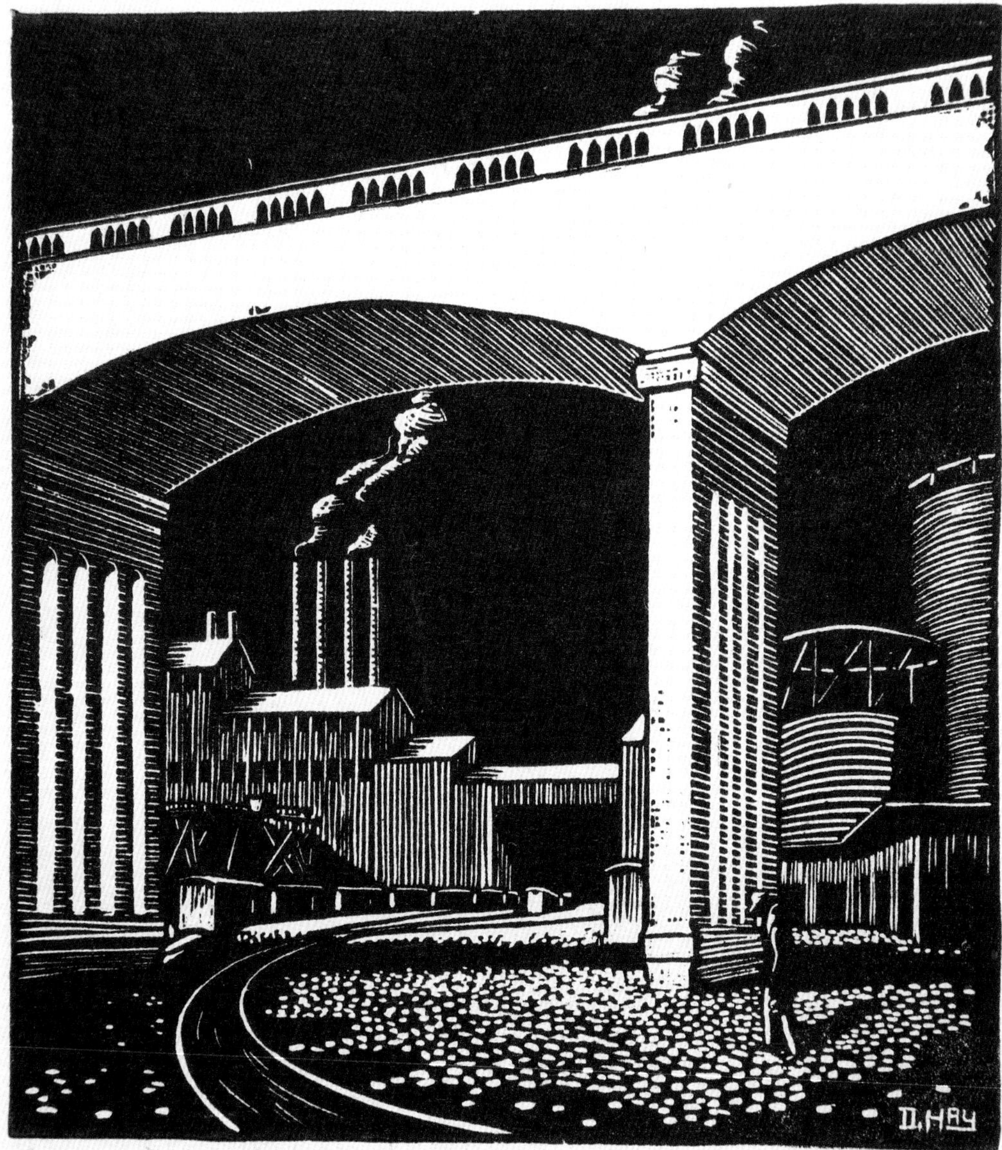

Plate 29

Dorothy Hay Jensen (1910–1999),

The Million Dollar Bridge, 1933, linocut, $6\frac{5}{8}$ x 6 in.

Courtesy of Neil Jensen

Several of the women artists belonged to the Hayloft Society (nicknamed the Haylofters), which met for sketching trips and critiques, a more modern version of the Brush'uns. A lively bohemian art scene in Portland was centered in studios on Congress and Exchange Streets and often included Alfred Morang (1901–1958), a colorful figure who was born in Ellsworth and was a classical violinist in addition to being a painter, writer, and occasional printmaker. In 1939 he settled in Santa Fe, New Mexico.

As already noted, the decade of the 1930s saw a tremendous increase in the so-called "American scene" in art, especially in printmaking. Rural scenes with modest motifs such as barns, churches, village streets, trees, streams, stone walls, and pastoral landscapes were prevalent. Seen by some critics (and artists) as a provincial reaction to modernist (i.e., "European") innovations, this trend represented for others a resurgence of a new style of truly American art. Some representatives of this genre were also reacting to the disastrous economic problems of the world, or even the increasing technological power of the cities.[2] In Maine, this quality is exemplified in the straightforward portrayals of Linwood Easton or Stow Wengenroth, rather than the expressionism of Walt Kuhn or George Bellows.

Despite the artistic upheaval during this period, such traditional printmaking achieved a significant level of public interest, with a large number of artists' and collectors' groups forming to foster the art. Among them were the Society of American Etchers (now the Society of American Graphic Artists [SAGA]), the Woodcut Society, the American Artist Group, the Miniature Print Society, and important print "clubs" in Philadelphia and Cleveland, among other cities.[3] Perhaps the most prominent was the American Institute of Graphic Arts, whose annual juried selection and traveling exhibition of the "Fifty Prints of the Year" was a focus of considerable attention. Aesthetic battles of the era were reflected in the struggles of progressive, modernist printmakers to be included in the "Fifty." Elaborate jurying rules evolved, at times resulting in an awkward annual division into "academic" and "modern" categories.[4]

The lithographs of Stow Wengenroth (1906–1978) are closely identified with the coast of Maine and are quintessential examples of the New England cultural construct. He was inspired to learn lithography while studying with George Pearse Ennis at the summer sessions of the Grand Central School of Art in Eastport. His earliest prints, dating from 1931–32, are a series of darkly rendered scenes in the area. Although he lived in New York (virtually all of his lithographs were printed there by George Miller and his son), Wengenroth returned to Maine almost every summer, variously based in Port Clyde,

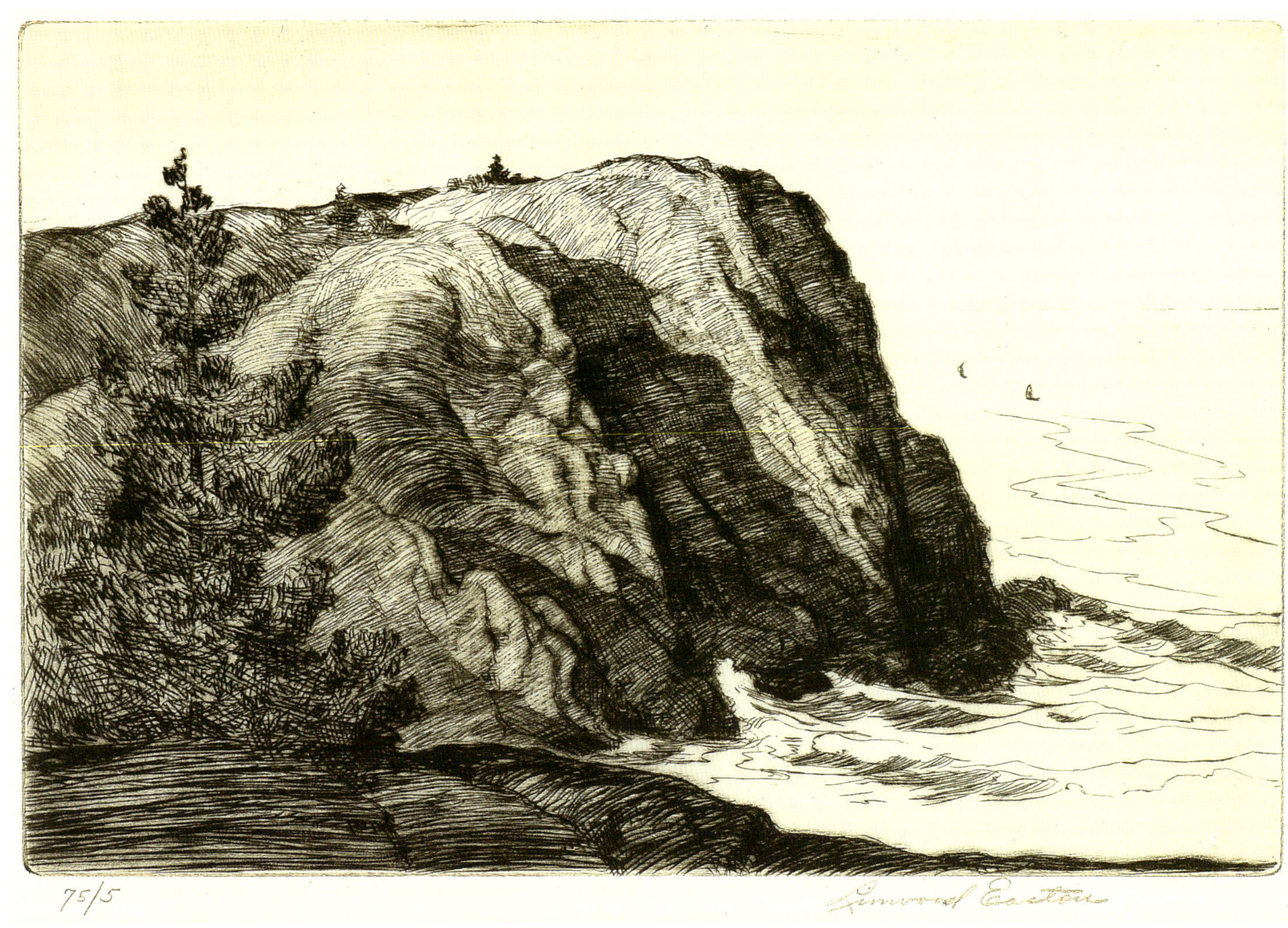

Plate 30

Linwood Easton (1892–1939), *White Head-Monhegan*,

1939, drypoint, 5 7/8 x 8 7/8 in.

Collection of the Portland Museum of Art

Gift of Roger and Katherine Woodman. 1994.23.2

Castine, Boothbay Harbor, Monhegan, Corea, Wiscasset, and Ogunquit. *Meeting House* (Plate 31) is one of his most noted images, an intricately composed interior of a classic New England church in Castine. It is no coincidence that such an iconic vision was drawn during a world war, nor that this print received second prize in the 1942 Metropolitan Museum of Art exhibition in support of the war effort, "Artists for Victory"—of 1,500 works exhibited, 581 were prints, selected from 6,000 submissions. *Meeting House* was the first lithograph in which Wengenroth used a second tone stone of very light greenish-gray in all areas of the print except the white highlights, slightly but very effectively increasing the depth of tone.

The view of Boothbay Harbor (*Street Scene, Maine Village*—Plate 32) of 1934 by John Heagan Eames (1900–2002), rendered in lines of carefully organized clarity, betrays the artist's original training as an architect. After a decade of practice in New York, Eames studied printmaking at the Royal College of Art in London. He spent the 1930s etching architectural views and landscapes in England and France before returning to New York, then eventually settling in Maine (he had spent childhood summers in Boothbay). *Street Scene* offers a fascinating contrast with similar motifs by American-trained printmakers. While thematically reminiscent of the quiet views of Hopper, Wengenroth, or Nason, Eames's vision comes from a different sensibility, derived from the exquisitely crafted draftsmanship perfected by English etcher-engravers such as his teachers Malcolm Osborne and Robert Austin. Eames's clear and delicate depiction of details such as shop signs, shingles, and electrical wires reflects a highly developed control of the etching medium.

Many artists at this time chose the technique of wood engraving to depict rural scenes, perhaps because of that medium's small, intimate scale and its ability to achieve great detail. Among engravers who worked at this time in Maine were Thomas W. Nason (1889–1971), Asa Cheffetz (1896–1965), Julius J. Lankes (1884–1960), Pauline Winchester Inman (1904–1990) and Kevin O'Callahan (1890–1977). Cheffetz cut an intricate scene of the *Fish Pier (Portland, Maine)* in 1935. In addition to creating individual images, Lankes illustrated three of Maine poet Robert P. Tristram Coffin's books. O'Callahan executed a series of strikingly patterned views of a boat under construction and a number of scenes in the Rockland area. Perhaps the two best-known Maine wood engravers, however, were Carroll Thayer Berry (1886–1978) and Leo Meissner (1895–1977).

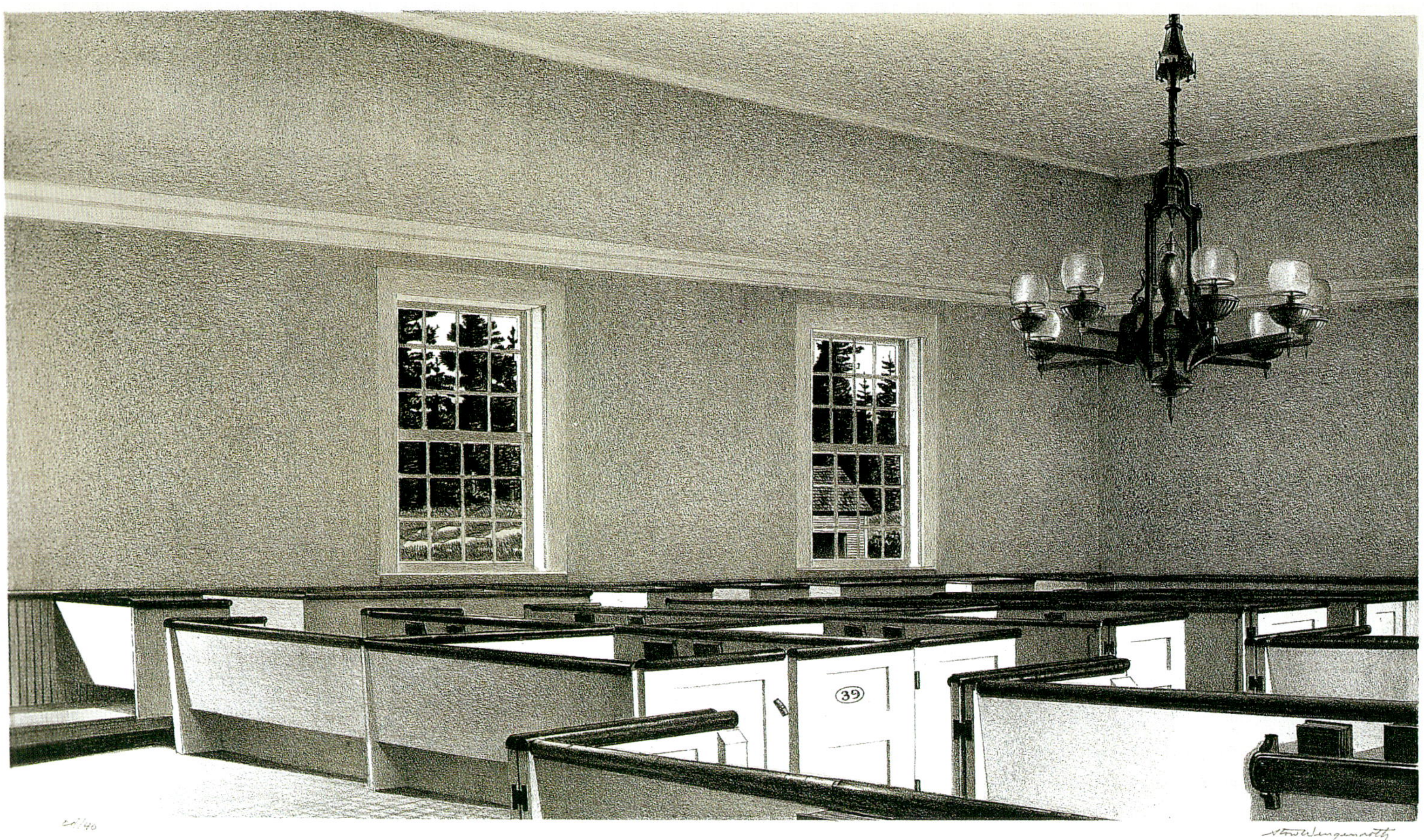

Plate 31

Stow Wengenroth (1906–1978), *Meeting House*, 1940,

lithograph, $9\frac{1}{4}$ x $16\frac{11}{16}$ in.

printed by George C. Miller, New York

Collection of the Boston Public Library, Print Department

Gift of Isabelle S. Knobloch.

Reproduced by permission of the artist's estate

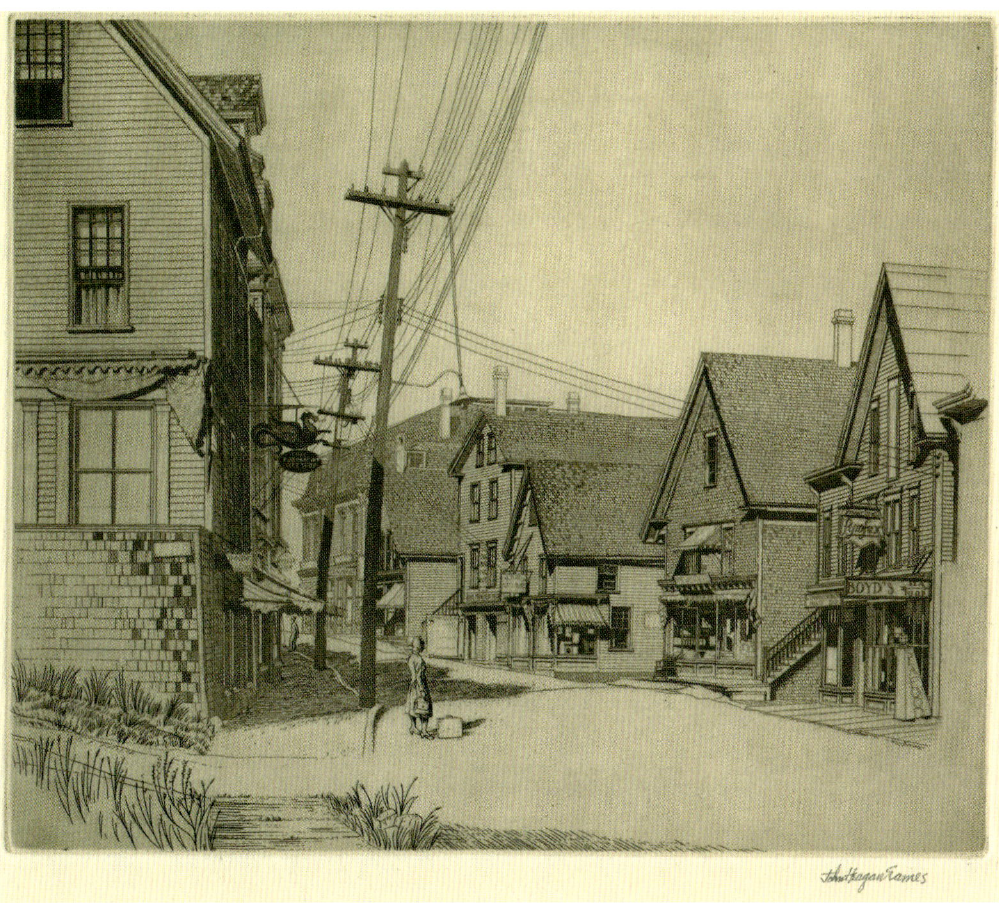

Plate 32

John Heagan Eames (1900–2002), *Street Scene, Maine Village*, 1934, etching, 6 5/8 x 8 in.
Collection of the Bates College Museum of Art
Gift of John Heagan Eames in memory of his wife, Muriel MacMicken Eames. 1992.1.17

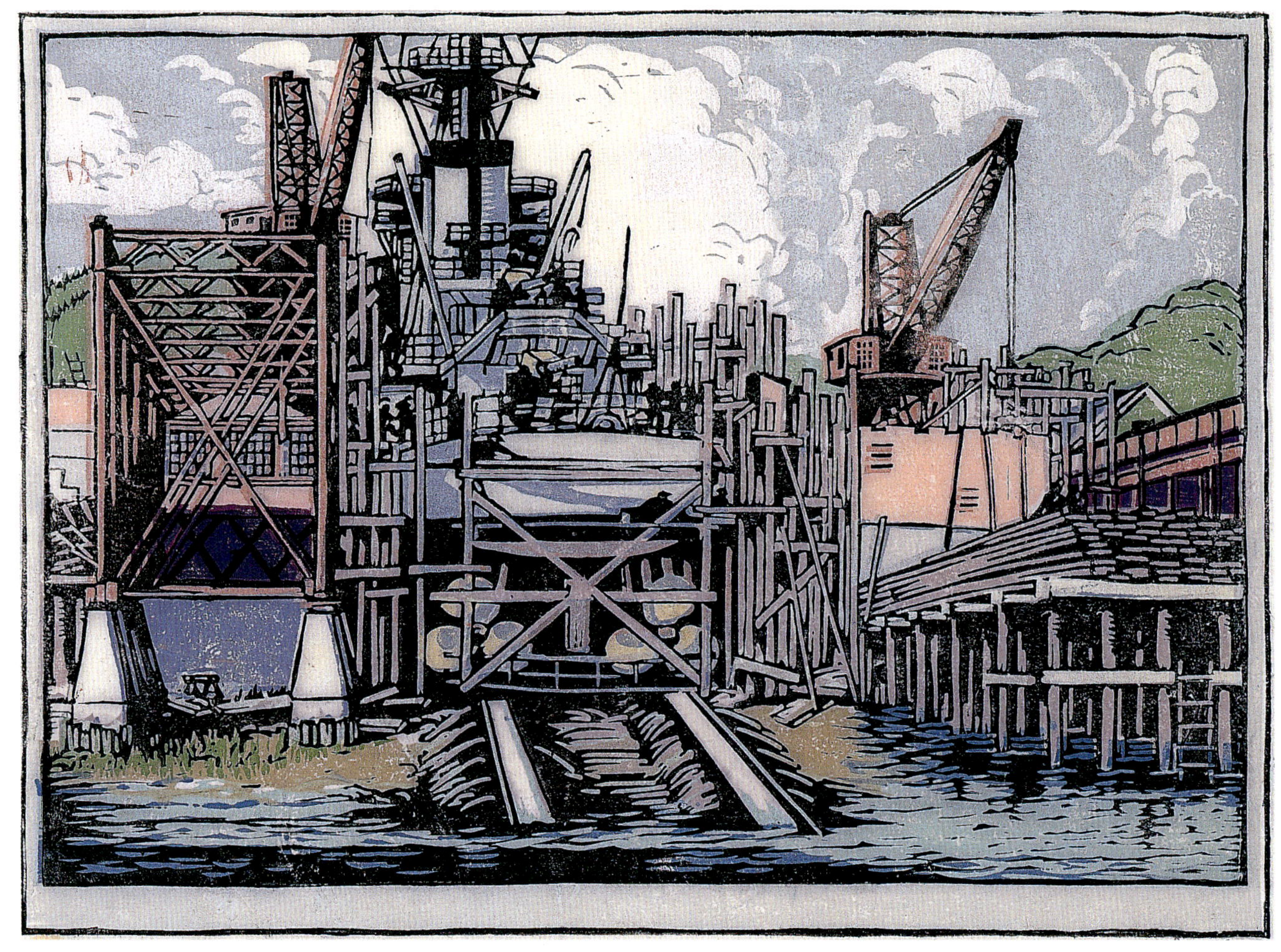

Plate 33

Carroll Thayer Berry (1886–1978), *Destroyer Lamson, Bath Iron Works*, 1935, color linocut, 11 3/4 x 16 1/4 in.
Collection of the Farnsworth Art Museum
Gift of Carroll Thayer Berry, 1971. 71.1777.21

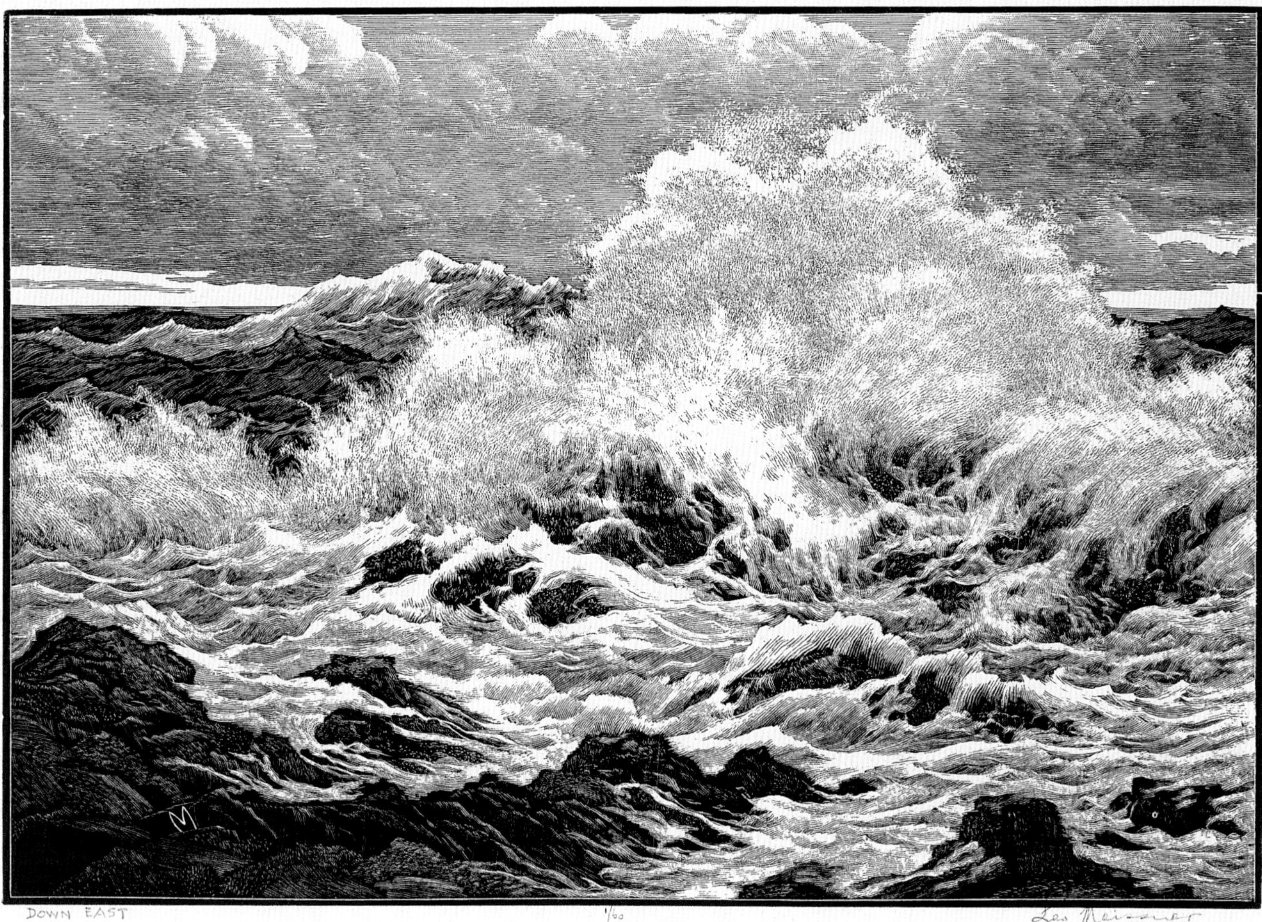

Plate 34

Leo Meissner (1895–1977), *Down East*, ca. 1971–72

wood engraving, 7 1/2 x 10 7/8 in.

Collection of the Farnsworth Art Museum

Gift of Mr. and Mrs. Leo Meissner, Cape Elizabeth, Maine,

1978. 78.63.245

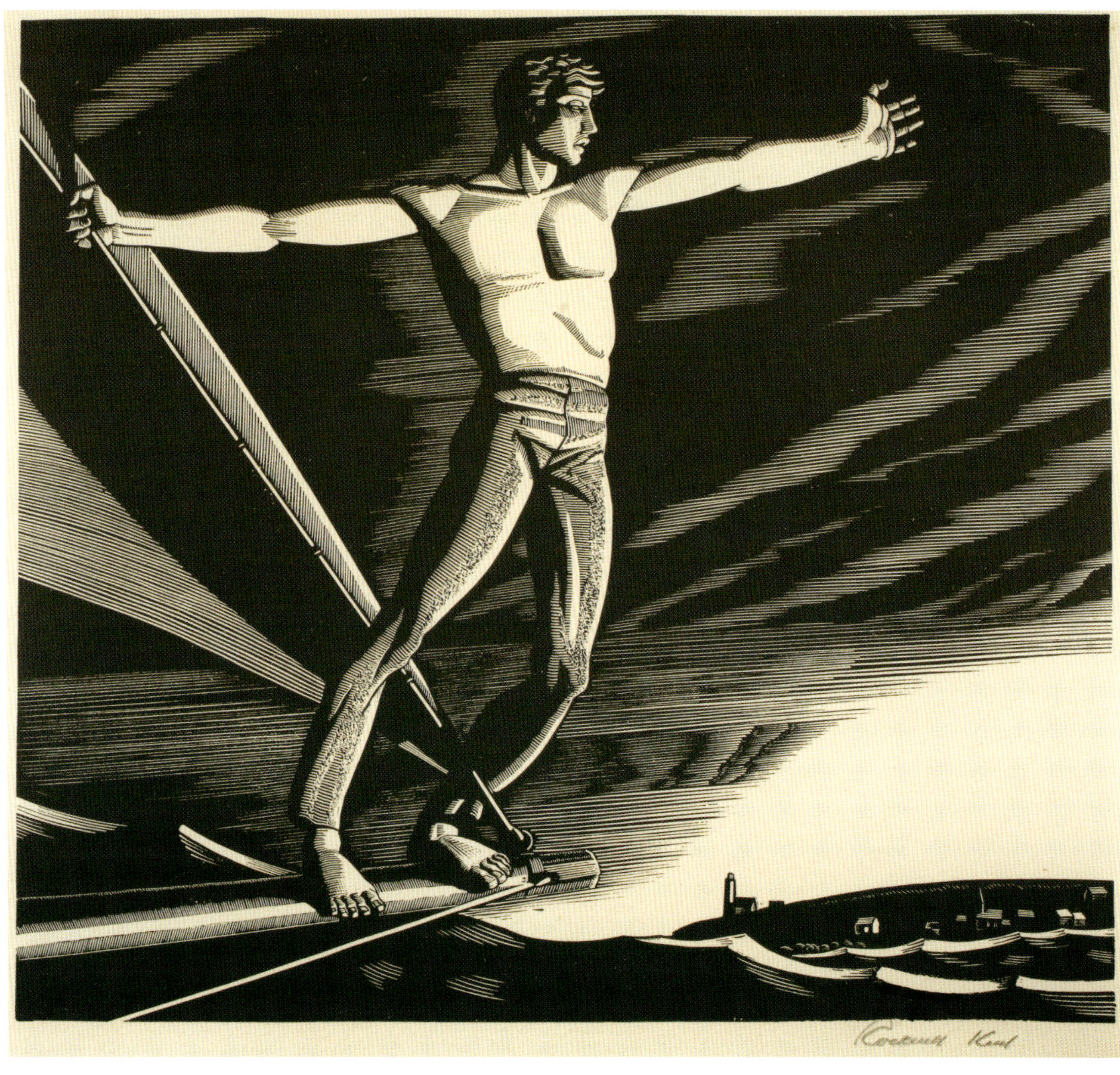

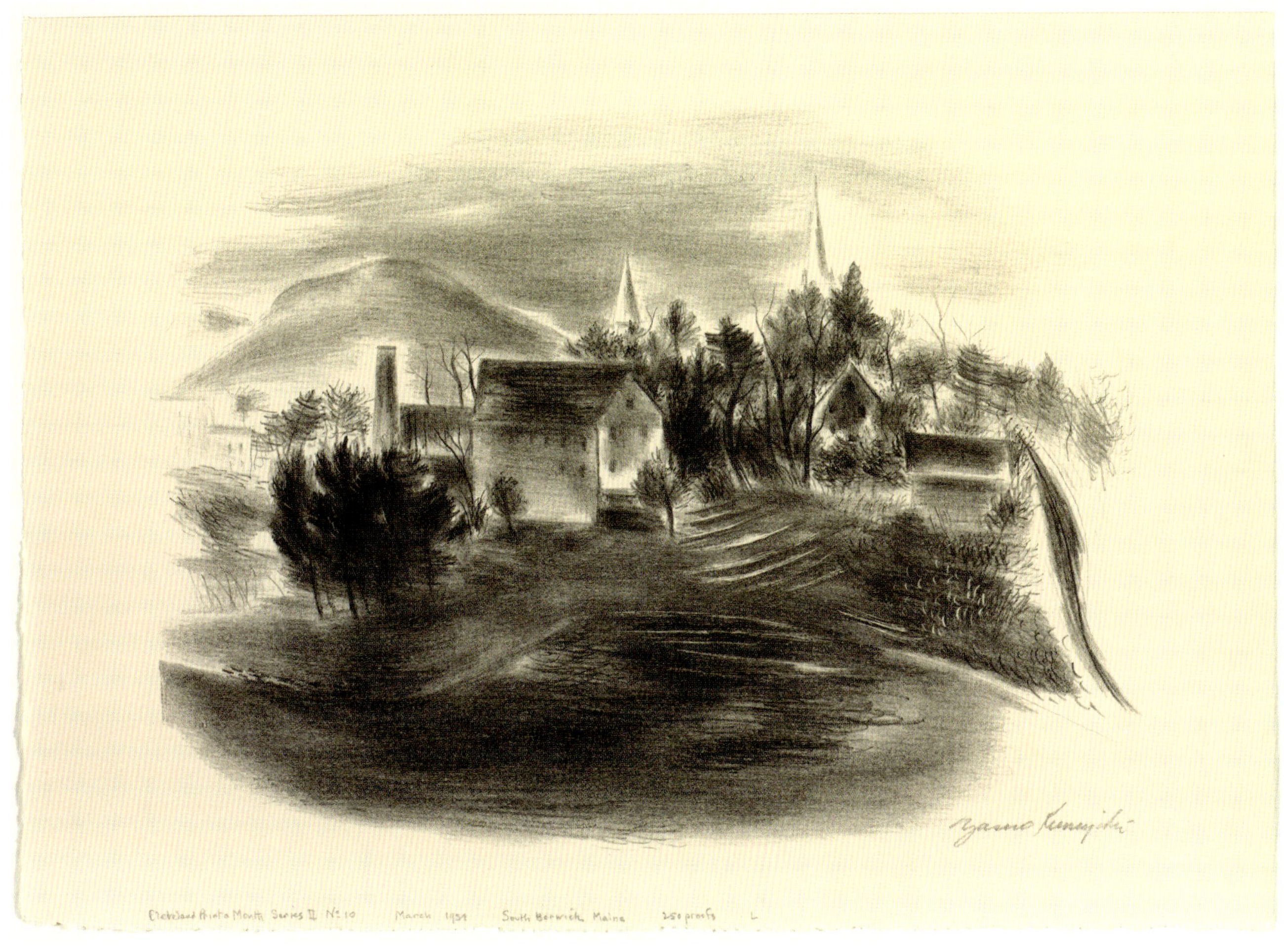

Plate 35

Rockwell Kent (1882–1971), *Home Port*, 1931

wood engraving, 6 1/2 x 7 3/8 in.

Collection of the Bowdoin College Museum of Art

Museum Purchase, Barbara Cooney Porter Fund. 2002.18.

By permission of the Plattsburgh State Art Museum,

Plattsburgh College Foundation, Rockwell Kent Gallery and Collection.

Bequest of Sally Kent Gorton

Plate 36

Yasuo Kuniyoshi (1893–1953), *South Berwick, Maine*, 1934

lithograph, 9 x 12 1/2 in.

published by Cleveland Print Makers

Collection of the Philadelphia Museum of Art

Purchased with the Lola Downin Peck Fund from the

Carl and Laura Zigrosser Collection, 1974. 1974-24-120.

Born in New Gloucester and raised in Portland, Berry trained as an engineer before turning to illustration in 1915 in New York and Chicago. Returning to Maine in 1932, he lived in Wiscasset and Rockport, devoting his career to paintings and prints of coastal villages, fishing boats, lighthouses, and rocky cliffs. His color linocut *Destroyer Lamson—Bath Iron Works* of 1935 (Plate 33) is, however, an atypical coastal scene portraying the largest shipyard in the state. Done early in his printmaking career, this image is printed in nine rather psychedelic colors.[5] After about 1950, Berry worked exclusively in woodcut and engraving for both his black-and-white and color prints.

Leo Meissner's *Down East* (Plate 34), though dating from the early 1970s, is a consistent example of his carefully executed realism. He was born in Detroit and studied there and in New York at the Art Students League. His earliest prints are linocuts from 1924, but ten years later Meissner switched exclusively to wood engraving. In addition to his favored subject of sea and surf along the Maine coast, especially Monhegan, he portrayed views of the southwest and, elsewhere in New England, urban scenes, still lifes, and tree studies. *Down East* is a tour de force of engraving detail and tonality, affording an interesting contrast in printmaking media with Paul Dougherty's monotype of the identical motif (see Plate 20).

Despite the prevalence of nostalgic scenes in wood engraving, as with most such categorizations, there are not always clear lines of demarcation between "modern" and "not modern," as exemplified by the prints and illustrations of Rockwell Kent (1882–1971). Kent first visited Maine in 1905, spending several years on Monhegan and returning a number of times throughout his life. In between his later wilderness journeys to such severe landscapes as Greenland, Alaska, Newfoundland, and Tierra del Fuego, Kent forged an enormously successful career as an author and illustrator (*Moby Dick* and *Candide* being among his most famous book projects). He utilized the sharp lines and strong contrasts of black-and-white wood engraving for his preferred print medium, though he also executed many lithographs. *Home Port* of 1931 (Plate 35) is one of twelve illustrations commissioned by the American Car and Foundry Company for a national magazine campaign advertising its motor yacht division. Kent's dramatic and smoothly delineated compositions were an influential presence in the advertising world, promoting a streamlined, industrial aesthetic.[6] *Home Port* echoes a theme of hope with the portrayal of an emerging dawn over an archetypal coastal village.

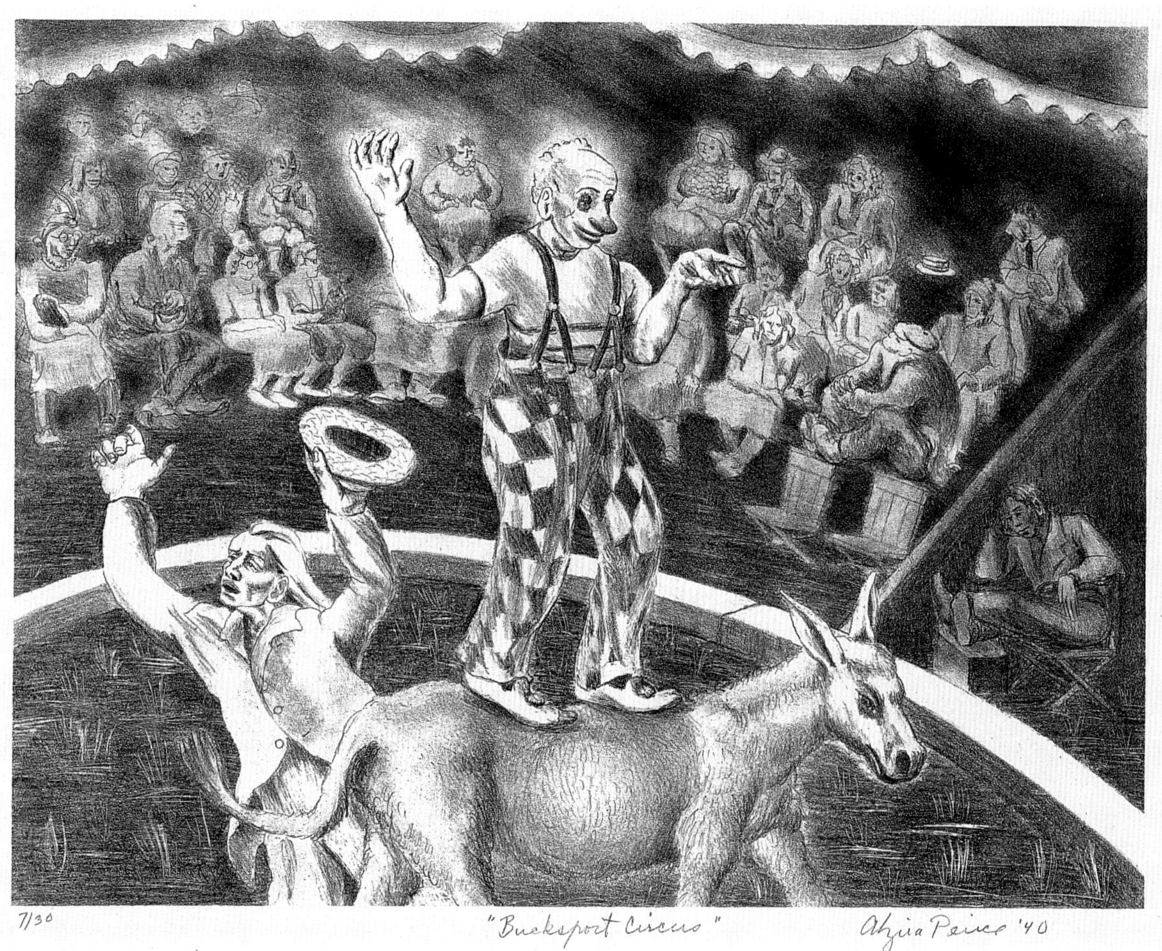

Plate 37

Alzira Peirce (b. 1908), *Bucksport Circus*, 1940

lithograph, 11 3/8 x 15 1/8 in.

Collection of the Farnsworth Art Museum

Gift of Anna Peirce, 1984. 84.8

Further modern takes on the Maine landscape at this time are seen in the flashing boldness of Jan Matulka's (1890–1972) lithograph of 1925 entitled *Sunrise (Landscape from Maine)* or the magic realism of Kyra Markham's (1891–1967) 1934 lithograph *Ogunquit Beach*, a disconcerting, uninhabited vision of a usually crowded space. Louis Lozowick (1892–1973) executed at least three lithographs of the Maine coast from 1939 to 1946, including an amusing view of himself and his wife sunbathing in the nude on the Monhegan rocks. The view of *South Berwick, Maine* of 1934 (Plate 36) by Yasuo Kuniyoshi (1893–1953) is an unsentimental, cubist-inspired treatment of a classic New England village. Born in Japan, Kuniyoshi studied in Los Angeles and New York and spent many summers in Ogunquit art circles, first visiting with Hamilton Easter Field in 1918.

A more personal view of life in Maine at this time is afforded by the prints of Alzira Peirce (b. 1908), Barbara Cooney (1917–2000), and Peggy Bacon (1895–1987). Peirce studied in New York and painted two murals for the WPA in the Ellsworth and South Portland post offices. Little is known of her printmaking activity, but *Bucksport Circus*, 1940 (Plate 37) is an amused view into small-town life, represented by audience and performers in a traveling circus clown act. Her husband, the Bangor-born painter Waldo Peirce (1884–1970), also executed a number of lithographs.

Cooney's *Island Home* (Plate 38) reveals her deeply skilled abilities as a famed illustrator of more than 100 children's books (several of which she also authored), though she maintained that she made picture books "for people, not children." Her most famous books with Maine settings are *Island Boy* and *Miss Rumphius*. *Island Home* is a somewhat realistic view of a teeming lobsterman's home and family perched on the edge of the rocky coast, that seems to encapsulate a great many stories itself. It was executed early in her career, in about 1940 as she was studying lithography and etching at the Art Students League in New York. Born in Brooklyn, New York, she summered in Maine as a child and eventually settled permanently in Damariscotta.

Peggy Bacon had early decided on a career as an illustrator, also studying at the Art Students League (crediting John Sloan as her most influential teacher). She illustrated more than 60 books (19 of which she also wrote) and became noted for her caricature portraits, many of which were drawn of her artistic circle. After a number of years living in the artists' colony around Woodstock, New York, Bacon and her husband, Alexander Brook, spent the first of several summers in Ogunquit in 1941, the year

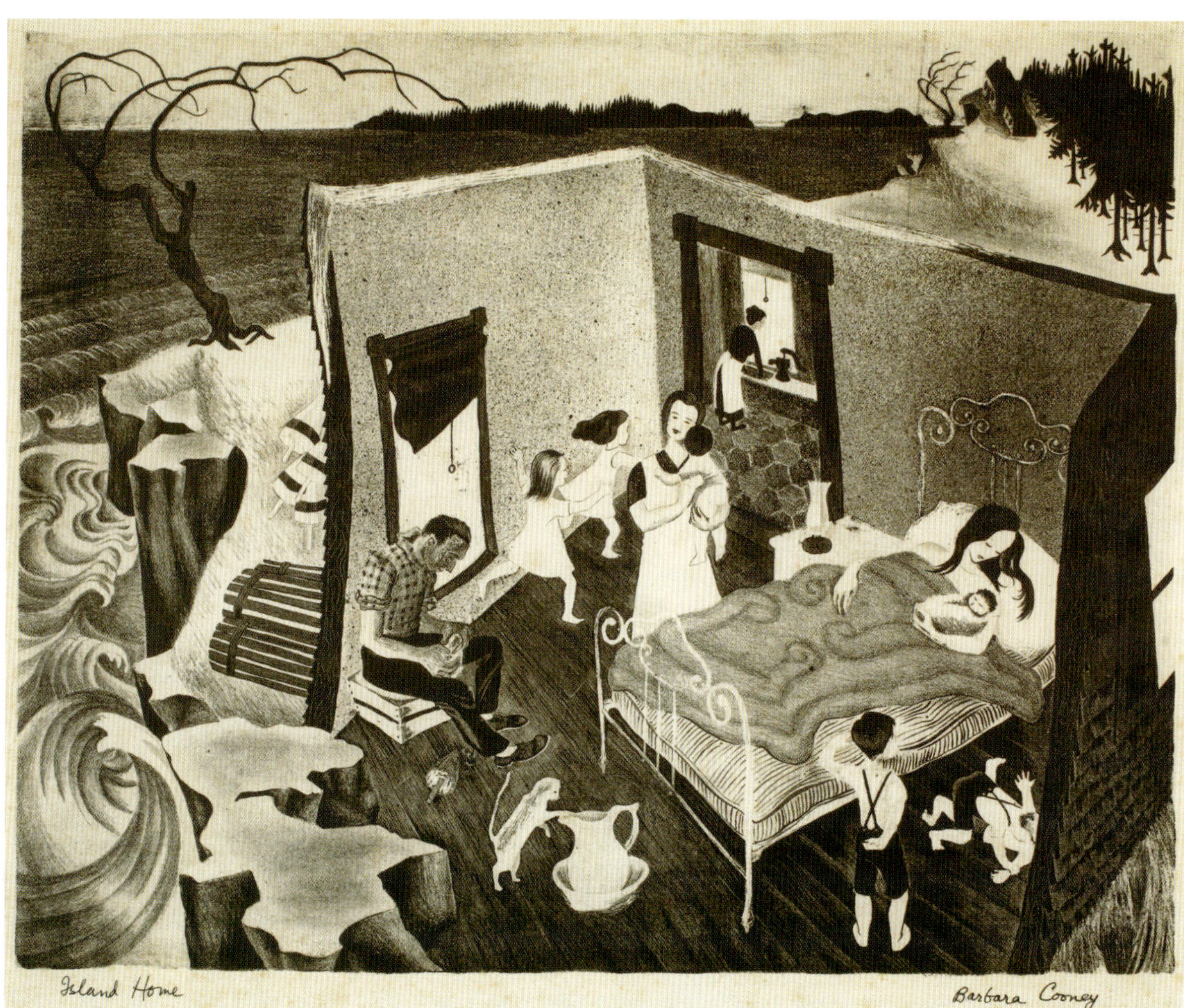

Plate 38

Barbara Cooney (1917–2000), *Island Home*, ca. 1940

lithograph, 11 1/16 x 14 1/8 in.

Collection of the Bowdoin College Museum of Art

Museum Purchase, Barbara Cooney Porter Fund. 2003.8.

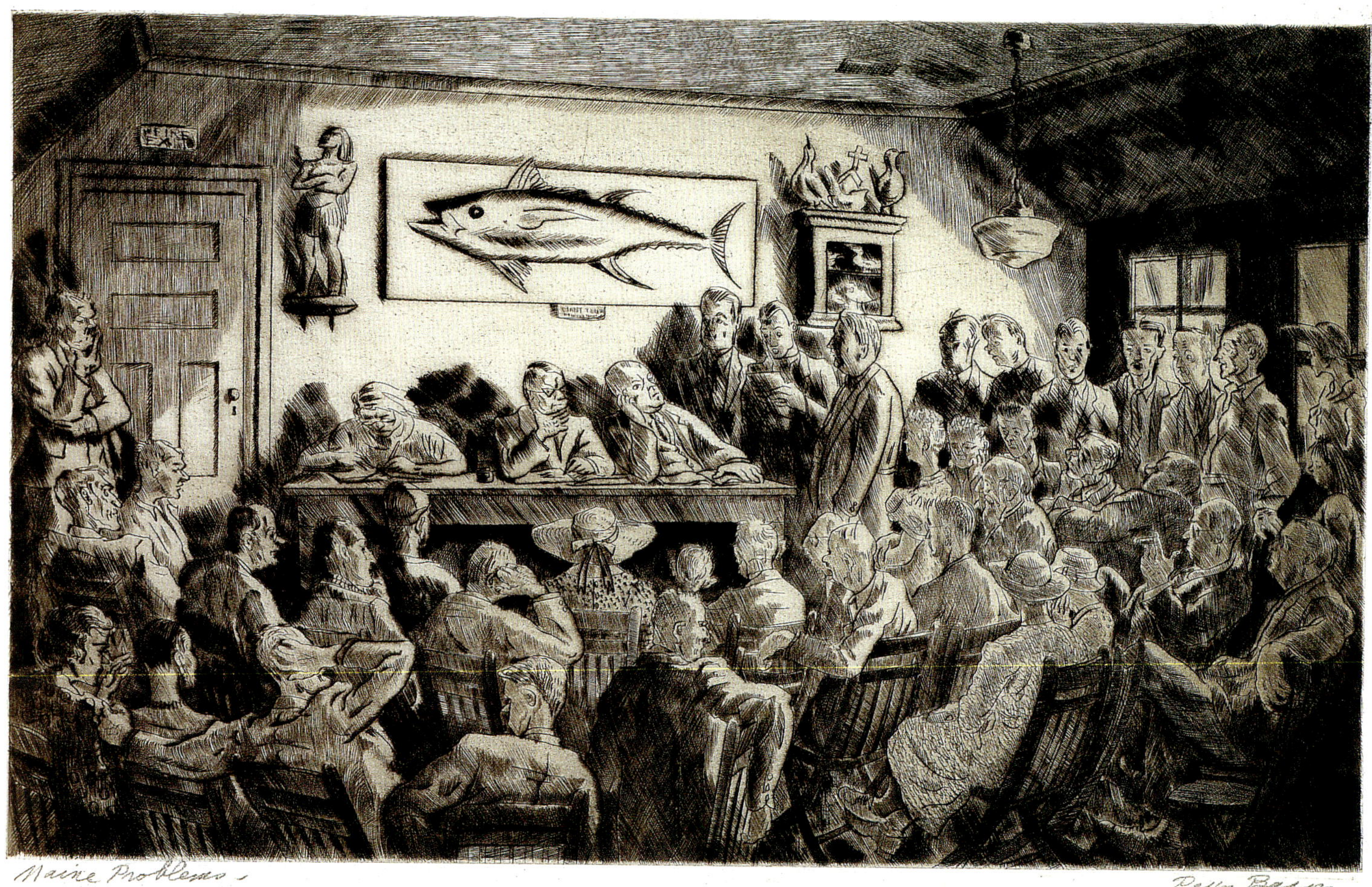

Plate 39

Peggy Bacon (1895–1987), *Maine Problems*, 1941

drypoint, 8 7/16 x 13 15/16 in.

Collection of the Portland Museum of Art

Gift of Harold Shaw. 1984.370

she executed *Maine Problems* (Plate 39). The image is executed in drypoint, which she taught herself in art school, before also learning etching and lithography. The resistance inherent in the drypoint medium, involving the action of scratching lines with a sharp needle into a bare metal plate, leads to a sharp angularity suitable to her incisive character portrayals, enlivened by the dark accents of ink left around the metal "burr" thrown up by the needle (see also the Washburn and Harris prints, Plates 13 and 61). While essentially apolitical in her depictions, she effectively found the comedy in daily life around her, as in this wry town meeting presided over by a large stuffed tuna. In 1961 Bacon settled permanently in Cape Porpoise, near Kennebunkport.

After a period of hardship, social engagement, and wartime sacrifice, the years following World War II would mark a period of tremendous economic growth, dominant conservative values, and at the same time opportunities for artistic freedom—occupied by the rise of abstraction, poetic innovation (the Beat generation and others), new materials and shapes in design, and new directions in music (jazz and rock).

NOTES

1. For a recent overview of this subject, see Elizabeth G. Seaton, "Want and War—Politics in American Fine Art Prints," in *American Identities—Twentieth-Century Prints from the Nancy Gray Sherrill, Class of 1954, Collection* (Wellesley [Mass.]: Davis Museum and Cultural Center, Wellesley College, 2004), pp. 60–73.
2. See, for instance, Richard S. Field, "Rural America—The Country," in Richard S. Field, et al., *American Prints 1900–1950* [exh. cat.] (New Haven: Yale University Art Gallery, 1983), pp. 89–94.
3. See Marilyn S. Kushner, "Genesis of the Twentieth-Century Print Club," in *American Identities—Twentieth-Century Prints from the Nancy Gray Sherrill, Class of 1954, Collection* [exh. cat.] (Wellesley [Mass.]: Davis Museum and Cultural Center, Wellesley College, 2004), pp. 82–95.
4. See James Watrous, *A Century of American Printmaking 1880–1980* (Madison: University of Wisconsin Press, 1984), p. 94.
5. The USS *Lamson* was launched on June 17, 1936, and served in the Pacific throughout World War II, before being purposely sunk in an atomic bomb test on Bikini Atoll on July 2, 1946. [http://www.destroyerhistory.org/goldplater/danfs367.html (accessed February 27, 2006)]
6. Jake Milgram Wien, *Rockwell Kent—The Mythic and the Modern* (New York: Hudson Hills, 2005), pp. 118–20.

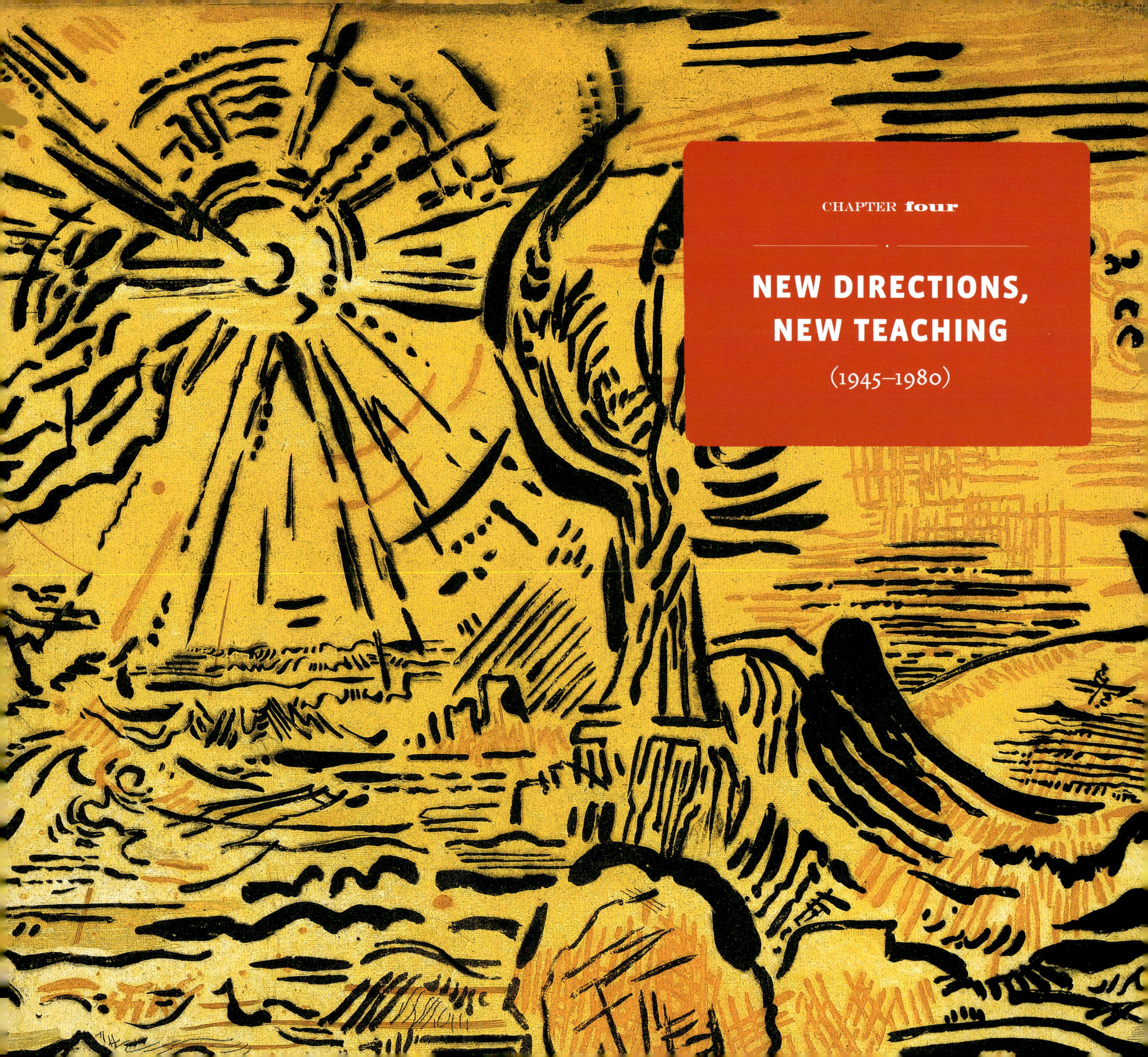

CHAPTER **four**

NEW DIRECTIONS, NEW TEACHING

(1945–1980)

A combination of factors led to a tremendous increase and freedom in printmaking after the end of World War II. These factors included the work and teachings of a number of European émigrés, larger enrollments in colleges and universities, and the growing economy (which admittedly always takes its time trickling down to artists). The establishment in 1940 of the British-born Stanley William Hayter's New York workshop, Atelier 17, was a major catalyst for introducing innovative methods of intaglio printmaking, while also shaking up the conservative printmaking tradition through its clear favoring of abstract and surrealist imagery. Atelier 17 was an uncommon example of printmaking taking the lead in introducing artistic ideas, rather than leaving such change for more "major" art forms. In addition to sponsoring visiting European artists as Joan Miró and André Masson, the workshop provided a stimulating atmosphere that began to attract younger American artists open to experimentation of form and technique. Four of these, all of whom happened to be émigrés, had close connections to Maine.

Though born in Russia, the noted sculptor Louise Nevelson (1900–1988) grew up in Rockland and returned there often through her life. *Landscape at Night (Trees)* (Plate 40) is one of her first prints, from a series of some thirty etchings and aquatints executed at Atelier 17 during 1953–55. These were strongly influenced by a recent trip she had taken to view the ancient ruins of Central America and Mexico. Nevelson etched her designs roughly, combining scratchy marks (some made on the plate while it was in the acid bath) and patterns applied from cloth and/or wire screens. She often printed impressions with varied layers of hand-manipulated inking; there is a second impression of *Landscape* in the Portland Museum that is almost totally covered in a thick layer of black ink, with only a small geometric area in the center wiped clean to reveal a fragment of the design. Both versions emphasize the undefined quality of the space around the design, abstracting the recognizable motifs of tree and figure.

Karl Schrag (1912–1996), whose first trip to Maine was in 1945, eventually chose Deer Isle as his summer home for the rest of his life. Born in Germany and trained there and in Geneva and Paris, Schrag moved to New York in 1938, first studying printmaking at the Art Students League. In 1945, he began working at Atelier 17 and was appointed its director when Hayter returned to Paris in 1950. Many of Schrag's prints, such as *Evening Radiance* of 1953 (Plate 41) reflect his lifelong engagement with the spiritual qualities of landscape. His meditations on seasons, trees, water, sun, and moon often do not depict specific locations. The bold black lines in this and many of his prints evoke Schrag's intense interest in Asian calligraphy, forming a counterweight to the intensity of his colors. Schrag printed *Evening Radiance* at Atelier 17 from three plates (yellow, orange, and black).

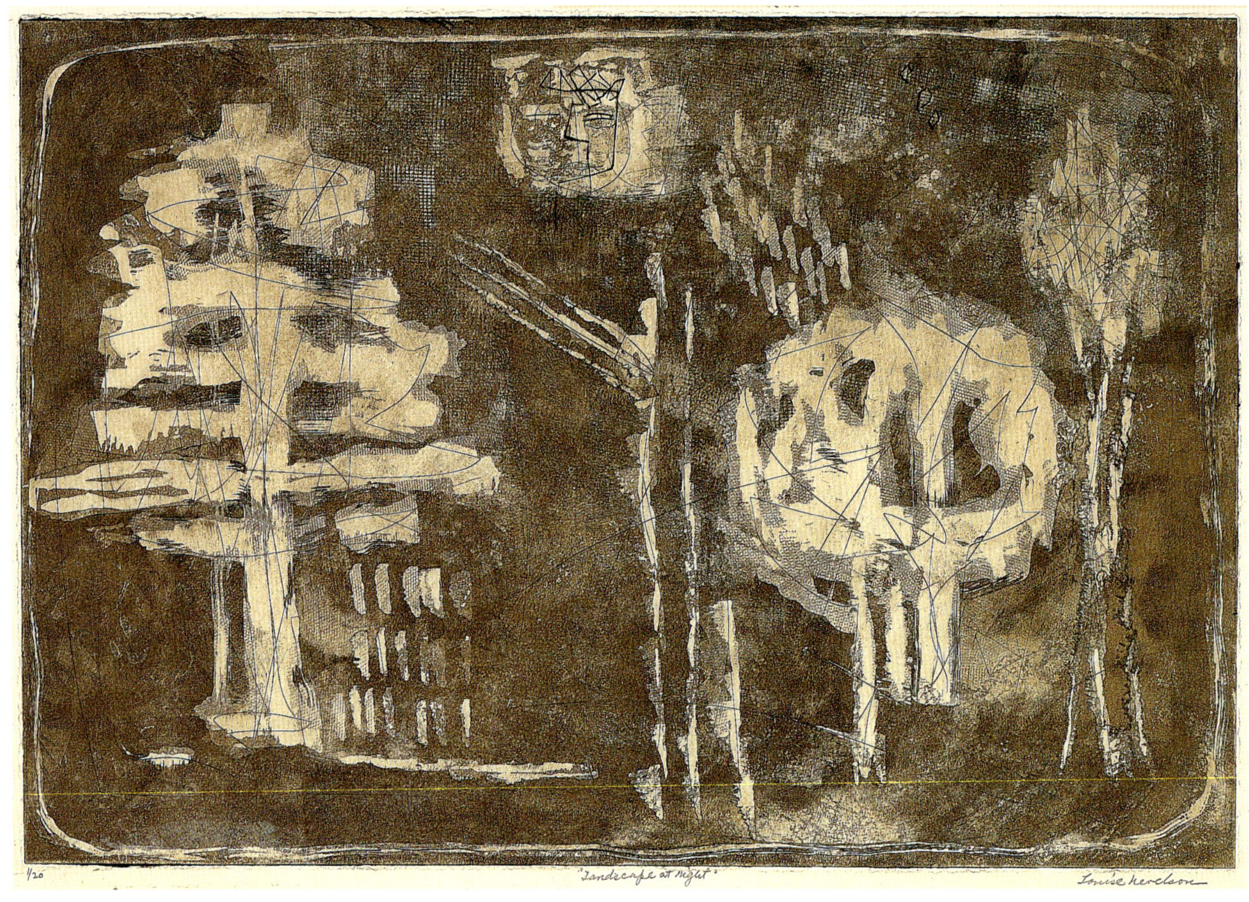

Plate 40

Louise Nevelson (1900–1988), *Landscape at Night (Trees)*, 1953–55
soft- and hard-ground etching, drypoint, 13 7/8 x 20 5/8 in.
Collection of the Portland Museum of Art, Museum Purchase with
support from the Friends of the Collection, 1996.55.

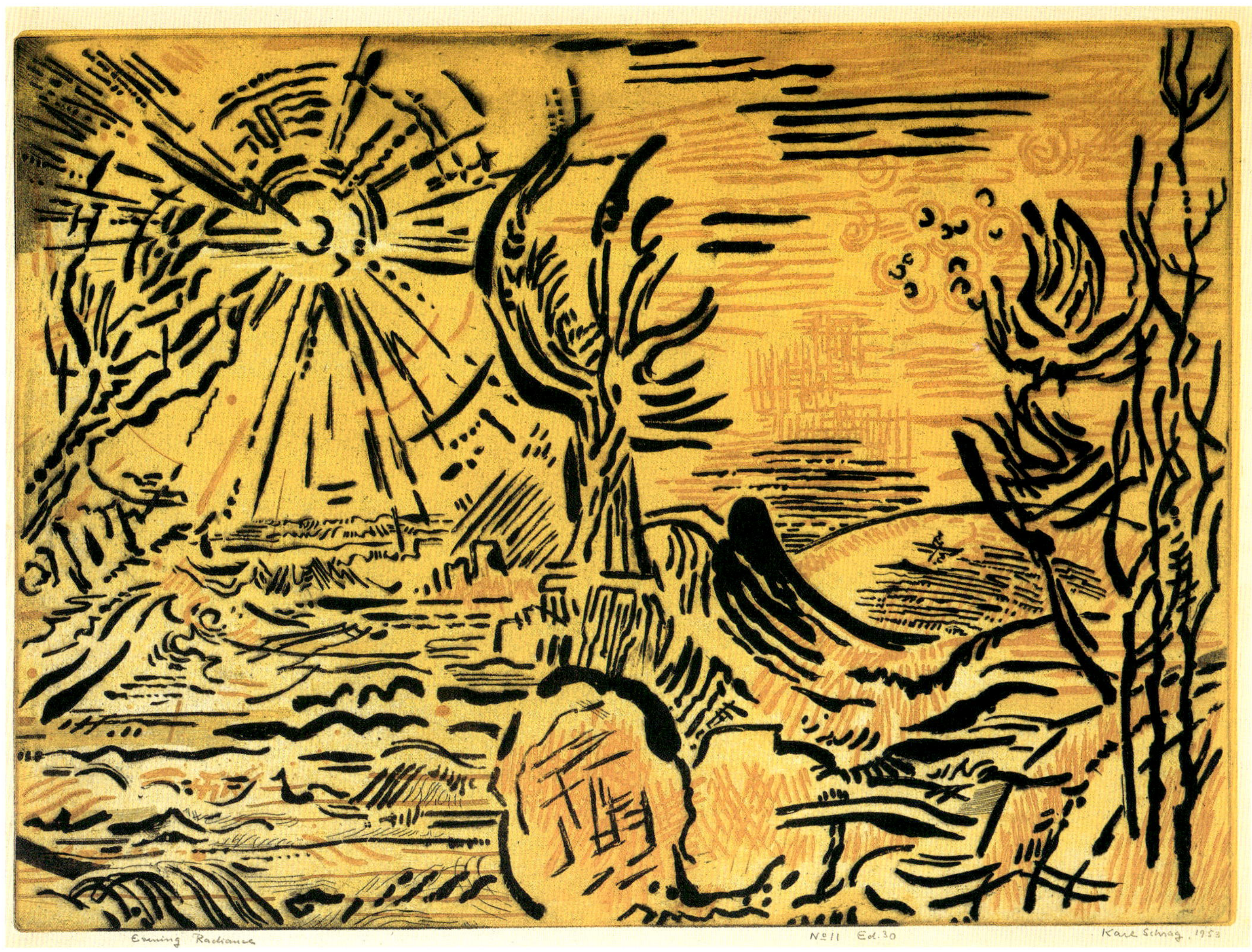

Plate 41

Karl Schrag (1912–1996), *Evening Radiance*, 1953

etching and aquatint with drypoint, 19 x 26 5/8 in.

Collection of the Worcester Art Museum

Anonymous Gift. 1988.99

A longtime summer resident of Vinalhaven, Mauricio Lasansky (b. 1914) was born and trained in Argentina and moved to the United States in 1943. After working in Hayter's workshop, he set up the printmaking department at the University of Iowa, training a large number of students, many of whom also went on to become influential teachers in their own right. Lasansky's often large-scale prints are usually multi-layered colorful mixtures of various intaglio methods. Working primarily in an expressionist figural mode, he is particularly noted for his *Nazi Drawings* of 1966, a series of 30 life-size portrayals of evil and suffering.

Another European émigré who became an influential printmaker and teacher, working in woodcut rather than intaglio media, was Werner Drewes (1899–1985), who studied in Stuttgart, Germany, and at the famous Bauhaus school in the 1920s. He moved to the United States in 1930, actively teaching and exhibiting in New York (including at Atelier 17), in addition to being an important advocate for abstract art. From 1946 to 1965 he taught at Washington University in St. Louis. First visiting Maine in the 1940s, Drewes made several color woodcuts of coastal views in Monhegan and Camden; in 1983 he also cut a portrait of Schrag. His expressionist, abstracted *Maine Sunset* of 1949 (Plate 42) is printed from four blocks (black, brown, blue, and yellow).

During the 1950s and 1960s, Maine shared in the nationwide growth of printmaking departments in universities and art schools. Programs were begun or revived at the Portland School of Art (now the Maine College of Art), Bowdoin College, the University of Maine, and elsewhere. Such teachers as John Muench and Allan Gardiner at Portland, Jeanna Dale Bearce and Lawrence Rakovan at the University of Maine at Portland-Gorham (now University of Southern Maine), George Burk at Nasson College, Thomas Cornell at Bowdoin, and Donald Lent at Bates were important influences on the encouragement and appreciation of printmaking in the state.

Summer programs such as those at Skowhegan and Haystack attracted new artists to the state, as did teaching residencies by visiting artists at undergraduate institutions. One of these is David Driskell (b. 1931), who has had a second home in Falmouth, Maine, since 1961, inspired by his own student residency at Skowhegan. In addition to his years of travel and teaching in the South, primarily at Talladega College, Howard University, Fisk University, and the University of Maryland, Driskell has taught in Maine at Bowdoin College, Maine College of Art, and the summer schools at Haystack and Skowhegan. He has made prints throughout his career, usually in relief methods of woodcut and linocut,

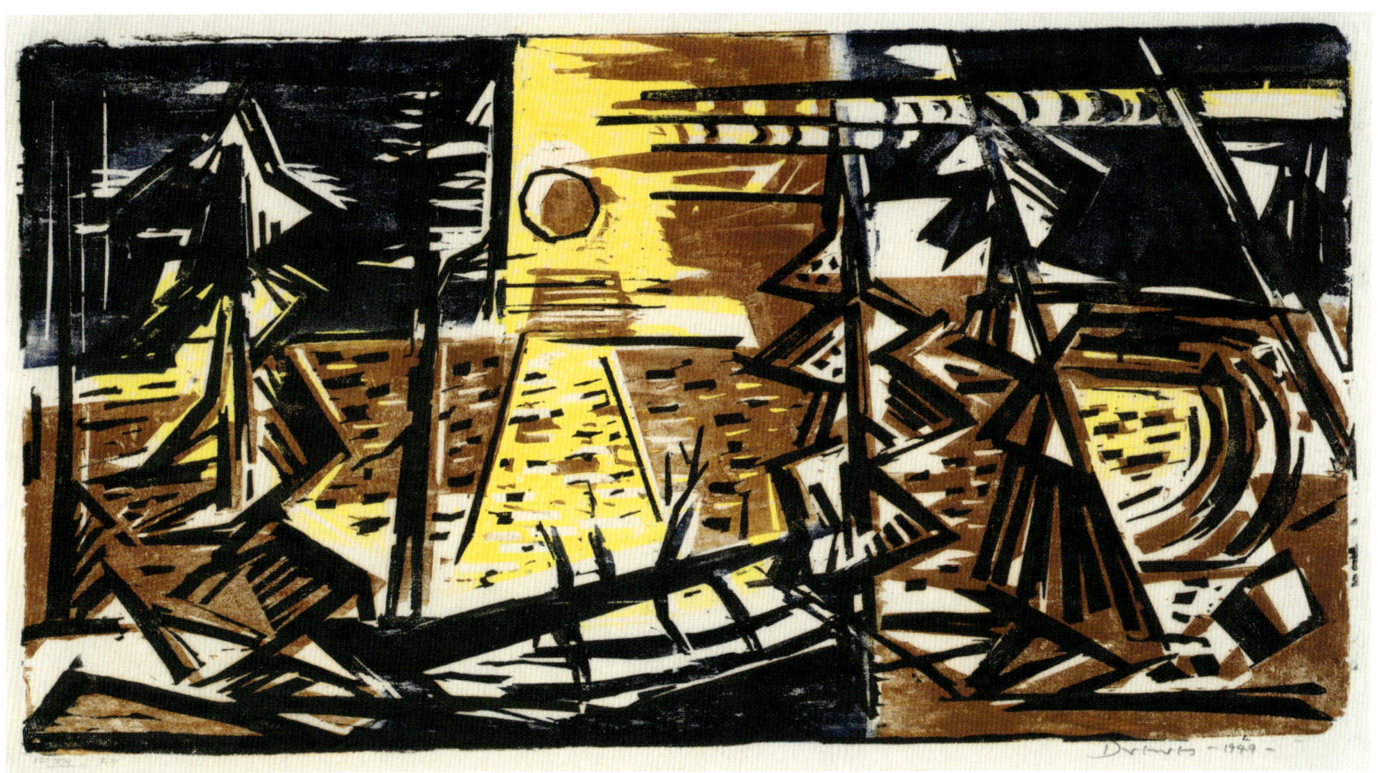

Plate 42

Werner Drewes (1899–1985), *Maine Sunset*, 1949,
color woodcut, 12 1/2 x 23 3/4 in.
Collection of the Fogg Art Museum,
Harvard University Art Museums
Louise E. Bettens Fund. M12970

but also lithograph and collagraph. Using multi-layered combinations of media and printings, Driskell explores themes of landscape, still life, religious parables, and African culture and art. *Mountain and Tile #2* of 1968 (Plate 43) incorporates a linocut block (the blue-green circle) executed several years earlier with a woodcut (the red-ochre rectangle), the pair placed on a layered cardboard base; the impressions are hand-printed by the artist with a wooden spoon. The composition, inspired by the artist's memory of a partial solar eclipse witnessed on the Maine coast in 1963, became an iconic and often-used motif of sun, sky, land, and water.

The influence of Leonard Baskin (1922–2000), through his art and his teaching (at Smith and Hampshire Colleges), has extended to many students and followers, especially in New England. An articulate and ardent advocate of humanism in an age of abstraction, Baskin most often celebrated the figure, but on occasion he explored nature in still-lifes, plant studies, and quiet landscapes, such as *View at Deer Isle* (Plate 44) from the mid-1960s. His reputation was first established with his monumental figural woodcuts of the 1950s; they were among the first truly wall-sized prints to be produced in this country. In addition, Baskin was a masterful wood engraver, etcher, and lithographer, and was widely recognized for his typography and illustrations in books from his own Gehenna Press. He summered for many years on Little Deer Isle.

One of Baskin's students, Thomas Cornell (b. 1937) has taught at Bowdoin College since 1962. He is especially noted for his acutely delineated portraits, human and animal—here represented by his *Snapping Turtle II* of 1968 (Plate 45). For many years he has closely explored figural compositions and arcadian landscapes in prints and many paintings. He has contributed many etched book illustrations, the latest a portrait of Edith Wharton for her novel *Ethan Frome* for an edition printed by the Ascensius Press in Portland in 2001.

Dahlov Ipcar (b. 1917) is a painter, author, and illustrator of more than thirty children's books published since 1947. She was consistently encouraged in her artistic studies by her parents, Marguerite and William Zorach. Ipcar admits to a lifelong love of animals, and they are a steady theme in her art, depicted in an overall abstracted, optically varied pattern, often in bright colors. She has executed a number of lithographs and woodcuts through her career, including *Unicorn Wood* in 1969 (Plate 46). She has also worked on a public scale, executing murals in schools, hospitals, and libraries in Maine and elsewhere, as well as on a smaller scale in her colorful fabric animal sculptures.

In contrast to the relative prominence of intaglio printmaking in the 1940s and 1950s, the period saw a comparative decline in the prominence of fine art lithography, due in part to the lack of trained printers (the artist-printers George Miller and Bolton Brown not having encouraged students). One of the few accomplished printers in this exacting medium was John Muench (1914–1993), who was prompted by the gift of a lithograph to learn the technique for himself, rather than relying on professional printers. In 1943, Muench bought a press and stones and essentially taught himself the necessary skills. By 1953, further inspired by a visit to the famed French printer Jacques Mourlot, he had set up a studio in New York and began printing editions for other artists, becoming well known for his skill in color printing. In 1958 Muench was appointed director of the Portland School of Art, followed in 1964 by a move to the Rhode Island School of Design. In 1976, he became artist-in-residence at Westbrook College in Portland and set up the Maine Printmaking Workshop there. Despite his teaching duties, Muench was a prolific

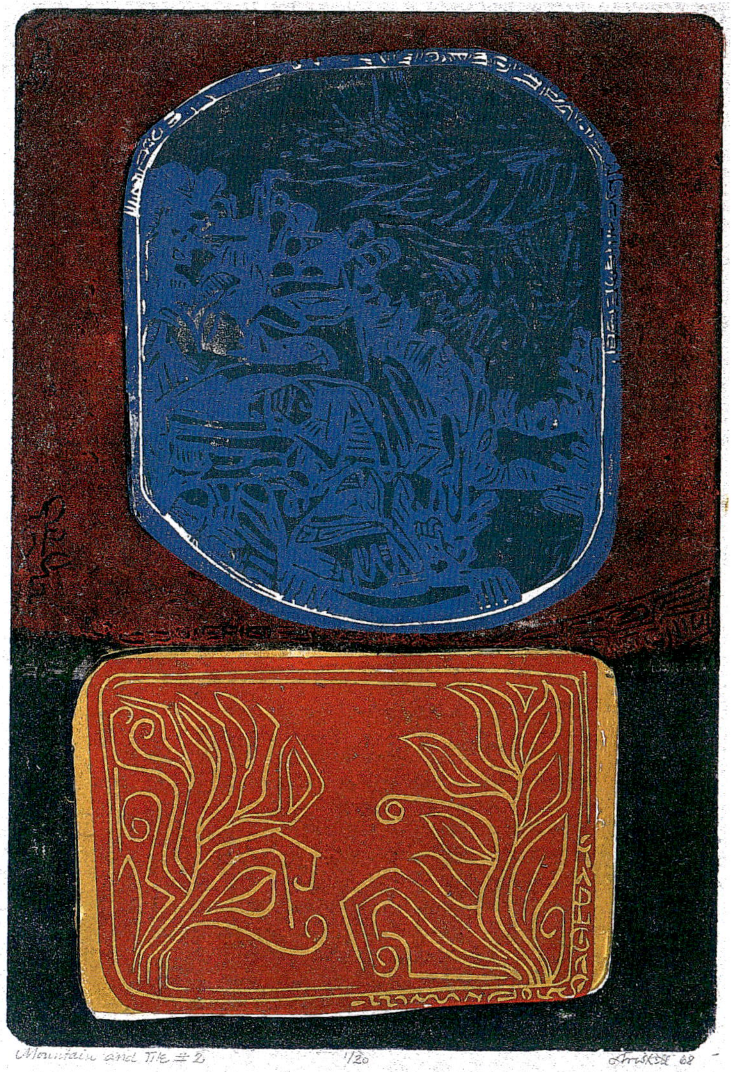

Plate 43

David Driskell (b. 1931), *Mountain and Tile #2*, 1968
color woodcut, linocut, and collagraph, 15 1/2 x 11 in.
Collection of the Bowdoin College Museum of Art
Museum Purchase, Art Objects Fund. 1969.32

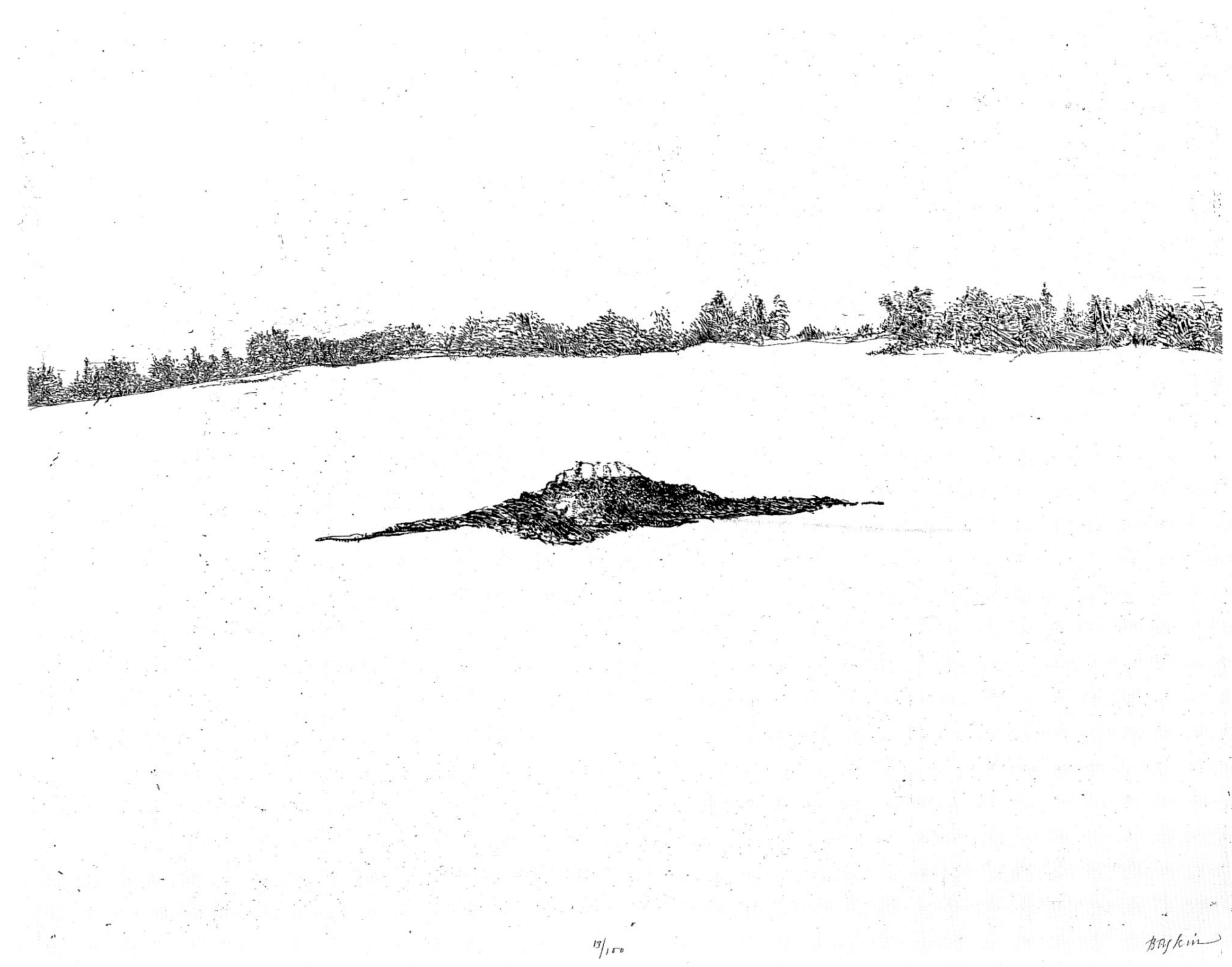

Plate 44

Leonard Baskin (1922–2000), *View at Deer Isle*,
ca. 1965, etching, 9 x 12 in.
Collection of the Portland Museum of Art
Gift of Kenneth N. Shure and Liv M. Rockefeller, 2005
2005.22.1. © Estate of Leonard Baskin

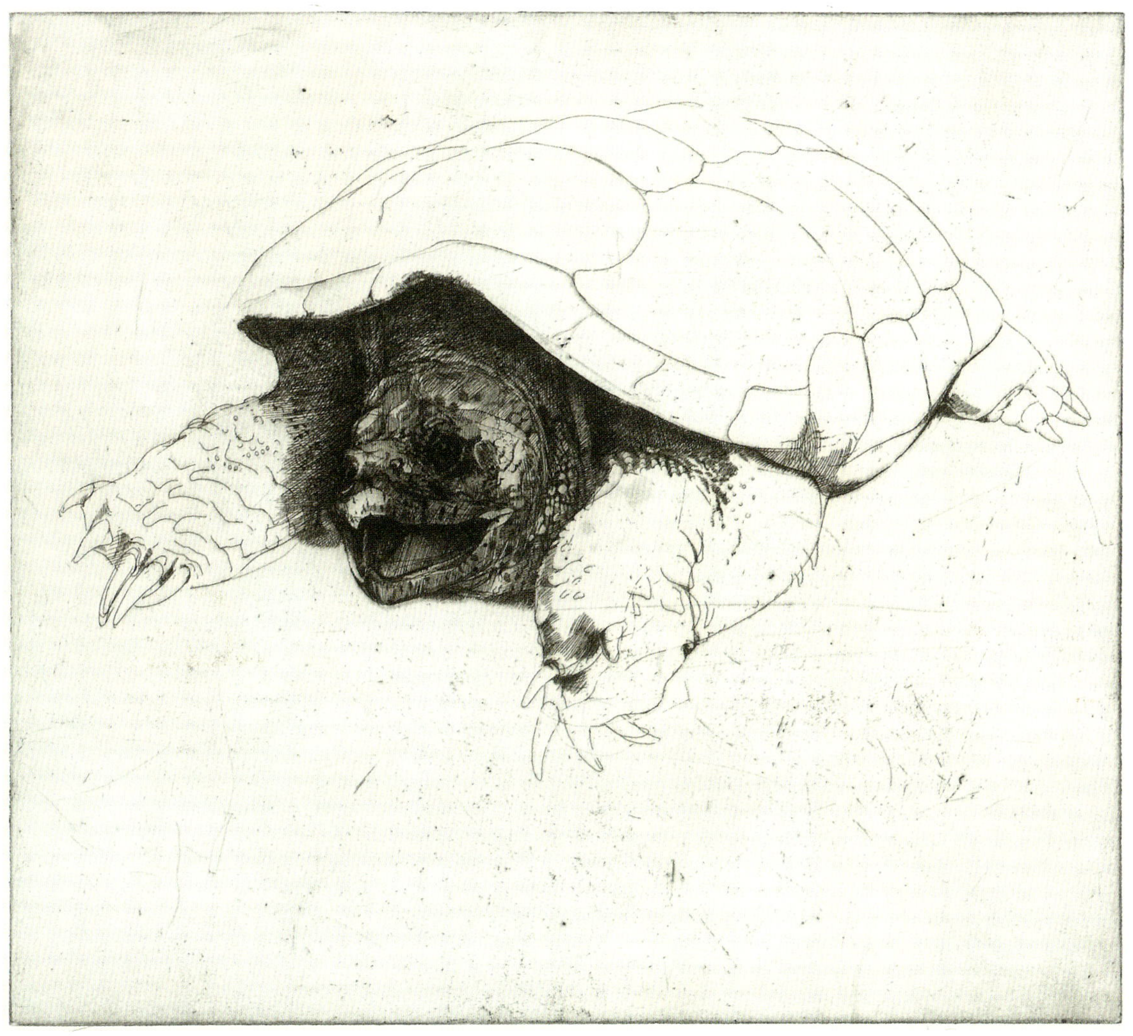

Plate 45

Thomas Cornell (b. 1937), *Snapping Turtle II*, 1968

etching, $15\,^{1}/_{2}$ x $17\,^{13}/_{16}$ in.

Collection of the Colby College Museum of Art

Museum Purchase with a grant from the

Charles E. Merrill Trust. 1973.221

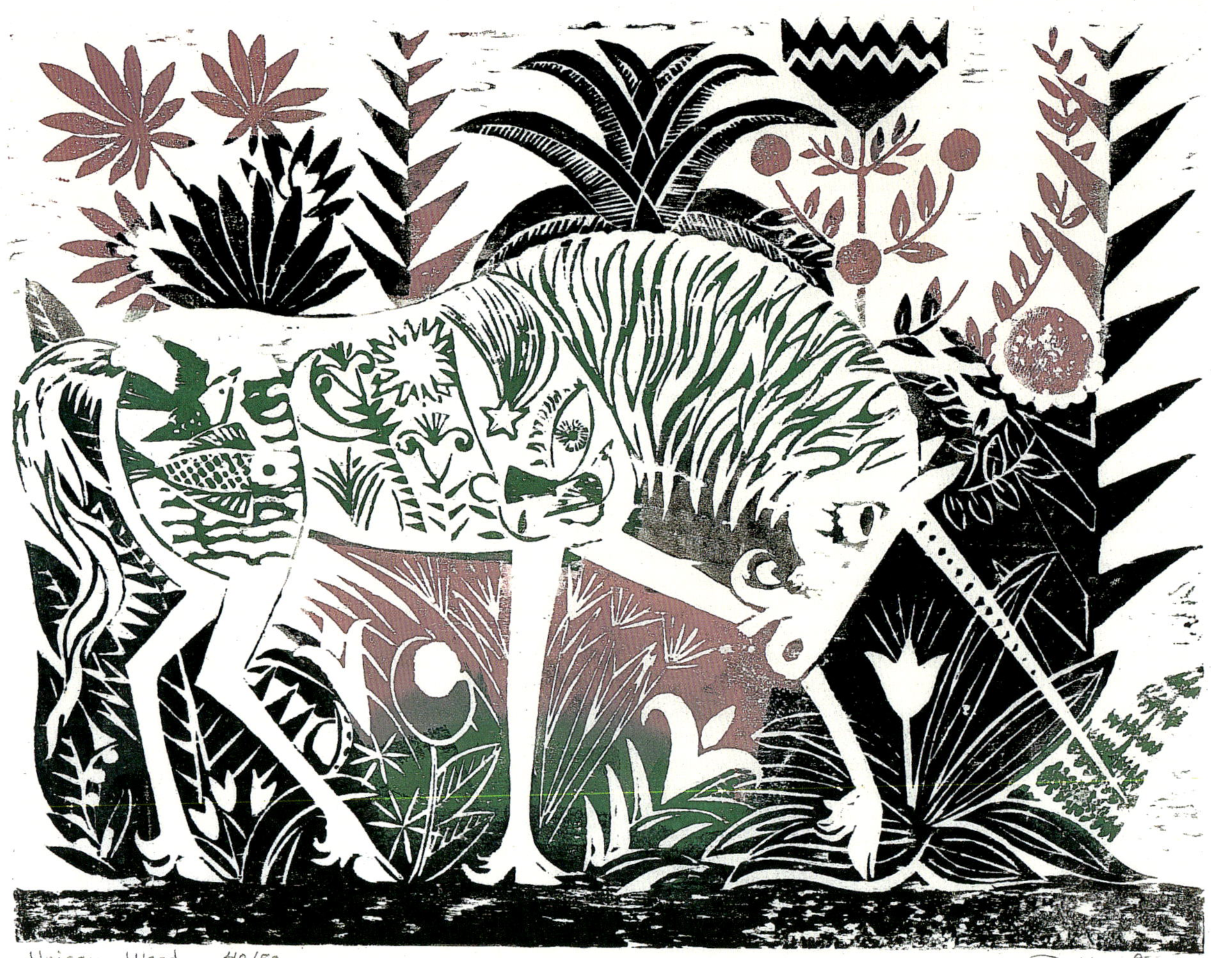

Plate 46

Dahlov Ipcar (b. 1917), *Unicorn Wood*, 1969

color woodcut, $16^{7}/_{8}$ x $22^{1}/_{2}$ in.

Collection of the Portland Museum of Art

Gift of Dahlov Ipcar in memory of her brother,

Tessim Zorach. 1995.37.2

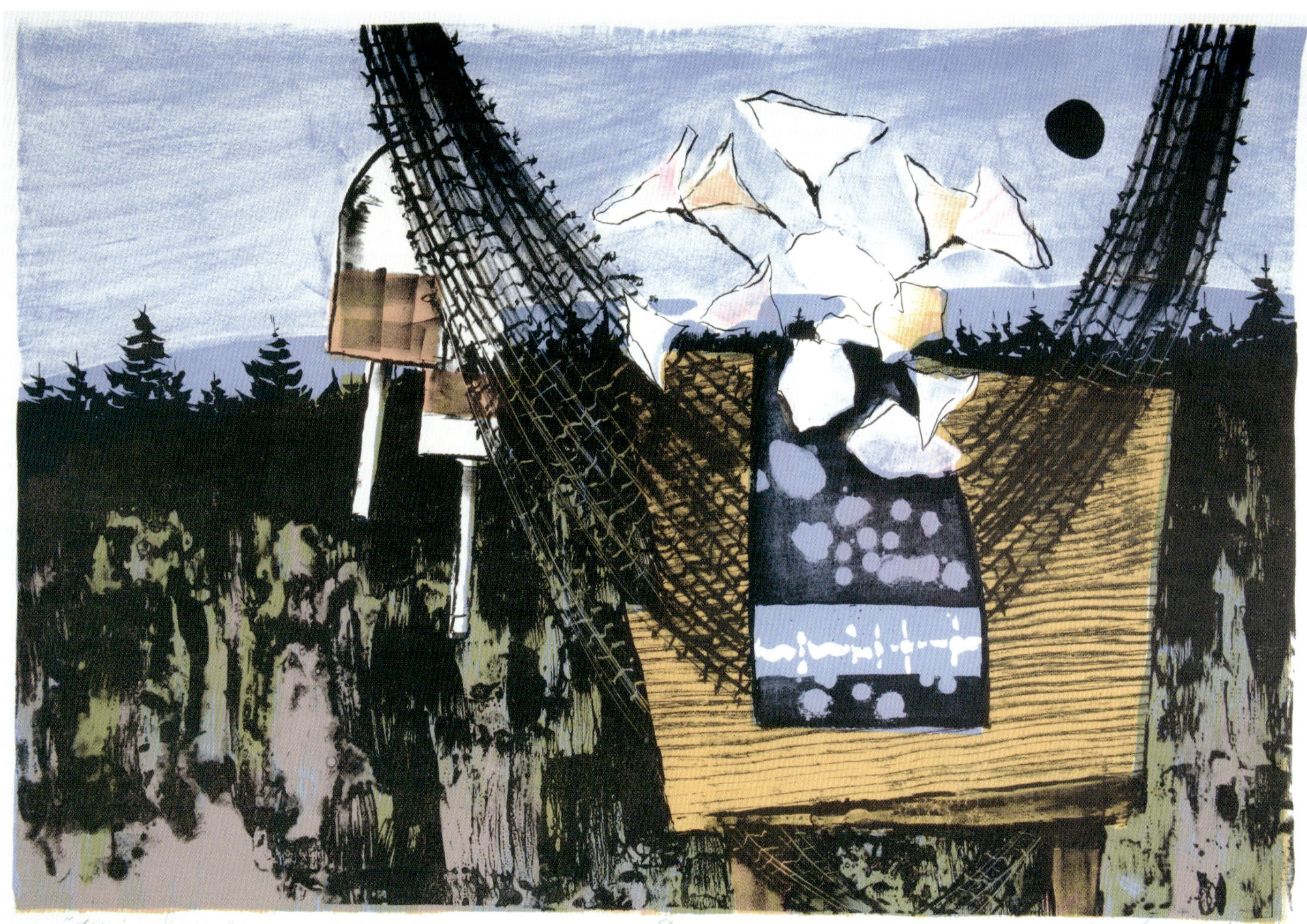

Plate 47

John Muench (1914–1993), *Maine Spring*, 1966

color lithograph, 14 1/8 x 21 1/8 in.

published by Impressions Workshop, Boston

Courtesy of the Muench family

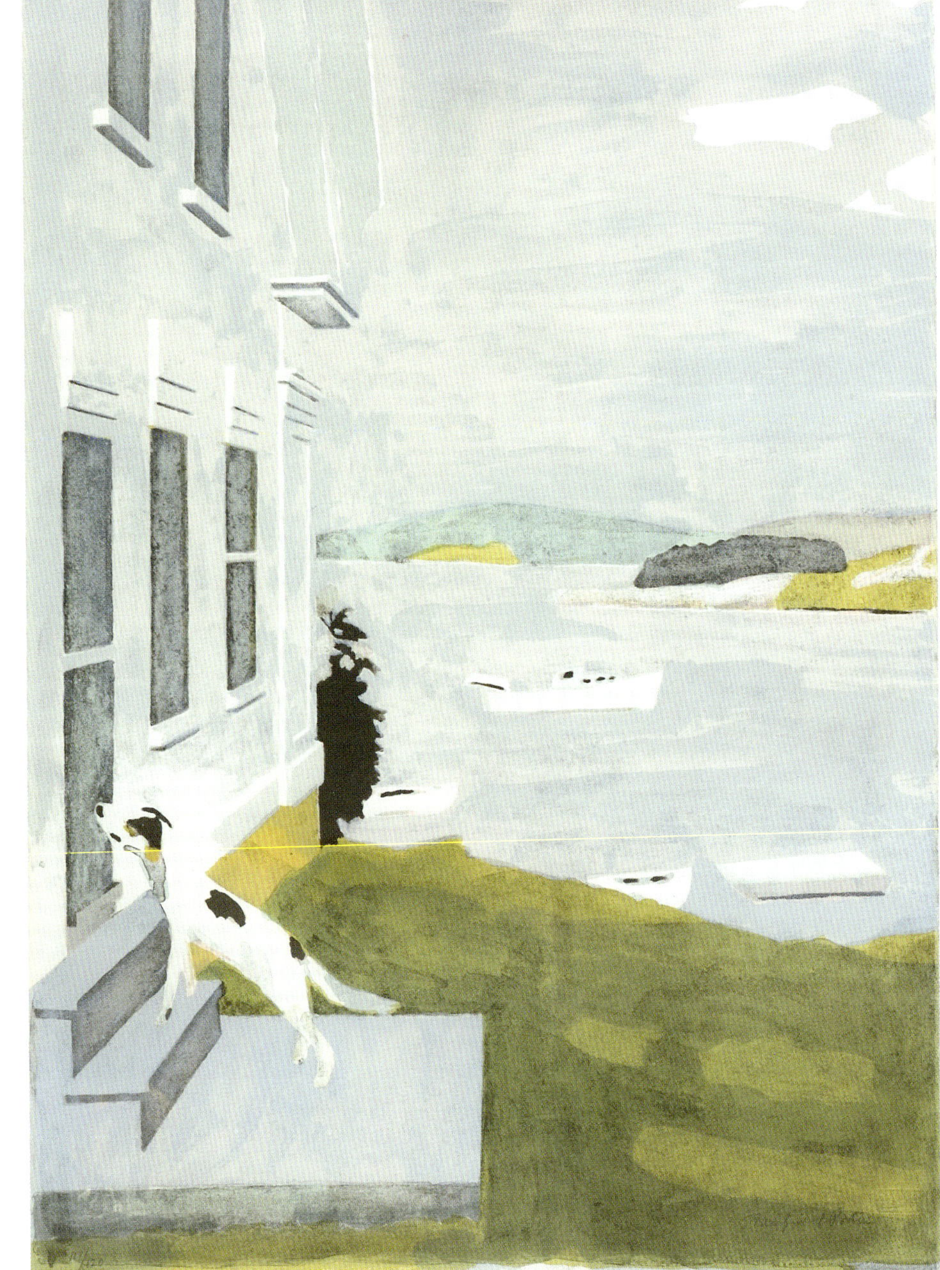

Plate 48

Fairfield Porter (1907–1975), *Dog at the Door*, 1971

lithograph, $29^{5}/_{8}$ x 22 in., printed and published by

Bank Street Atelier Ltd., New York

Collection of the Colby College Museum of Art

Gift of Ada and Alex Katz. 1972.66

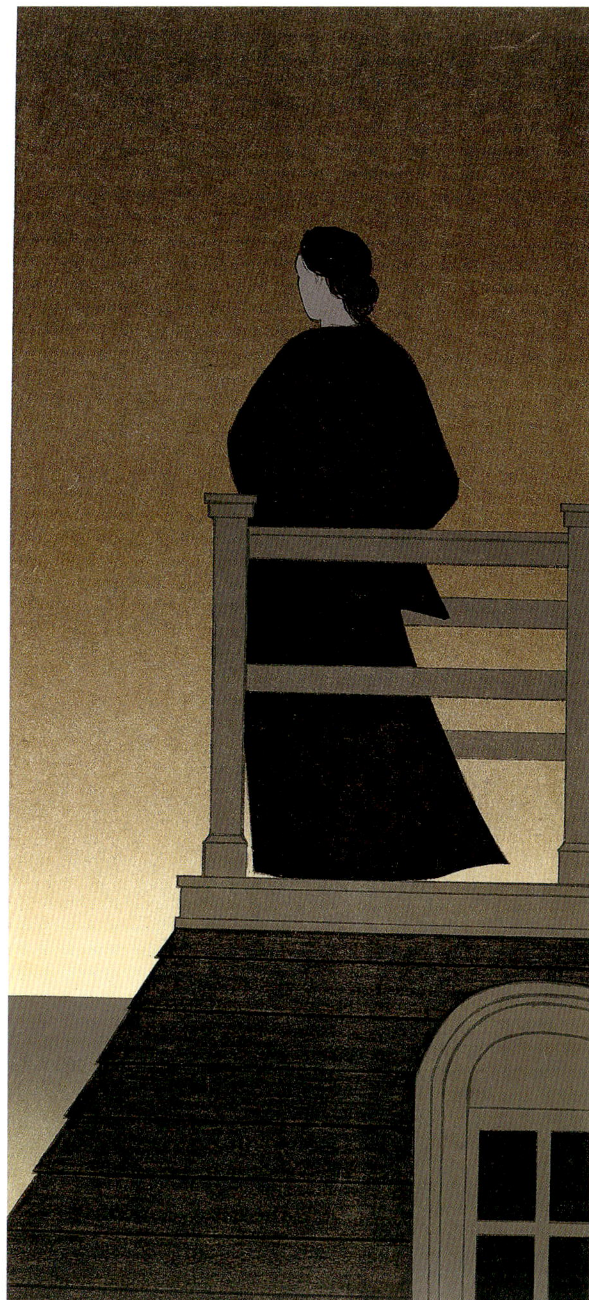

Plate 49

Will Barnet (b. 1911), *Dawn*, 1975
color lithograph, 23 7/8 x 11 1/8 in., printed at Mourlot, Paris
Collection of the Portland Museum of Art
Museum Purchase with support from the
Friends of the Collection. 1996.52.1.

lithographer. He published *The Painter's Guide to Lithography* in 1983, an attempt to help demystify the process for artists. Many of Muench's themes of layered abstraction, still life, the Maine landscape, and a favored inclusion of a black, gibbous moon, are present in his *Maine Spring* of 1966 (Plate 47). Printed at Impressions Workshop, Boston, in four colors (black, blue, ochre, and red), it is one of a portfolio of four lithographs, *Maine Seasons*, with poetry by the Rockland-born Edna St. Vincent Millay.

It is generally agreed that the establishment of several collaborative printmaking workshops in the United States, beginning about 1960, greatly changed the face and public status of printmaking in the following decades. These workshops created an atmosphere in which many innovative painters and sculptors tried their hand at the process, often for the first time. The results were so successful that prints began competing successfully in scale and visual impact with paintings and sculpture. Prints by Jasper Johns, Robert Rauschenberg, Helen Frankenthaler, Jim Dine, and Andy Warhol, for instance, occupy a prominent place in any survey of art during the 1960s and 1970s. The market for such prints grew to such an extent, as the Museum of Modern Art's curator of prints Deborah Wye has pointed out, that whereas in the 1960s artists not already printmakers had to be coaxed to do prints, by the 1980s artists were often eager to try it, and often realized printmaking's potential for making connections with their works in all media.[1]

Three of the most important workshops were Tamarind Lithography Workshop, Universal Limited Art Editions, and Crown Point Press. Each was founded for slightly different purposes, but their combined influence in producing classic prints and training fine printers was crucial. June Wayne founded Tamarind in 1959 in Los Angeles (it moved to Albuquerque in 1970), largely to address the lack of trained lithographic printers in the United States. At about the same time, Tatyana Grosman founded Universal Limited Art Editions on Long Island as a more specialized shop catering to a limited number of artists. Finally, Kathan Brown established Crown Point Press in 1962 in San Francisco, specializing at first in fine intaglio printing. While no workshop on their scale arrived in Maine until Patricia Nick's Vinalhaven Press in 1985 (for which see the next chapter), several Maine artists have worked at workshops around the country. Among the first were John Muench and John Hultberg (1922–2005), who both worked at Tamarind in the early 1960s.

The painter and critic Fairfield Porter (1907–1975) executed a group of some 17 color lithographs at the end of his life, collaborating with Mourlot-trained printers at the Bank Street Atelier in New York. He worked from watercolor studies of his subject, painting directly on the lithographic stone with a brush filled with tusche, a dilute lithographic ink wash. For his 1971 print, *Dog at the Door* (Plate 48), Porter used seven colors in a subdued palette: light gray, medium gray, blue, black, pink, green, and yellow. Many of Porter's works in all media depict Great Spruce Head Island in eastern Penobscot Bay, where he summered for his entire life.

The painter and printmaker Will Barnet (b. 1911) has chosen to depict a more allegorical vision of the Maine coast, where he has spent summers since 1971. Barnet has often explored the theme of female strength and endurance through single figures and groups set against timeless skies—a motif originally inspired by the silhouette of his wife on the deck of a house they were renting in Chamberlain. His 1975 lithograph, *Dawn* (Plate 49 and cover) is rendered in a somber palette that Barnet feels reflects the harsher qualities of Maine light. Regardless of specifically local allusions, the implied stance of viewer watching a solitary figure who is also watching recalls many similar nineteenth-century depictions by such artists as the German painter Caspar David Friedrich, or, even more relevant to the Maine coast, Winslow Homer.

During this period, too, the number and visibility of exhibitions devoted exclusively to new varieties of printmaking began to increase in the state and around the country. Many cities around the country established national print invitational exhibitions, including ones from 1952 to 1958 at the Portland Museum of Art. Jurors for the Portland exhibitions included Cadwallader Washburn, Leo Meissner, Carroll Thayer Berry, Francis Merritt, John Muench, and Vincent Hartgen. Director of the University of Maine Museum from 1946 to 1983, Hartgen sponsored print exhibitions and actively purchased prints for the university collection through this period. During the 1960s and 1970s, the Bowdoin College Museum of Art lent exhibitions of nineteenth- and twentieth-century prints through its Traveling Print Program to libraries and public schools around the state.

The significant increase in printmaking activity in Maine during the postwar years through the 1960s and 1970s is of course also reflected in the sheer number of artists working in the medium, too numerous to encompass in this short survey. The coastal artistic communities, both summer and year-round, saw the greatest production of prints, consistent with earlier history. For instance, many artists on Monhegan at this time were involved in printmaking, among them James Elliott, Henry Kallem, Charles Martin, Louise Freedman, Jacqueline Hudson, Morton Grossman, and Reuben Tam, to name only a few. Other significant print artists are John Laurent, Beverly Hallam, William and Stell Shevis, Francis Merritt, Francis Hamabe, and William Manning.

NOTE

1. See interview with Wye in *The Print Collector's Newsletter*, vol. 27 (May–June 1996), p. 59.

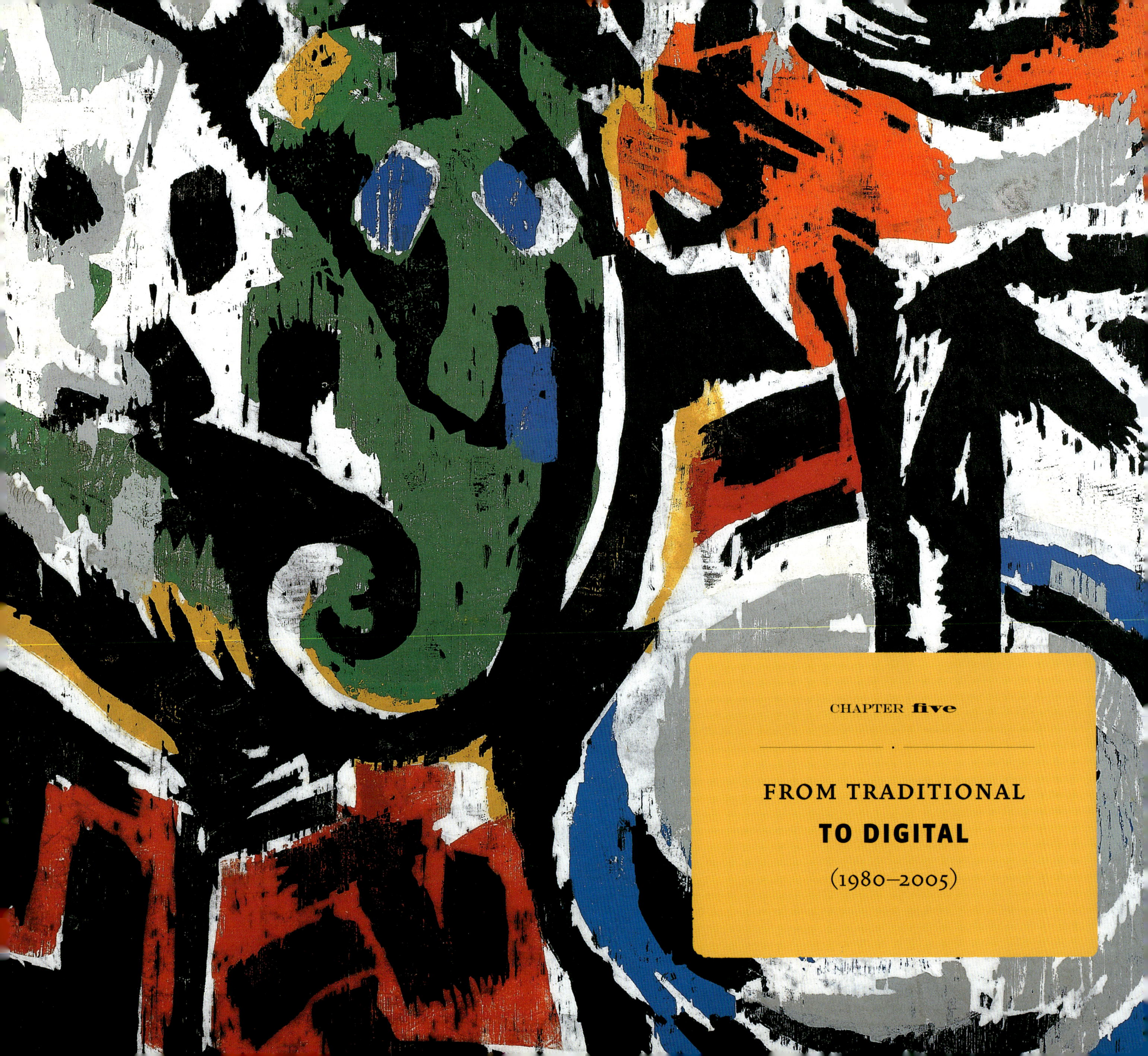

CHAPTER **five**

FROM TRADITIONAL **TO DIGITAL**

(1980–2005)

The last twenty-five years in Maine have seen ever-growing interest, experimentation, and acceptance of printmaking. Reflecting a national trend, no longer can printmaking be marginalized as a secondary medium in Maine. As the art historian Susan Tallman wrote in an influential history in 1996, "Not only do the best artists of our time make prints, some of the best artworks of our time are prints."[1] In addition to the inherent vitality of printmaking, its growth within the state has resulted from several factors, such as an increase in the number of exhibition venues (museums, galleries, and urban alternative spaces) and academic programs; the establishment of independent print workshops; the in-migration of artists; increased critical attention; and, to a degree, economic growth.

As in previous decades, the "mix" of Maine prints during this period includes the work of artists who live in the state year-round and those who visit for lesser or lengthier stays. However, the boundaries are in reality more fluid, as artists spend a period of time teaching at a Maine institution before moving elsewhere, a "local" artist achieves a significant national reputation, or an "outside" artist spends more and more time in the state or is commissioned to do a print edition by a Maine workshop. As in previous decades, this insider/outsider dichotomy still has its occasional awkwardness, but the mix of culture(s) and outlook has enlivened the artistic atmosphere and left its distinctive imprint on the art that results.

The print workshops in the state demonstrate this mix of influences. There are individual master printers such as the Jefferson lithographer Frances Hodsdon or the Portland silkscreen and etching printer Richard Wilson. Many printers and printmakers (oftentimes both in one individual) travel throughout the state teaching, demonstrating, or exhibiting, thus establishing a more active and collaborative printmaking community. Other collaborative efforts have included Pearl Street Printmakers, founded by Porge Buck in Camden and in operation from 1978 to 1983, and John Ames's 1980s informal workshop in Belfast associated with his Gallery 68, where artists such as Katherine Porter, Judy Pfaff, Harold Garde, and Scott Reed worked on their prints. The Peregrine Press, founded in 1991 by Alice Spencer, Kate Mahoney, Lin Lisberger, and others, has thrived as an active collaborative print community in Portland. Today numbering 30 members, the group organizes workshops, exhibits widely together, sponsors an annual scholarship for young printmakers, and actively pursues new techniques and safer ways of practicing them.

The Vinalhaven Press, founded by Patricia Nick in 1985, was a particularly ambitious effort to raise the profile of collaborative printmaking in Maine. Attracting master printers and artists from around the country (and internationally) to an island off the coast was not an easy task, but the press achieved a remarkable record of over 130 editions by some 30 artists before ending its productions in 1997.[2] In addition to working with Maine-based artists such as Charlie Hewitt, Robert Indiana, Carolyn Brady, and Yvonne Jacquette, the press also was the midwife for signal works by visiting artists Robert Morris, Leon Golub, Robert Cumming, Alison Saar, Mel Chin, Komar and Melamid, Grisha Bruskin, and José Bedia, among others. Many notable master printers worked at the press, including John C. Erickson, Randy Hemminghaus, Jonathan Higgins, Brenda Zlamany, and Orlando Condeso.

Another important workshop category in Maine that can only be mentioned here is that of the production of fine illustrated books, from traditional letterpress printing shops to individual book artists exploring variations of the historical codex form of the book. The state has had a rich tradition of fine book printers, such as Thomas Bird Mosher, Frederick Anthoensen, both in Portland, and more recently August Heckscher (The Printing Office at High Loft, Seal Harbor), Michael Alpert (Theodore Press/Sarah Books, Bangor), George Benington (Coyote Love Press, Portland), Scott Vile (Ascensius Press, Portland), Walter Tisdale (Landlocked Press, Bangor), and David Wolfe (Wolfe Editions, Portland).[3]

Print exhibitions have also proliferated, along with a significant growth in collections of contemporary prints. As the price of paintings skyrockets, many academic museums have been able to successfully represent contemporary trends with prints. Several institutions have attracted significant individual archives, such as complete collections of the prints of Charlie Hewitt at the Bates College Museum of Art, Alex Katz and Terry Winters at the Colby College Museum of Art, and the Vinalhaven Press at the Bowdoin College Museum of Art. The Portland Museum signified its commitment to the medium by hiring Aprile Gallant as its (and the state's) first full-time curator of graphic arts in 1996.

Obviously, the great number of significant printmakers in the state during this period cannot hope to be judiciously covered in this all-too-cursory overview. Contemporary Maine printmaking deserves a book of its own. However, one lens through which to sketch such a survey is to examine the range of different printmaking techniques, traditional and not, that artists have been using to such great effect.

WOODCUT

Woodcut is the oldest printmaking technique, dating in the western tradition from the late fourteenth century, but in a world of abstraction and Pop and Conceptualism, its influence had waned by the later twentieth century. Certain artists had always used it, especially those, like Leonard Baskin, who were familiar with the historical printmaking tradition. However, the appearance in the 1980s of a number of monumental, roughly executed woodcuts by German artists such as Anselm Kiefer and Georg Baselitz coincided with a search by many artists for a more personal expression in their art at the time. Many American artists took to the woodcut medium, both in directly expressionist fashion (Jim Dine, Susan Rothenberg, Charlie Hewitt) and more refined manners (Helen Frankenthaler, Alex Katz).

Appropriately, perhaps, for the "pine tree" state, woodcut has been quite evident in Maine in recent years. Lewiston-born Charlie Hewitt (b. 1946) has energetically exploited what he refers to as woodcut's "muscular" quality, producing a major body of work in the medium, often on a monumental scale (his *German Music* of 1990 measures six feet in height). The rough gouges and large scale of his forms reflect the new expressionism seen in recent German work, but are entirely consistent with his own equally forceful paintings. Hewitt combines numerous personal and religious symbols in his colorful works, such as *Iago II* of 1986 (Plate 50), which Hewitt drew and cut in a burst of activity during a single week of his first residency at the Vinalhaven Press, where it was printed with Chris Erickson. The objects that he combines in his imagery, including spinning tops, rolling dice, lobster pots, floating eyes, or rough fragments of reinforced steel bars, all combine in a tumbling sense of movement.

Primarily a sculptor and installation artist, Alison Saar (b. 1956) had done very little printmaking before spending two summer residencies at Vinalhaven in 1993 and 1994, after a stint as visiting artist at the Skowhegan School. Saar's strong desire to honor forgotten or suppressed cultural histories is represented by her use of evocative found materials in her sculpture and as printing surfaces, as in the piece of cracked linoleum retrieved from the Vinalhaven dump that was used to create the figural element in this print. Based on a 1985 sculpture, *Snake Charmer*, her *Snake Man* of 1994 (Plate 51) features a textured background and snake, lips, and nipples that are printed from woodblocks; the snake-man figure is actually printed from a lithographic transfer from the linoleum, which was not itself able to stand up to the printing pressure of the press.

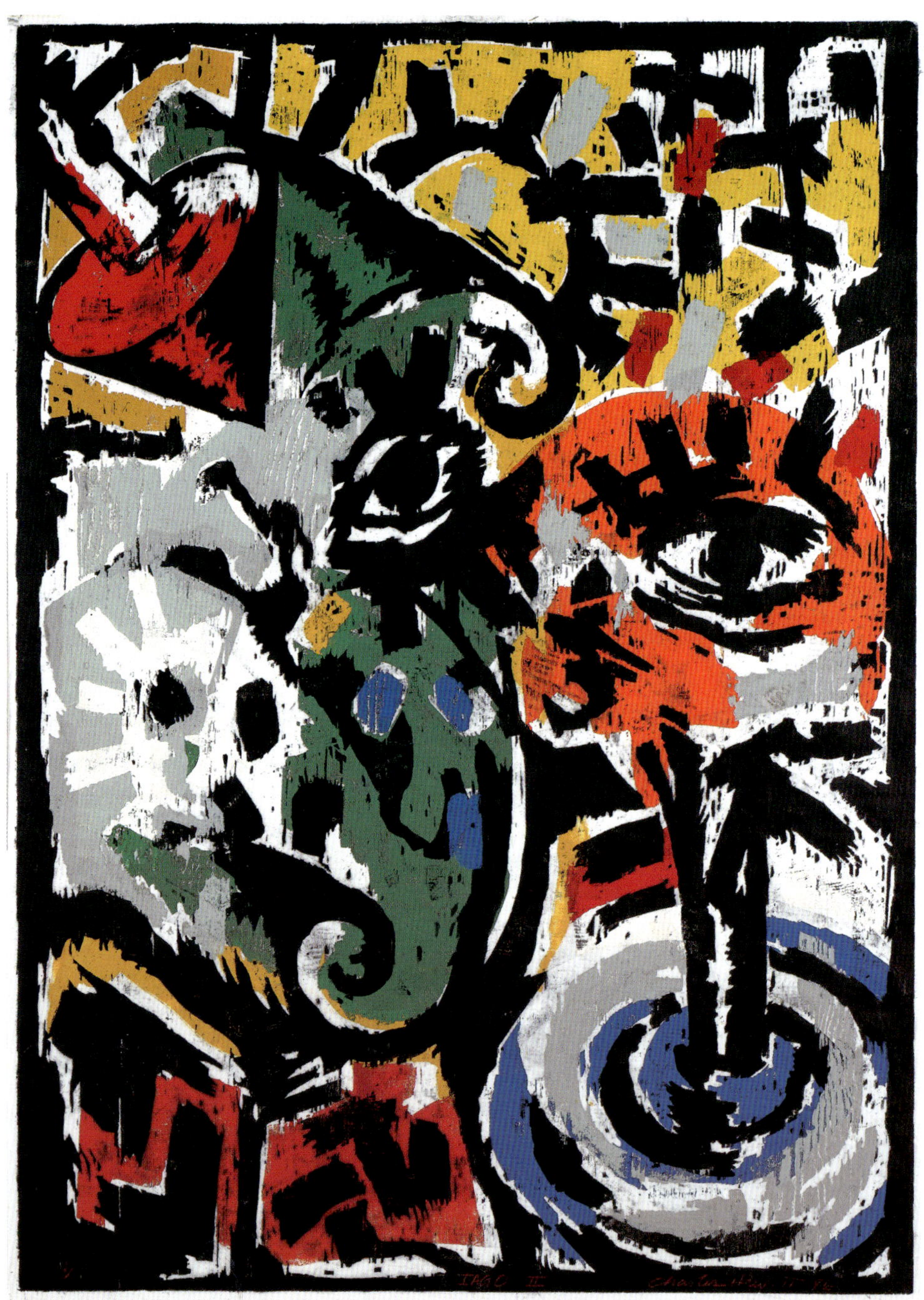

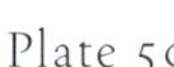

Plate 50

Charlie Hewitt (b. 1946), *Iago II*, 1986

color woodcut, 46 7/8 x 34 7/8 in.

printed by Anthony Kirk, George Bartko, and Marie Arcand,

published by Vinalhaven Press

Collection of the Portland Museum of Art

Museum Purchase with support from Joan B. Burns. 1986.249

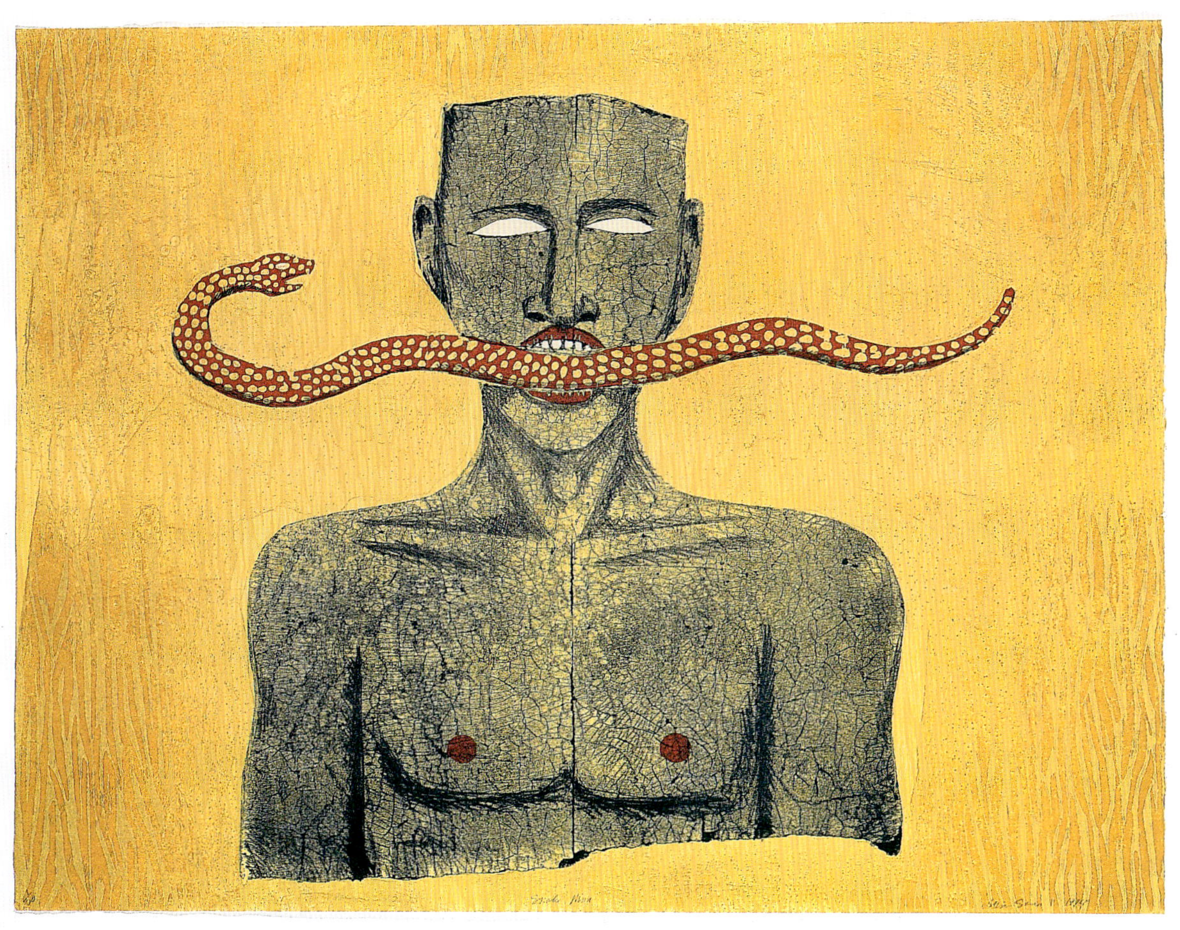

Plate 51

Alison Saar (b. 1956), *Snake Man*, 1994
woodcut and lithograph, 27 3/4 x 37 1/16 in.
printed by Jonathan Higgins, Kathleen Beckert,
and Scott Smith, published by Vinalhaven Press
Collection of the Bowdoin College Museum of Art
Anonymous Gift and Museum Purchase. 1995.10

Guilford resident Tom Staley (b. 1942) is also unafraid to gouge deeply into a woodblock. He prefers to work negatively from black to white (in reverse of the normal woodblock process of cutting around the lines of a drawing) by cutting into a block painted black in order to expose the lighter areas of his compositions. When printed, these areas become highlights that achieve a surprising sense of movement, as in the sparkling water surface depicted in his *Stream. Reflection* of 1992 (Plate 52). It is one of a series of woodcuts of the northern woods and mountains, some of which are portrayed under black skies and which include white trees swaying in black winds.

Alex Katz (b. 1927) has executed more than seventy woodcuts since 1951, in addition to working extensively in lithography, etching, and silkscreen. After his first small-format cuts of the 1950s, Katz did not return to the medium again until 1985, through an invitation from Crown Point Press, which had established an innovative collaboration in Japan with Tadashi Toda, a printer trained in the traditional *ukiyo-e* woodcut technique. Beginning with a watercolor sent by the artist, the printer and woodcutters evolved a multi-block color woodcut of the image that was then refined through a series of further proofs in a collaborative, back-and-forth process with Katz, adjusting numerous details of color and shading. The subtle tonal modeling and smooth "texture" of *The Green Cap* (Plate 53) is strikingly different from more expressionist contemporary woodcuts. Since then, many of Katz's woodcuts have taken up a simpler, monochromatic style, often worked from dark to light, defining forms and surfaces through outline and highlight, including a notable series of forest landscapes of 2001.

Although he is best known for his intricate silkscreen prints of urban scenes beginning in the 1970s, Northeast Harbor summer resident Richard Estes (b. 1932) has recently used the seemingly improbable technique of color woodcut to interpret his photorealist vision. *Post Office, 33rd and 8th* of 2004 (Plate 54) is printed in sixteen colors using eleven blocks cut by the master printer Karl Hecksher of K5 studios. In contrast to the more transparent Japanese woodcut style of the Katz print (Plate 53), Hecksher works in the European color woodcut tradition, which uses opaque oil-based inks to build up the complex spaces and reflections of Estes's subject. His close-up vantage point portrays a skewed cityscape in the reflections of puddles and car windows, themselves revealing intriguing abstractions of their own.

A more traditional outlook is seen in the work of Siri Beckman of Deer Isle (b. 1942), who executes small-scale wood engravings that fit into a long illustrative tradition, but whose clarity and openness of line bring a new sensibility to the medium, as in her *Otter Cove* of 1999 (Plate 55). She has

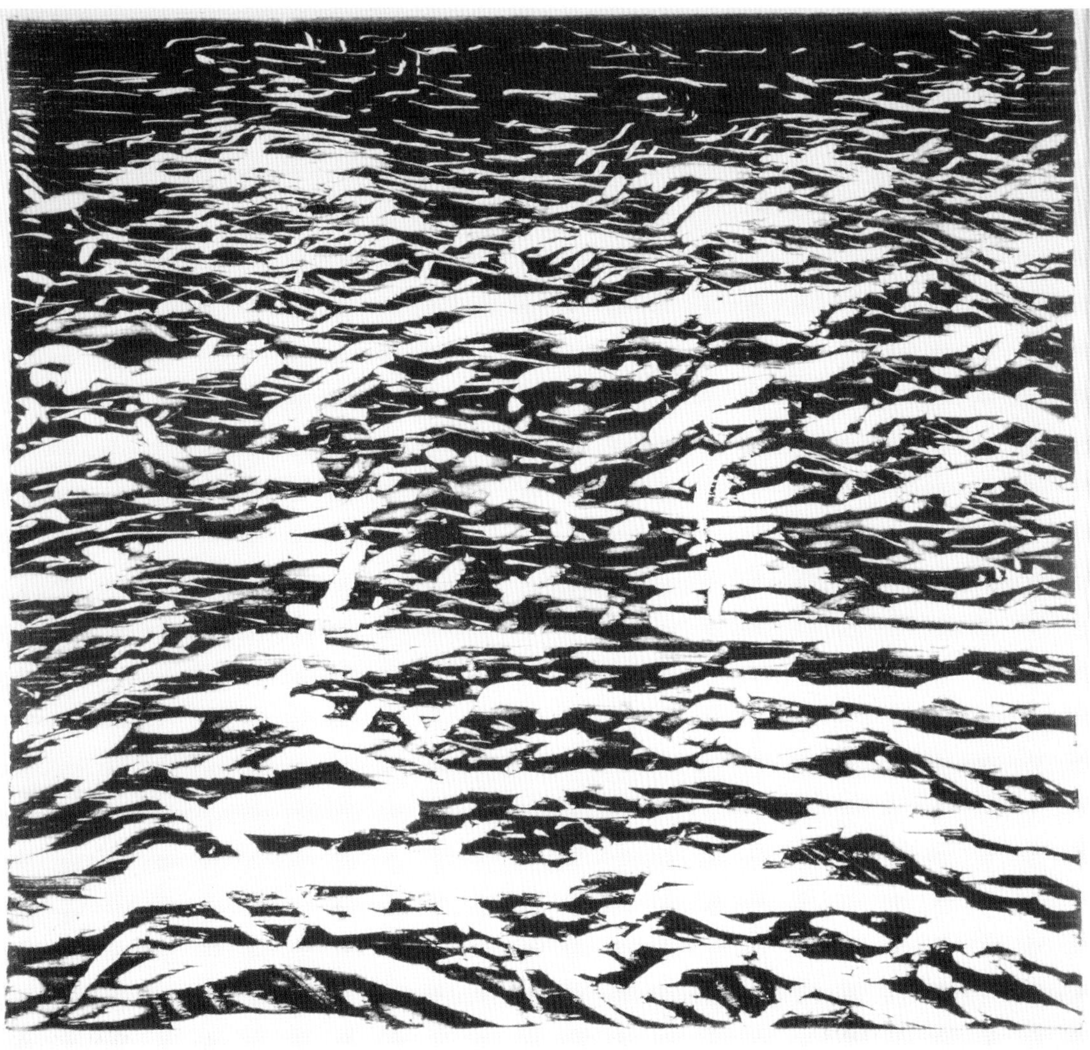

Plate 52

Tom Staley (b. 1942), *Stream. Reflection*, 1992

woodcut, 11 1/8 x 12 in.

Courtesy of the artist

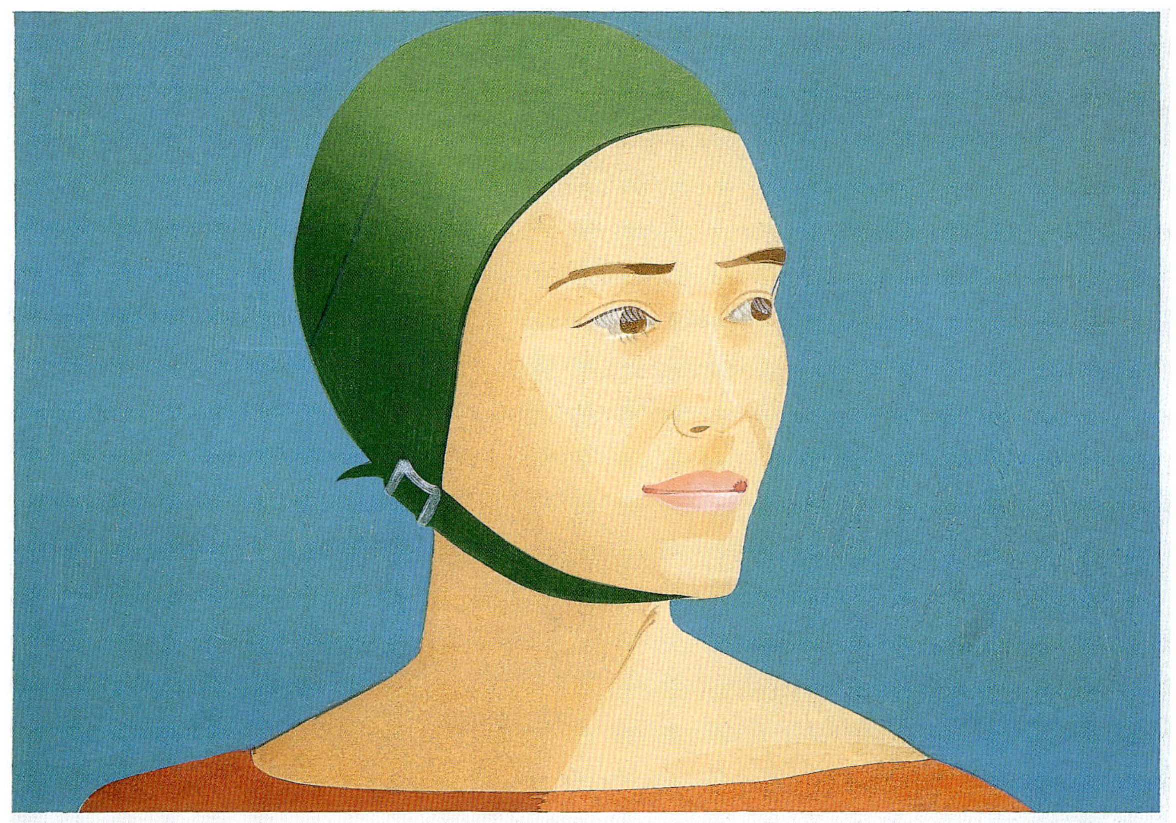

Plate 53

Alex Katz (b. 1927), *The Green Cap*, 1985

color woodcut, 12 1/4 x 17 7/8 in.

printed by Tadashi Toda, Shiundo Print Shop, Kyoto, Japan

published by Crown Point Press, San Francisco

Collection of the Colby College Museum of Art,

the Paul J. Schupf Wing. Gift of the artist. 1995.459.

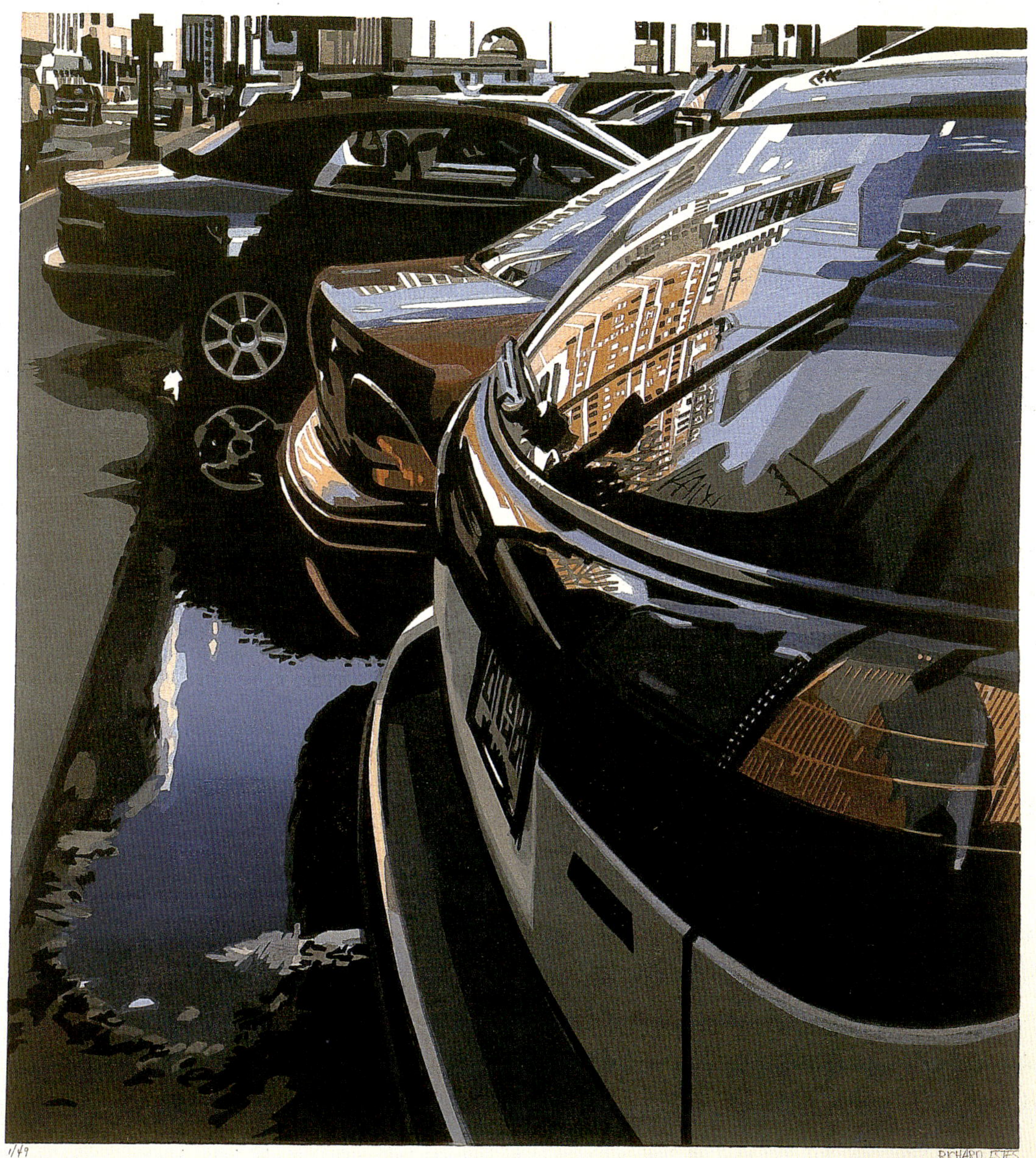

Plate 54

Richard Estes (b. 1932), *Post Office, 33rd and 8th*, 2004
color woodcut, 16 x 14 3/4 in.
printed by Karl Hecksher at K5 Studios
New Paltz, New York, published by Marlborough Graphics
© Richard Estes, courtesy of
Marlborough Gallery, New York, N.Y.

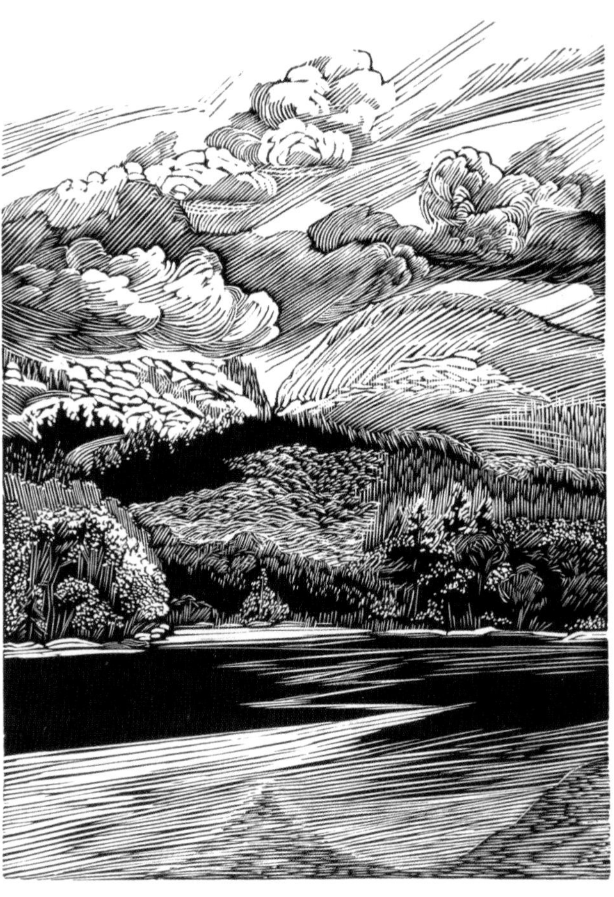

Plate 55

Siri Beckman (b. 1942), *Otter Cove*, 1999

wood engraving, 4 5/8 x 3 3/8 in.

Private Collection

illustrated a number of books set in the Maine landscape, such as *Week at the Lake* (1997). Among many others in the state working in a variety of woodcut styles today are Ashley Bryan, Wendy Kindred, Barbara Putnam, Don Gorvett, Scott Reed, Paulette Nejko, Dorothy Schwartz, R. Keith Rendall, and Gillyin Gatto.

ETCHING/DRYPOINT

Anyone working in the intaglio medium is usually acutely aware of the iconic etchings and engravings by such artists as Dürer, Rembrandt, Goya, and Picasso. Fair or not, etching has at times been seen as the true test of a printmaker, and it, along with woodcut/linocut, constitutes the primary and most accessible medium for teaching and practice of printmaking, in Maine and elsewhere. Following its own rich tradition, Maine has exhibited a continuing spirit of experimentation in recent intaglio technique and imagery, and has also pioneered significantly safer studio practices.

Speaking for the primacy of drawing as an essential foundation for printmaking is the bravura etching from the late 1970s by Berwick resident Pat Hardy (b. 1940), *Bench with Cacti* (Plate 56). It was printed at Lakeside Studio by the Massachusetts intaglio specialist Robert Townsend, who first printed a solid "roll" of silver-toned ink on the paper before printing the etched plate in a darker gray ink. The effect is reminiscent of the evanescent still-lifes of Giorgio Morandi or Alberto Giacometti. Steadily committed to drawing, Pat studied at Syracuse University and the Ogunquit School of Painting and Sculpture. She and her husband DeWitt Hardy (also an active printmaker) have honed their practice by taking part in a weekly drawing group since 1963, the year after they moved to Maine.

Robert Indiana (b. 1928) had not worked in etching since his student years, but returned to the medium in 1986 at the Vinalhaven Press. *Mother of Exiles* (Plate 57) is both in homage to the Statue of Liberty's centennial celebration and an exemplar of Indiana's preoccupation with the "American Dream" — the statue's melancholy tear also evoking a note of contemporary political commentary. Indiana is best known for his strictly two-dimensional, boldly colored, crisply outlined silkscreen prints of numbers and words, and this print stands out among his printed œuvre for its subtle tones and sculptural treatment of the figure. The inherent grittiness of the aquatint medium also slightly resists the precision of the artist's draftsmanship.

A more intimate view of the Maine landscape preoccupied Marvin Bileck (1920–2005), who explored from the 1940s the forest and shoreline of Cranberry Island. Bileck's intricately observed etchings

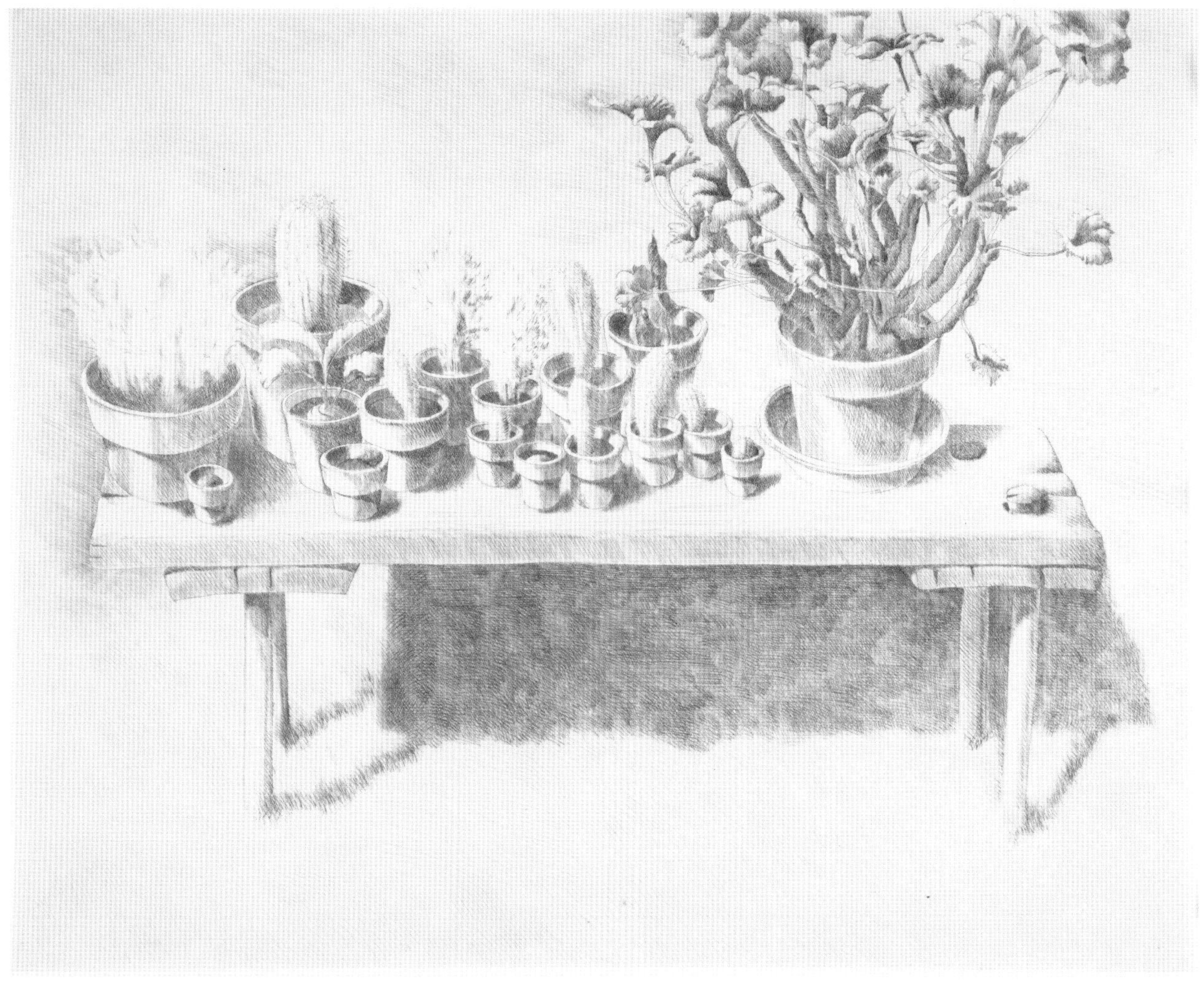

Plate 56

Patricia Hardy (b. 1940), *Bench with Cacti*, late 1970s
etching, 15 7/8 x 20 in., printed by Robert Townsend
published by Lakeside Studio, Lakeside, Michigan
Courtesy of the Burk Collection

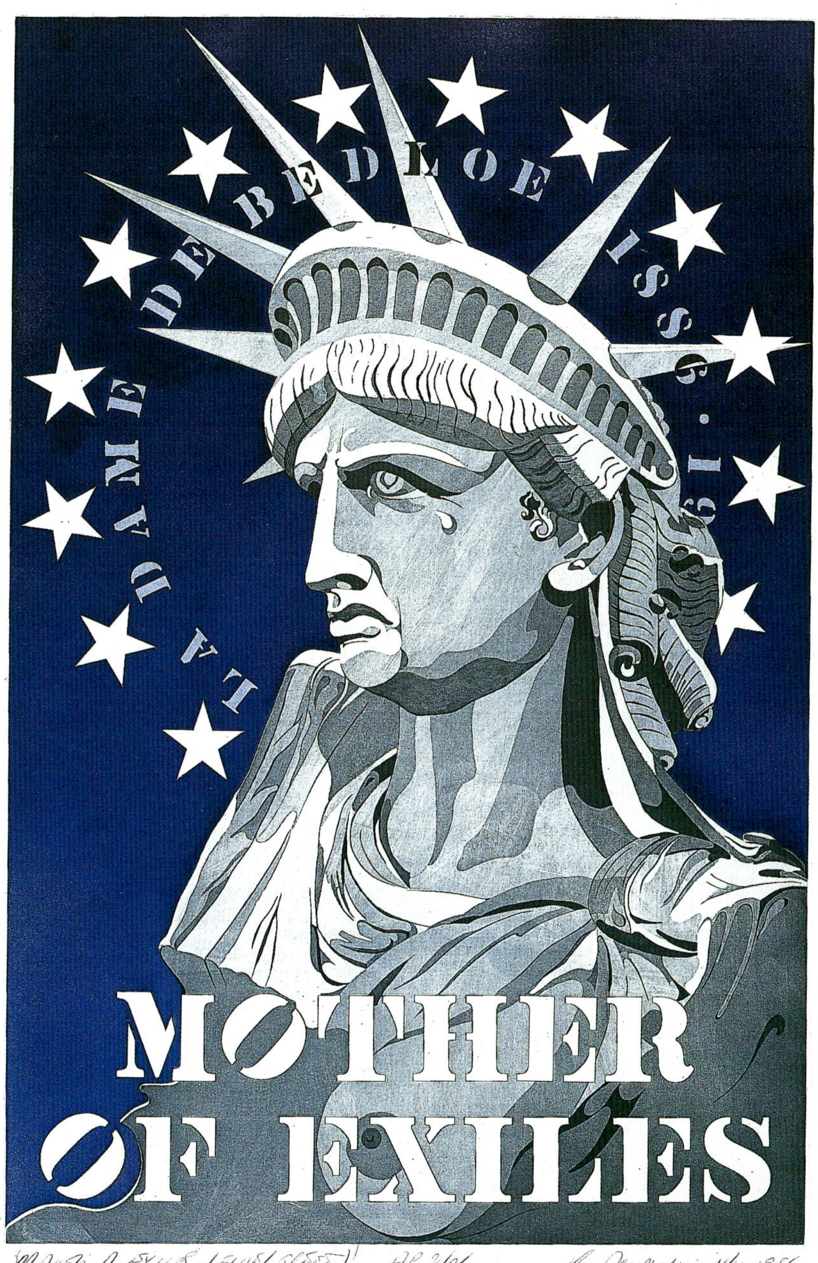

Plate 57

Robert Indiana (b. 1928), *Mother of Exiles*, 1986
hard-ground etching and aquatint, 36 x 24 in.
printed by Anthony Kirk, Orlando Condeso,
and Susan Volker, published by Vinalhaven Press
Collection of the Portland Museum of Art
Gift of Vinalhaven Press and Patricia Nick, 2000.30.2.

recall the inextricable visions of Rodolphe Bresdin or—more recently—Hyman Bloom, who portrayed the moss-laden woods of Lubec for many years in drawings and paintings. *Fallen Trees* (Plate 58) does not offer a broad view or try to depict every branch or knot, but examines the interlocking strengths and decays of a small corner of a lush forest. The Portland artist Brett Bigbee has done very few prints, but similarly has portrayed a small patch of grass in a subtly detailed lithograph, *Ground Cover*, of 1997.

John Walker (b. 1939) shares this intense examination of a small portion of the Maine landscape, but instead monumentalizes and abstracts it. His second home and studio face a small midcoast cove, which he has rendered in painting, drawing, monotype, lithography, and etching to explore different times of day, different seasons, different tides. *John's Bay II* of 2003 (Plate 59) is one of three extremely gritty carborundum "aquatints" he executed with Susan Hover Oehme at Riverhouse Editions in Colorado. He built up the image by drawing with a mix of acrylic and carborundum (an abrasive mixture of carbon and silicon used to grind smooth the surface of lithograph stones) directly on the printing plate. When inked and printed, the hardened, rough granular surface produces a very rich tonal image. The translucency of the mixture of black and opaque white inks used in printing the plate imparts the bluish tone, appropriate for a moonlit scene over water.

Another painter who has deeply committed herself to printmaking is Alison Hildreth (b. 1934). While also exploring woodcut and lithography at various times, she has particularly devoted herself to etching and drypoint, often in combination, as in her triptych *Timepiece* of 1994 (Plate 60), printed by Jonathan Higgins and Randy Hemminghaus at the Galamander Press. As with Walker's prints, Hildreth's technique reveals a complex layering of image and history and a deep engagement with the printing surface. A rich mix of etching, aquatint, and drypoint (the latter most visible in the central panel), the imagery in this print hovers on the fine line between representation and abstraction, revealing only dreamy hints of recognizable shapes of vessels in the right panel. She has recently executed an extensive series of small drypoints of bats, and is currently working on a series of combination polymer etching plates.

The technique of drypoint is inherently not delicate; it consists of drawing a sharp steel (or often diamond-tipped) point across the surface of a metal printing plate, in the process pushing up ridges of metal on each side of the furrow. When the plate is inked, these ridges (referred to as "burr") catch amounts of ink that when printed appear as soft, more or less velvety lines. This quality of softness combined with the tension necessary to control the drypoint tool has attracted many artists (Rembrandt and Beckmann come to mind, as do Washburn's landscapes [see Plate 13]). Charlie Hewitt has also used drypoint on both intimate and monumental scales, as in his six-foot long *Portland Tumble* of 1996–97. The technique's energetic qualities are able to convey extremely lively depictions, vividly revealed by *Twin Study* of 1999 (Plate 61) by Anne Harris (b. 1961), who taught for several years at Maine College of Art and Bowdoin College. An artist known for her unflinching portrayals of the nude, Harris succeeds in creating the vulnerable, yet insistent, presence of a newborn baby.

Trees Reflected on Ice of 2002 (Plate 62) was in fact the last print completed by Neil Welliver (1929–2005). Previously, the majority of his prints were either color woodcuts or etchings with aquatint. The latter usually comprised detailed areas of aquatint tones outlined by etched lines, imparting an overall textured and contained feel. This print, however, utilized a looser, more draftsmanly technique in which the artist painted on the surface of the plate with a brush filled with a sticky sugar solution. The plate was then covered with an acid-resistant ground and washed with water (in this case from the artist's garden hose), melting the hardened sugar and lifting the ground off those areas. An aquatint powder was then sprinkled on the plate and etched, creating bitten tones corresponding to the artist's brushstrokes. Printed in colors from seven different plates by Peter Pettengill at Wingate Studio, the broad aquatint strokes effectively reveal the artist's fluid draftsmanship, resembling a watercolor (in fact, an early term for aquatint was "wash manner"). *Trees Reflected on Ice* becomes a moving image of the evanescent effects of light and shadow.

The Portland artist Anna Hepler (b. 1969) often utilizes minute gestures in her sculpture and drawings, which in the aggregate combine to create a larger presence, as in three lithographs of circles and spirals produced at Tamarind in 2005. Her most recent series of intaglio prints are, in contrast, very loose renderings of apparently organic, cellular forms, although based on a group of hanging sculptures made of thin wire. She drew her white-on-black aquatint *Sphere Study #5* (Plate 63) directly on a copper plate with a Sharpie® marker, which constituted enough of a resist to retain her lines while applying an aquatint tone. When the plate was printed, her gestures remained perfectly highlighted. The print embodies Hepler's delight in the intersection of drawing, printmaking, and sculpture.

James Davies Cambronne (b. 1952), who taught at the Maine College of Art for ten years, has intently explored the realms between the visible and invisible, perception and conception, combining a modernist training with a strong childhood influence from Native American aesthetics and culture.

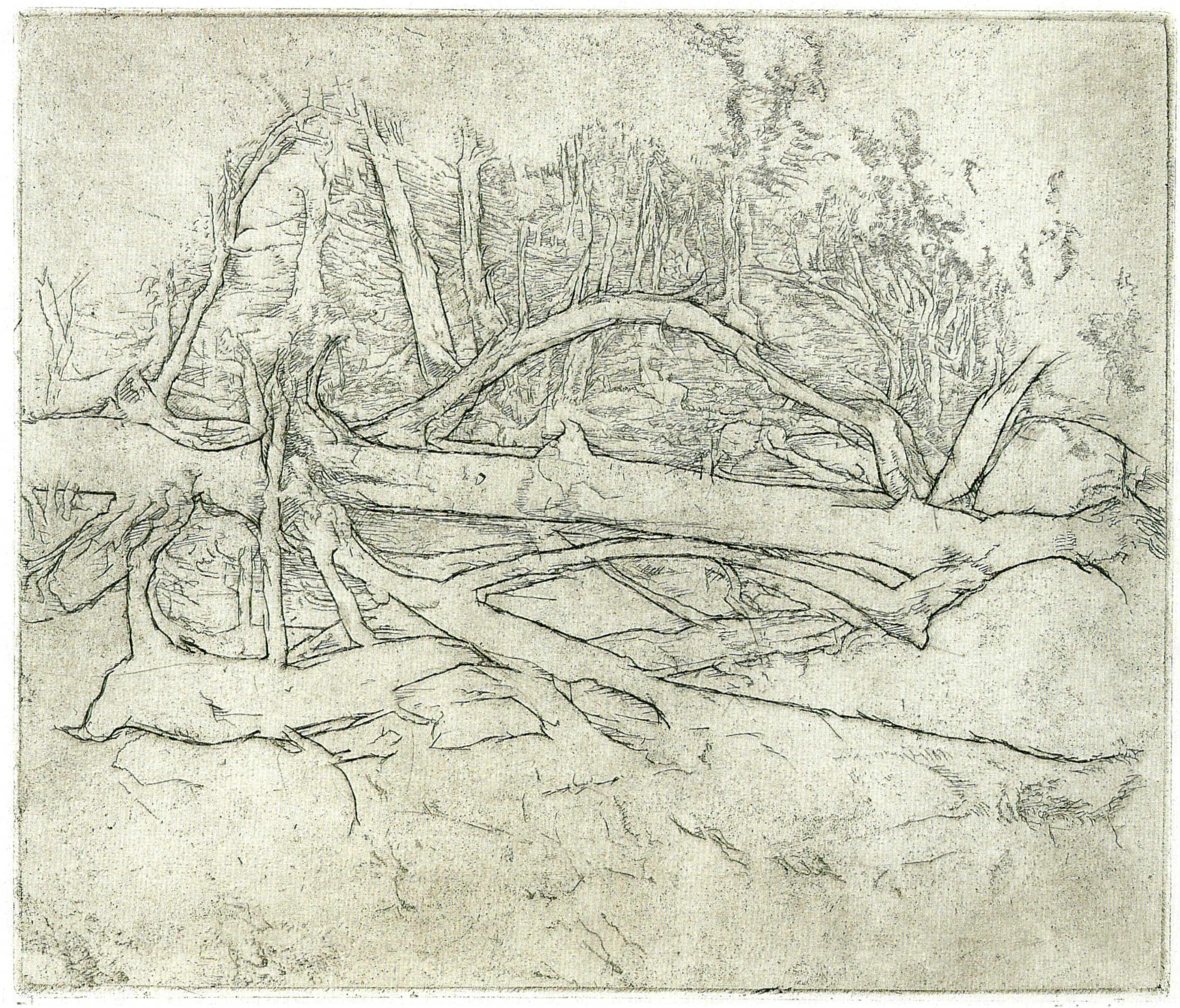

Plate 58

Marvin Bileck (1920–2005), *Fallen Trees*, n.d.,

etching and aquatint, 8 x 9 3/4 in.

Courtesy of the Alexandre Gallery, New York

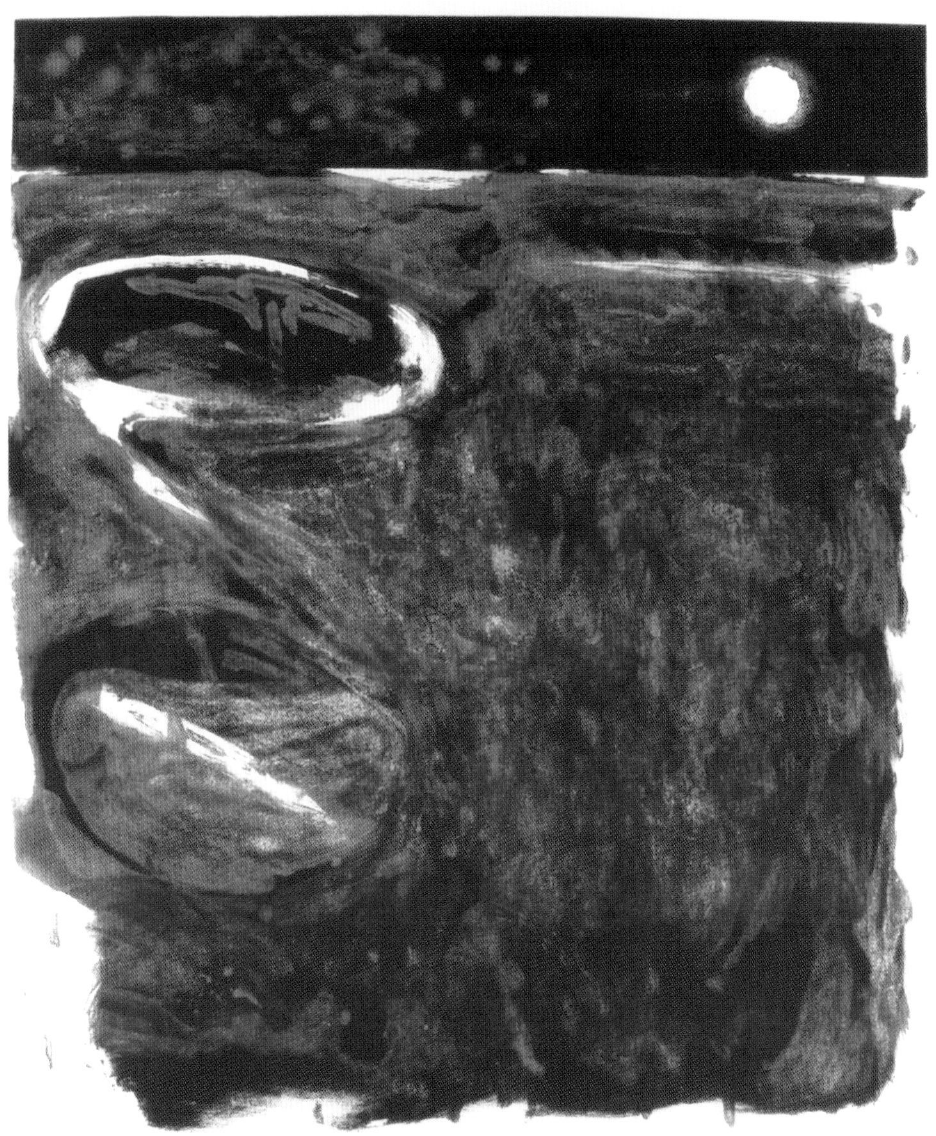

Plate 59

John Walker (b. 1939), *John's Bay II*, 2003

carborundum aquatint in two colors, 49 7/8 x 40 3/4 in.

printed by Susan Hover Oehme

published by Riverhouse Editions (William and Jan van Straaten), Steamboat Springs, Colorado

Courtesy of Riverhouse Editions

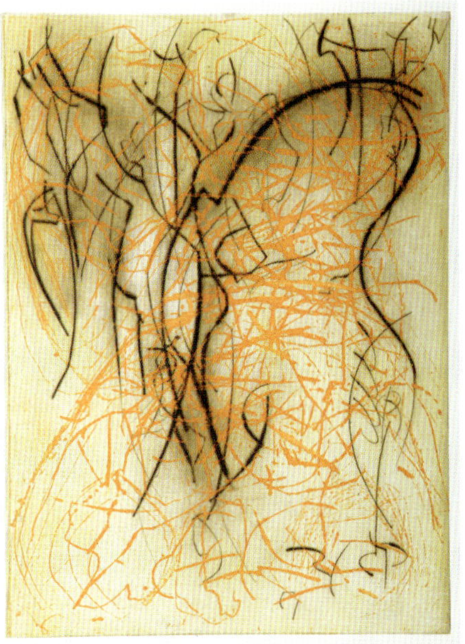
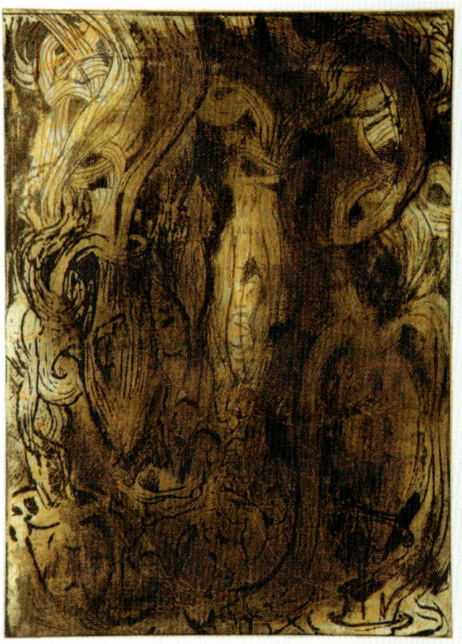
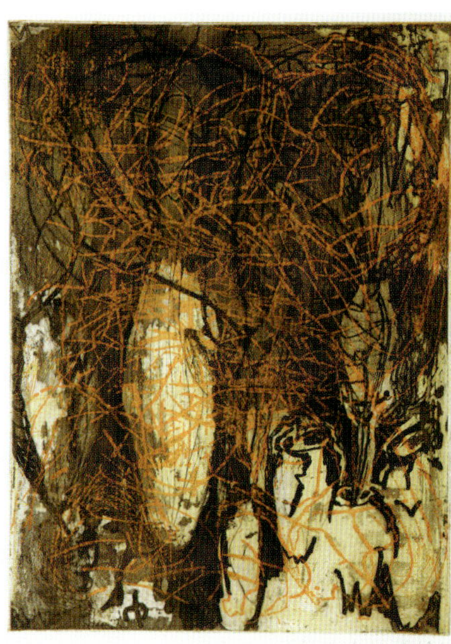

Plate 60

Alison Hildreth (b. 1934), *Timepiece*, 1994

etching and aquatint, 12 x 30 3/4 in.

printed by Randy Hemminghaus and Jonathan Higgins

at Galamander Press, New York

Courtesy of the artist

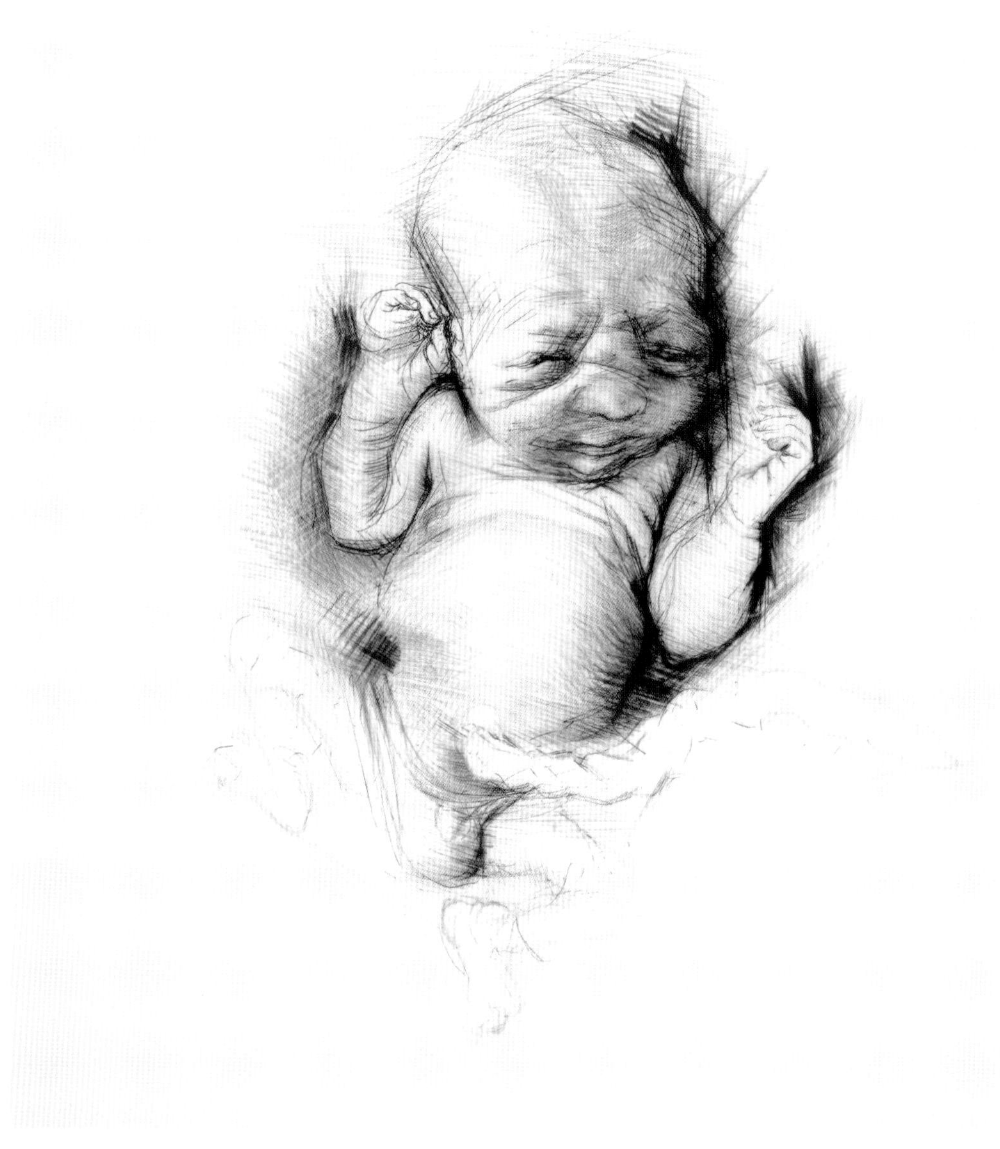

Plate 61

Anne Harris (b. 1961), *Twin Study*, 1999

etching and drypoint, 17 x 15 in.

Private Collection

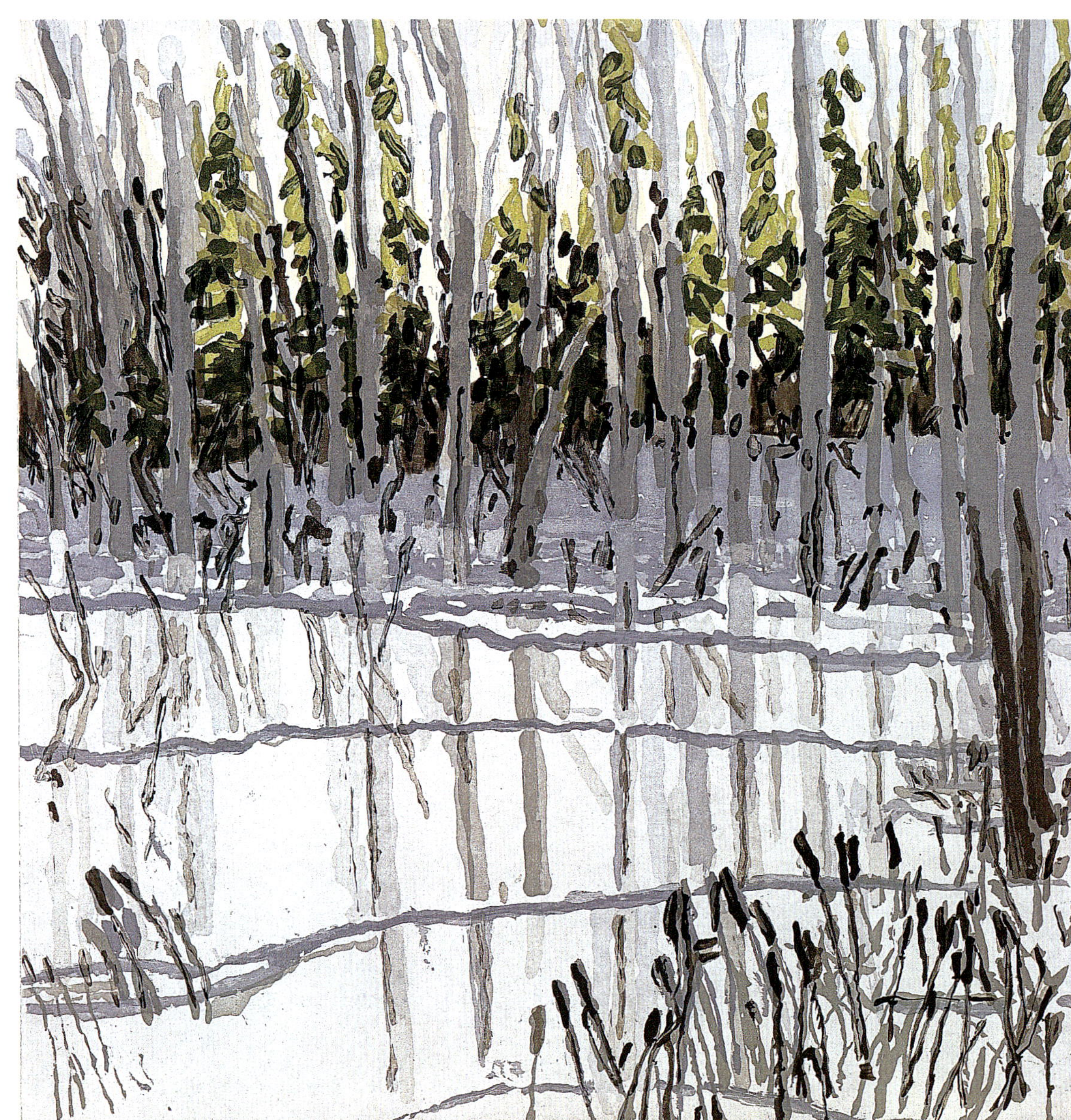

Plate 62

Neil Welliver (1929-2005), *Trees Reflected on Ice*, 2004

aquatint, 22 1/2 x 23 3/4 in.

printed by Peter Pettengill at Wingate Studio, Hinsdale, New Hampshire

published by Alexandre Fine Art, Inc.

Courtesy of the Alexandre Gallery, New York

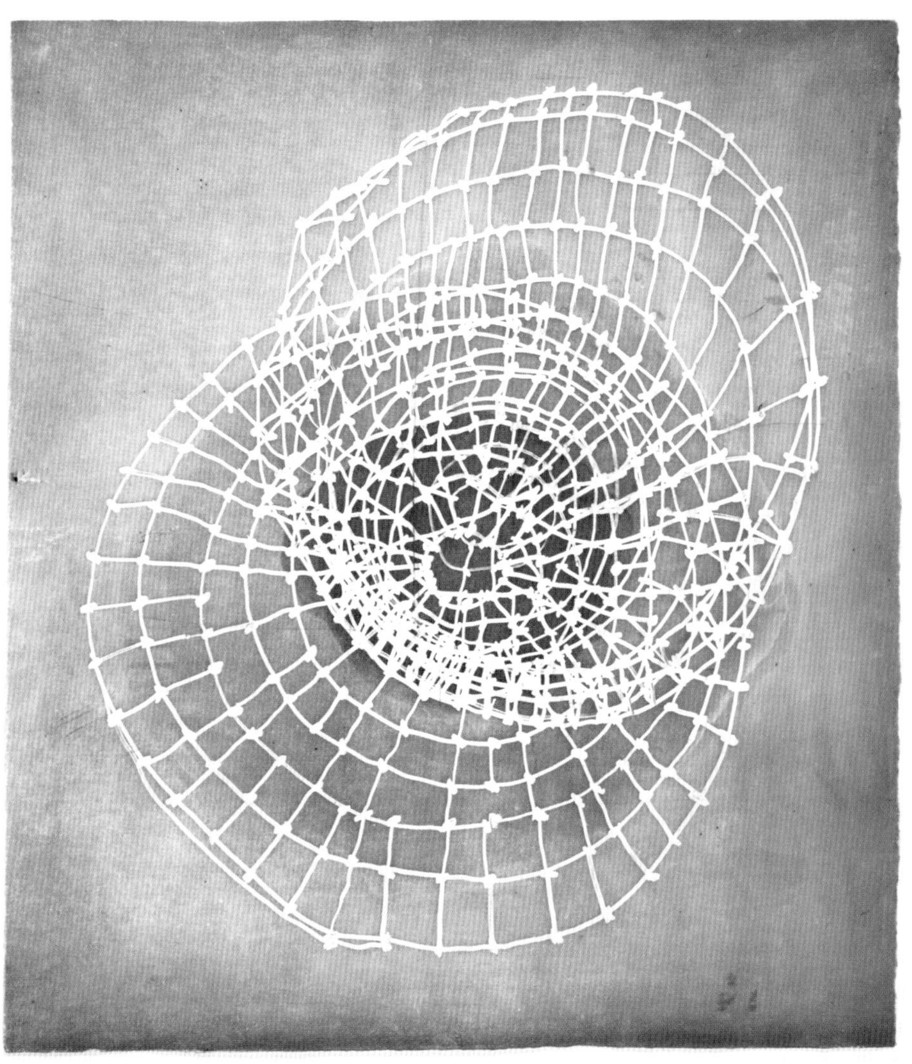

Plate 63

Anna Hepler (b. 1969), *Sphere Study #5*, 2005

aquatint and spitbite, 19 3/4 x 17 5/8 in.

Courtesy of the artist

Languidere of 1994 (Plate 64) references the Princess Languidere, a character in Frank Baum's Wizard of Oz books who owns a cabinet of thirty heads that she is able to exchange according to mood or occasion. Cambronne exploits this interchangeability through reversals of perspective, depth, and perception. Although deceptively simple in appearance, the three plates of this print were intensely worked by the artist, building up circles with carborundum, cutting a circle entirely through the plate, deeply etching the lines, burnishing and scraping, and using aquatint, drypoint, softground, and drypoint—not to forget transparencies of layered inkings. Cambronne worked on this print at the time he was developing his first room-sized installations of scrims, colored lights, and painted lines and dots.

Only recently have efforts been concentrated on finding alternatives to the toxic materials historically used in etching, especially acids, grounds, and oil-based inks. Susan Groce (b. 1954) has been a leader in this research at the University of Maine, also collaborating with scientists and printmakers in Canada and Scotland. Groce and her colleagues developed the Orono Ground, an acrylic resist increasingly used in studios around the world. She has also fostered the use of photo-polymer intaglio plates for printing. She has lectured and demonstrated her techniques and materials as far away as Australia.[4] In her large (itself space-invasive) wall installation, *Invasive Species* (Plate 65—detail), Groce intersperses photopolymer-etched electron microscopic images of leaf surfaces and seed pods (scanned on the electron microscope at the Royal Botanic Garden in Edinburgh), satellite views of secret military airfields, and images of hurricanes. Intentionally stretching the limitations of visual perception, she illuminates a potential dialogue of destruction and construction through man's effect on the natural world and climatic change, while referencing the human and natural costs of war, the "ultimate invasive act." The detail illustrated here is composed of 16 from a total of 288 etchings, arranged in a wall installation measuring nine by fourteen feet.

As with other techniques, only the smallest survey of the work of intaglio printmakers working in Maine is possible here, including a mention of others such as DeWitt Hardy, Gideon Bok, Alice Spencer, Elizabeth Peak, Donald Lent, Lesley Dill, Scott Schnepf, Stephen Burt, Vivien Russe, Rob Shetterly, Ron Slater, Charles Wadsworth, Valerie Zint, and Andrea van Voorst van Beest.

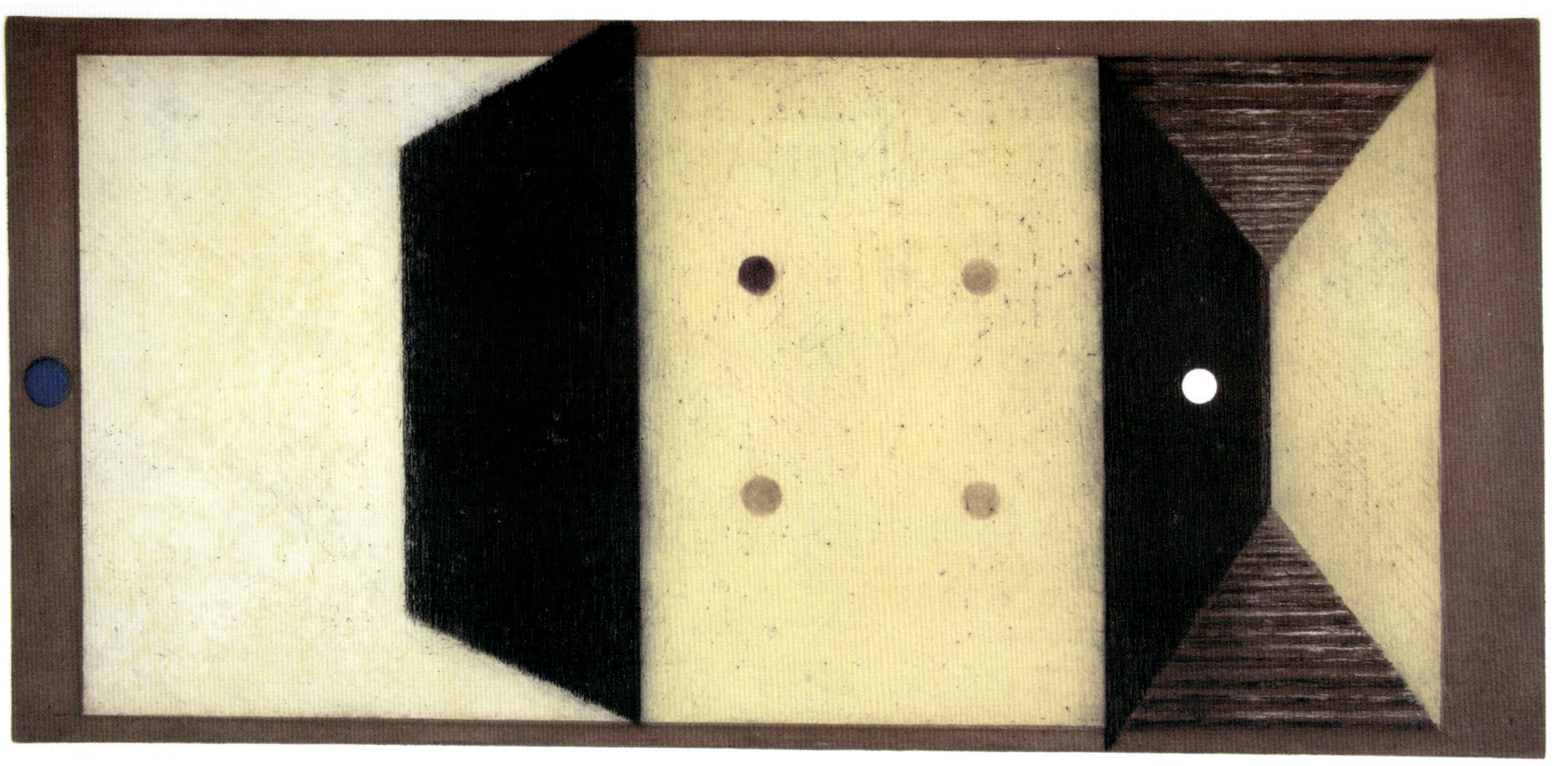

Plate 64

James Cambronne (b. 1952), *Languidere*, 1994
etching, engraving, aquatint, spitbite, drypoint,
with burnishing, 10 3/8 x 22 3/8 in.
Private Collection

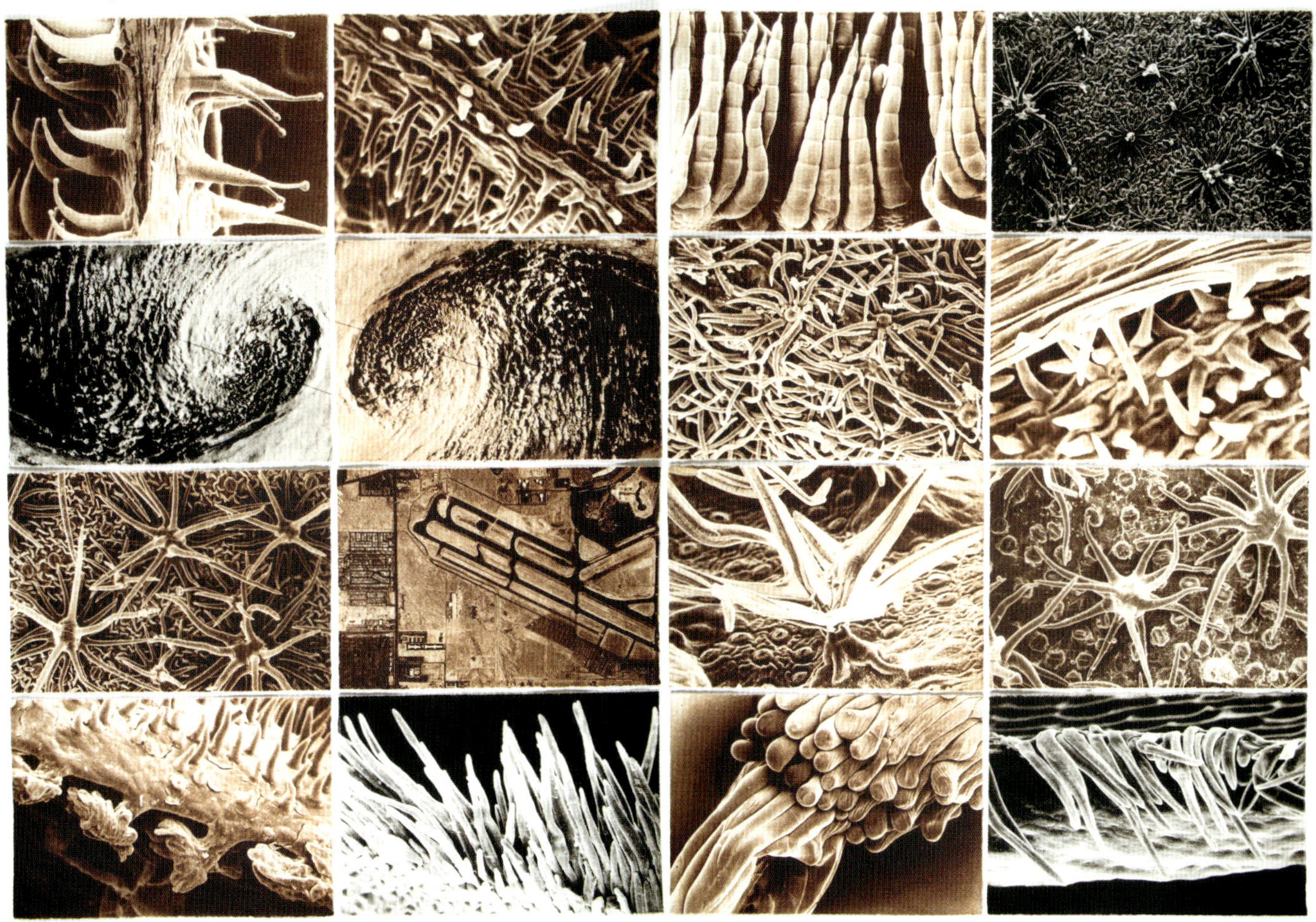

Plate 65

Susan Groce (b. 1954), *Invasive Species*, 2005, photopolymer etchings (16 from an installation of 288), 6 x 9 in. each.

LITHOGRAPHY

Compared to woodcut and intaglio prints, lithography does not seem to hold as prominent a place in printmaking practice within the state. The expertise and material investment necessary for printing on lithographic stones in particular is not easily acquired, and quite often artists have chosen to work with professional printers rather than tackle the task by themselves. While lithography is being taught at a few colleges and universities, there are relatively few professional art printers in the state. One such artist/printer is Frances Hodsdon (b. 1926), who was born in Wilton and studied at Kent State University and the Boston Museum School with Ture Bengtz before returning to Maine in 1975. In addition to working in intaglio and silkscreen, Hodsdon has her own lithographic press in her Jefferson studio, where she prints her own and others' lithographs (including those of Dahlov Ipcar and Jacqueline Hudson). Her *Self-Portrait* of 1994–95 (Plate 66) is rendered in broad areas of lithographic ink wash (tusche). What at first seem drawn outlines are in fact pooled areas of pigment at the outer edges of the tusche washes; crayon is used only to define subtle shading in her face. Hodsdon is an active teacher around the state and established the printmaking studio at the Round Top Center for the Arts in Damariscotta.

Another devoted teacher and lithographer was Allan Gardiner, who taught the technique at the Maine College of Art for 37 years after learning it there as a student. He executed exquisitely detailed land- and seascapes with a complete control of lithographic draftsmanship and printing. Alan Magee has executed color lithographs based on watercolors of his characteristic superrealist stones and still-lifes. As mentioned elsewhere, in addition to other print media, a number of Maine artists have collaborated with print workshops for lithographic productions, among them Alex Katz, Robert Indiana, Carolyn Brady, Anna Hepler, DeWitt Hardy, Yvonne Jacquette, Richard Wilson, and Brett Bigbee.

Recently, a remarkably low-tech alternative to the complexities of traditional lithography has appeared, often referred to as "xerox lithography" or "paper plate lithography." Using a xerox photocopy or laser print that has been treated with gum Arabic to protect the areas not to be printed, the paper "plate" is then moistened, rolled with ink (which only adheres to the image—identical to the principles of traditional lithography), and printed in a roller press, or even by hand. Subject to manifold variations through transfers, collage, layered printings, etc., the process is not as precise or controllable as traditional lithography, and the paper original is only able to produce a very few printings. Yet this

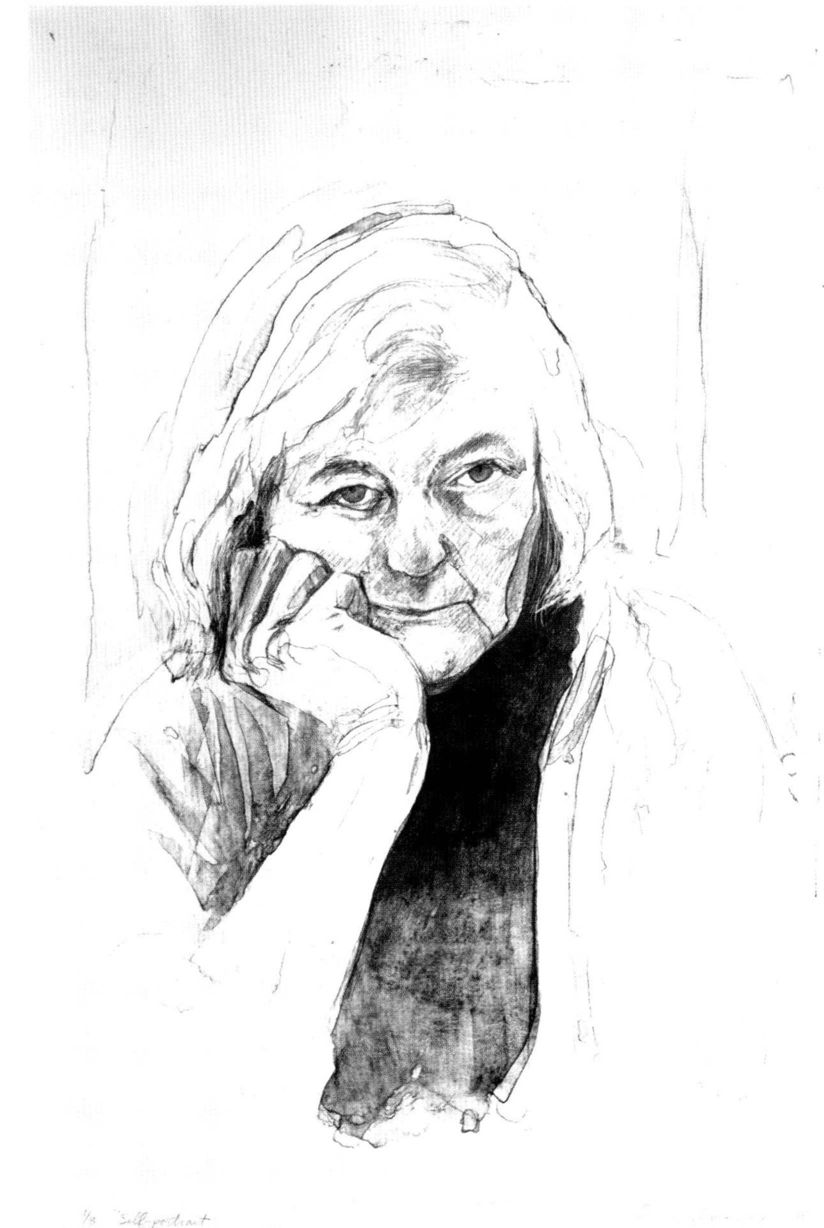

Plate 66

Frances Hodsdon (b. 1926), *Self-Portrait*, 1994–95

lithograph, 23 1/2 x 16 in.

Collection of the Bates College Museum of Art.

Museum Purchase. 1995.24.1

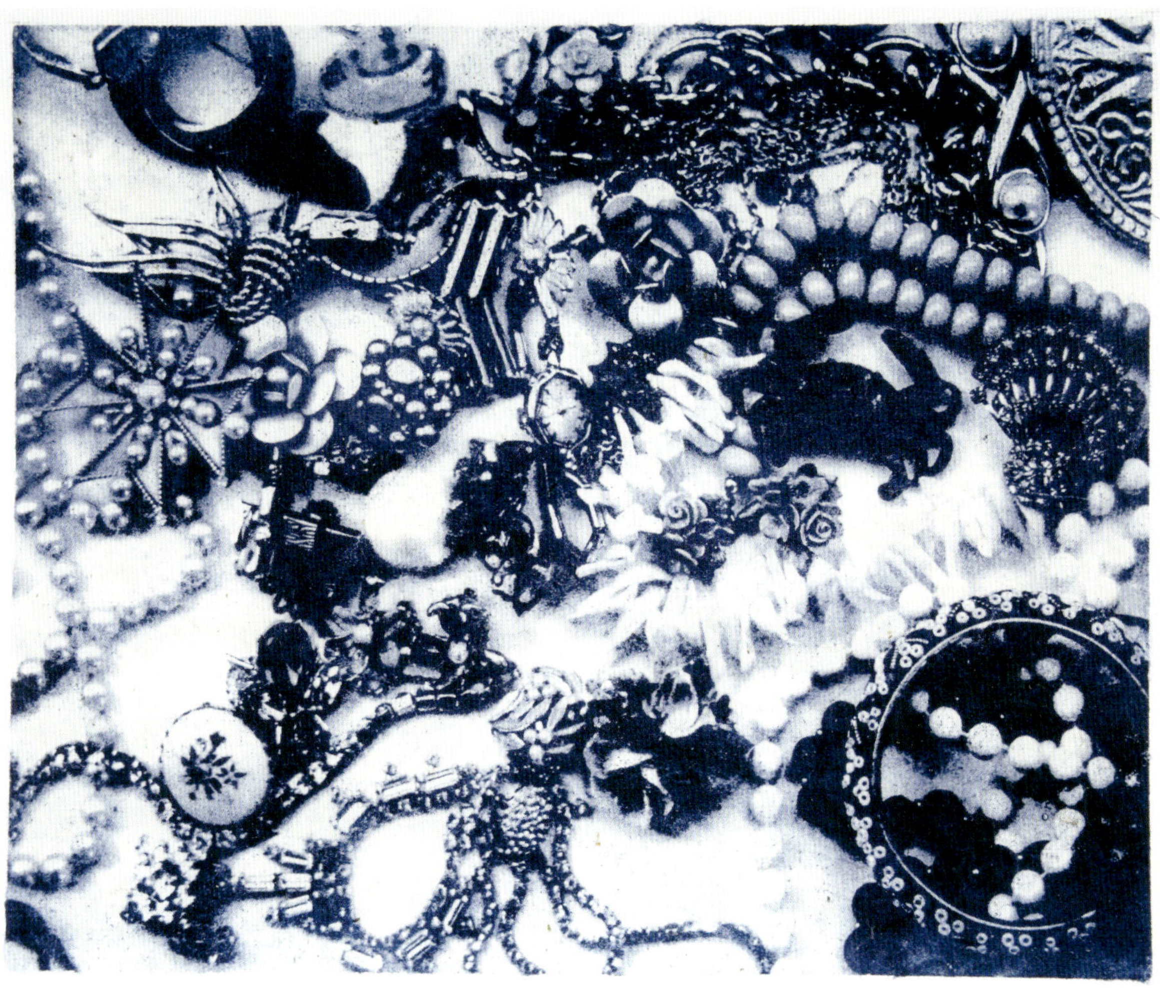

Plate 67

Judith Allen-Efstathiou (b. 1945), *The Contents of Betty's Jewelry Box*, 2003, xerox lithograph, 10 5/8 x 13 1/8 in.

Courtesy of the artist. © 2003 Judith Allen-Efstathiou

unpredictable, often rough, yet versatile and technically easy printmaking method has attracted many artists, notably at the Peregrine Press. For instance, Judith Allen-Efstathiou [b. 1945] has used it extensively, adapting digital photographs and photocopies and reveling in the deterioration of the images through repeated printings and transfers. She has printed extensively on cloth, creating wall-sized installations. *The Contents of Betty's Jewelry Box* of 2003 (Plate 67) is one of a series of similar evocations of her own and other family members' memories through material objects. This print shows her mother's jewelry, some of which came from her grandmother. Allen-Efstathiou comes from a Maine family with five generations (at least) of artists. She and her mother and daughter all are graduates of the Boston Museum School.

MONOTYPE

The practice of monotype is one of the easiest, quickest, and least technical forms of printmaking, and it has a particularly large presence in studios around Maine. This fascinating combination of drawing, painting, and print is often used as a "warm-up" exercise for artists who have never done prints (Vinalhaven Press made a regular practice of this), but equally often as a continuing exploration and primary medium throughout an artist's career (as, for instance, in the highly resolved and often large-scale compositions of Susan Amons). Often, too, monotype techniques are used to create variant printings within an edition from an etched plate or carved woodblock, in which hand-manipulated inking can produce impressions of strikingly different effects. (Impressions in these cases are usually referred to as "monoprints.")

The variations in monotype are seemingly limitless, allowing for the use of different types of ink (even watercolor), printing surface, and technical approach. Yvonne Jacquette (b. 1934) has experimented with printing multi-layered monotypes from pastel crayon drawings. During a residency at the Vinalhaven Press, she produced a group of related monotypes from a fine-grained wood surface. Using a basic outline on mylar as a guide, Jacquette would render a drawing that the printer, Chris Erickson, would then print, having laid down a roll of colorless acrylic medium in order to adhere the pastel medium to the printing paper. Further printings of new drawings on the same sheet would produce a many-layered monotype. Repeating the process on another sheet with a different palette, Jacquette produced a group of nine variations on *Vinalhaven Shelves and Ledges*, of which Plate 68 is the ninth. It consists of three layers of pastel

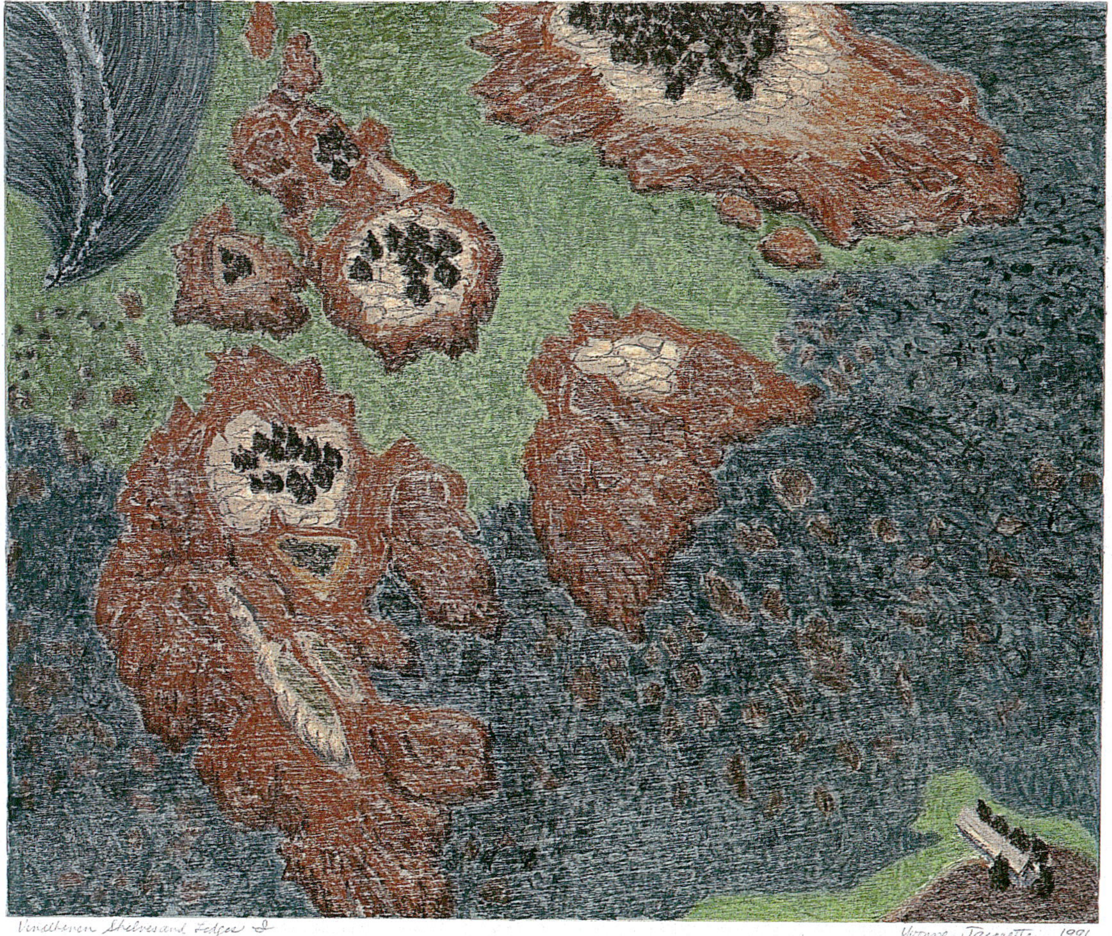

Plate 68

Yvonne Jacquette (b. 1934), *Vinalhaven Shelves and Ledges I*, 1991

color monotype, 16 1/2 x 20 17/16 in.

printed by John C. Erickson

published by Vinalhaven Press

Collection of the Bowdoin College Museum of Art

Courtesy of the artist and Mary Ryan Gallery, New York

between four layers of transparent acrylic. Other notable practitioners of more traditional forms of monotype in Maine include Beverly Hallam, Lois Dodd, Robert Cumming, and Alan Magee, who executed a series of particularly haunting black-and-white masks.

SILKSCREEN

Many artists have been attracted by the smooth surfaces and saturated colors possible with the silkscreen technique, which first achieved popularity during the Depression as a cheaper and less technical print medium. Emerging from the advertising industry, it became particularly popular for political and artistic posters. Pop artists such as Andy Warhol and Robert Indiana made major works in the medium, as did later photorealists such as Richard Estes. Silkscreen also represented a major crossroad of the printmaking and photographic aesthetics as light-sensitive emulsions were adapted to the technique, especially in the 1960s and 1970s.

While silkscreen is perhaps most often seen these days on T-shirts, several Maine artists have worked in the medium, in addition to Indiana and Estes. As mentioned above, Richard Wilson, in addition to his own printmaking, has made a specialty of printing silkscreens for artists such as Philip Barter, George Burk, Eric Hopkins, Francis Merritt, Marjorie Moore, Italo Scanga, and Juris Ubans. Rebecca Goodale has used the technique for a large number of illustrated books and prints, often in innovative formats, such as her current multi-year project illuminating the plight of endangered animal and plant species in the state, in which she has constructed pop-up books, free-standing "star" forms, and print/book animal forms. The low-tech photosilkscreen "gocco" process, a recent Japanese import, has become increasingly popular among printmakers.

DIGITAL AND OTHER FRONTIERS

The appearance of the first Macintosh computer in 1984 marked one of the most revolutionary inventions in image-making, comparable to the advent of the printing press in the fifteenth century and photography in the nineteenth. At the turn of the twenty-first century, the traditional boundaries of printmaking are no more. Abetted by the adaptability of digital imagemaking, artists are willing to try all sorts of materials, surfaces, scales, and presentations for works incorporating print techniques, whether virtual

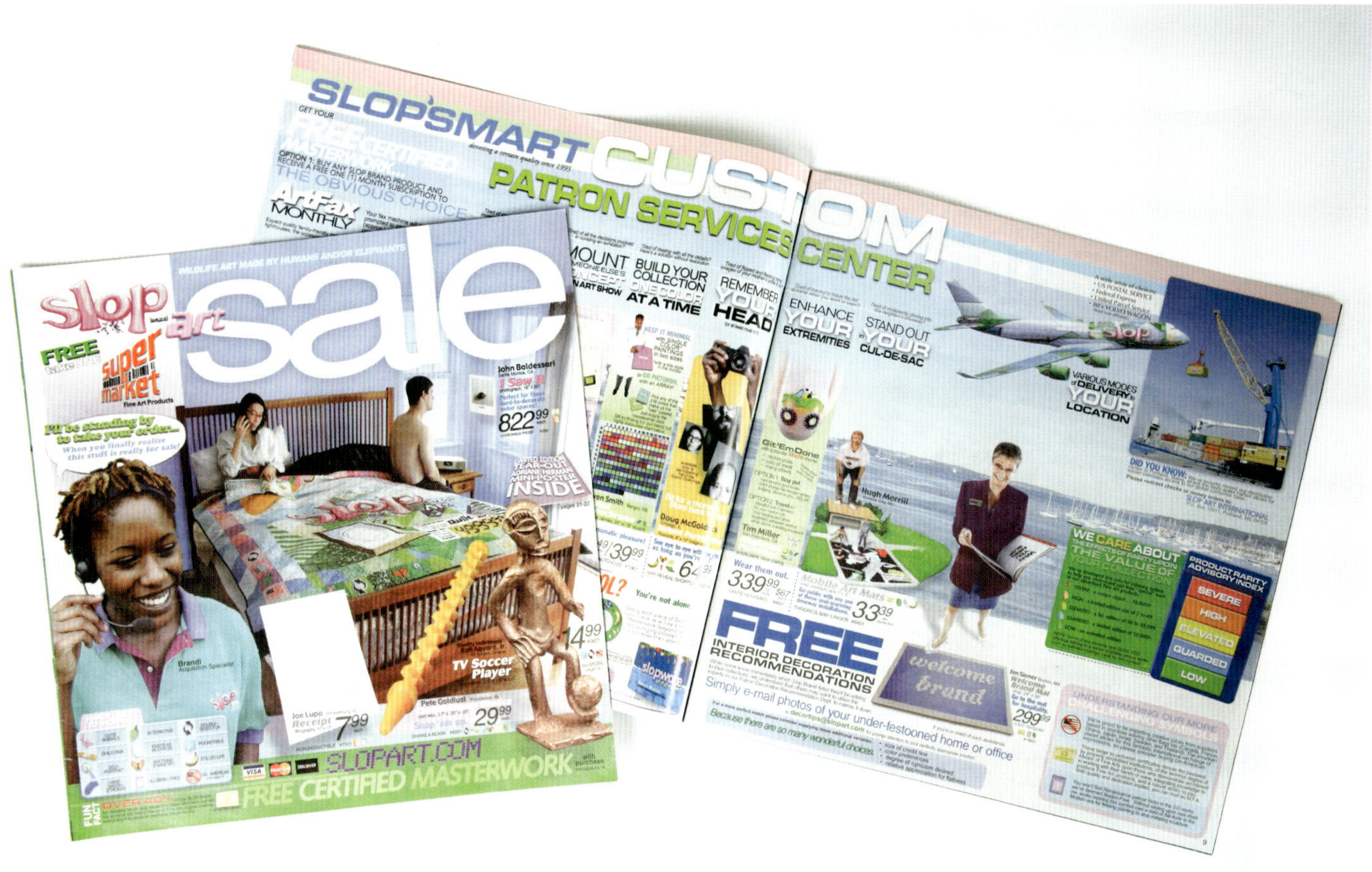

Plate 69

Adriane Herman (b. 1966) and **Brian Reeves** (b. 1969)

Slop Art Catalogue, 2003, photo-offset lithograph,

10 1/2 x 10 1/2 in. (page size). Courtesy of the artists.

or material. The current spirit is reminiscent in ways of the German expressionist printmakers of the early twentieth century, who took pride in disobeying the rules, hacking away at rough planks of wood, biting their etchings heedlessly in bathtubs, or mixing watercolor pigments in the water used to dampen lithographic stones before printing. It is also heir to the revolutionary Dada "anti-art" movement that flourished from 1916 into the 1920s.

Beginning in the 1960s, the incorporation of photographic imagery in printmaking has become an increasingly major element, previously seen in the low-tech lithographs of Judith Allen-Efstathiou, the photopolymer etchings of Susan Groce, and the photo-based imagery of Richard Estes. With the ease of image manipulation and variation possible in digital modes, all boundaries and technical constraints have been superseded. Much of recent digital printmaking has used photography as a starting point, as in the work of such Maine artists as Katharina Weslien, William Pope.L, William Wegman, and Joel Seah.

Inexpensively produced artists' books are yet another very large category of printed art, beginning in the 1960s, and they have been much in evidence in Maine, notably in the work of Bern Porter and Carlo Pittore. This category is represented in this survey with the *Slop Art* mail-order catalogue (Plate 69) of Adriane Herman (b. 1966) and Brian Reeves (b. 1969), a multi-layered take on the art world and its accessibility and market structure. Herman and Reeves use their professional graphic design skills to break down the elitist position of the "artwork" and to bring art into people's lives, whether through a Sunday newspaper supplement or a converted ice cream delivery truck on the streets of Portland. Purposely reminiscent of Claes Oldenburg's hand-made storefront of 1961 and an obvious pun on Pop Art, their Slop Art products recall the subversive democracy of the Fluxus movement. Herman herself has exploited numerous high- and low-tech printmaking techniques for her art, including traditional color woodcuts, bubble gum intaglio prints, temporary tattoos, and digital cookie decorations.

Perhaps the lowest-tech print in this survey is the collaborative effort of Portland sculptors Meghan Scribner (b. 1969) and Aaron Stephan (b. 1974). Their untitled print of 2001 (Plate 70) was printed with house paint applied to a worn mattress, in a varied edition of some thirty or so monoprints in different colors of ink. Each impression conveys different transparencies and auras, for instance in the ever-increasing size of the hole in the fabric that exposes the foam "innards" of the mattress. Reminiscent of Robert Rauschenberg's famous *Bed* painting of 1955 (the Museum of Modern Art), these prints carry layers of "remains, historical remnants, and inherent stories," as expressed by Scribner, to say nothing of the imprint of the artist.

NOTES

1. Susan Tallman, *The Contemporary Print from Pre-Pop to Postmodern* (London and New York: Thames & Hudson, 1996), p. 7.
2. See Aprile Gallant and David P. Becker, *In Print: Contemporary Artists at the Vinalhaven Press* (Portland: Portland Museum of Art, 1997)
3. For a selection of contemporary book artists, see Aprile Gallant, *Perspectives—The Art of the Book* [exhibition brochure] (Portland Museum of Art, 1997).
4. For a recent sourcebook on non-toxic printmaking, see Keith Howard, *The Contemporary Printmaker—Intaglio-Type & Acrylic Resist Etching* (Write-Cross Press, 2003).

Plate 70

Aaron Stephan (b. 1974) and **Meghan Scribner** (b. 1969),

Untitled, 2001, printed from mattress, 48 x 72 in.

Courtesy of the artists

SELECTED REFERENCES

Art—Maine—General

Artists Active in Maine in the Twentieth Century (Waterville: Archives of Maine Art at Colby College, 1963).

Beem, Edgar Allen. *Maine Art Now* (Gardiner: Dog Ear Press, 1990).

Little, Carl, and Arnold Skolnick. *More Maine Paintings* (Camden: Down East Books, 2006).

Maine and its Role in American Art 1740–1963, eds. Gertrude A. Mellon and Elizabeth F. Wilder (New York: Viking Press [1963]).

Maine Artists 1850-1899, "Artists Listed in City Directories in Maine," *Maine State Museum Checklist Series* ([Augusta: Maine State Museum, 1976]).

The Mirror of Maine—One Hundred Distinguished Books that Reveal the History of the State and the Life of Its People, ed. Laura Fecych Sprague (Orono and Portland: University of Maine Press and Baxter Society, 2000).

On the Edge—Forty Years of Maine Painting, 1952–1992, exh. cat. by Theodore E. Wolff (Rockport: Maine Coast Artists, 1992).

Traggard, Louise, Patricia E. Hart, and W. L. Copithorne. *A Century of Color 1886–1986—Ogunquit, Maine's Art Colony* (Ogunquit: Barn Gallery Associates, 1987). Includes [pp. 133–34] list of "Painters, Sculptors and Graphic Artists Who Have Worked in Ogunquit."

Women Pioneers in Maine Art, exh. cat. by William David Barry (Portland: Joan Whitney Payson Gallery of Art, Westbrook College, 1981).

Women Pioneers in Maine Art 1900–1945, exh. cat. by William David Barry and Joan P. Uraneck (Portland: Joan Whitney Payson Gallery of Art, Westbook College, 1985).

Printmaking—History and Techniques

Castleman, Riva. *Prints of the 20th Century—A History* [rev. ed.] (London: Thames & Hudson, 1988).

Gascoigne, Bamber. *How to Identify Prints—A Complete Guide to Manual and Mechanical Processes from Woodcut to Ink Jet* (New York: Thames & Hudson, 1991).

Griffiths, Antony. *Prints and Printmaking—An Introduction to the History and Techniques* (Berkeley and Los Angeles: University of California Press, 1996).

Ivins, William M., Jr. *How Prints Look—Photographs with Commentary*, rev. ed. by Marjorie B. Cohn (Boston: Beacon Press, 1987)

Tallman, Susan. *The Contemporary Print from Pre-Pop to Postmodern* (London and New York: Thames & Hudson, 1996).

Printmaking—United States

Acton, David, with Clinton Adams and Karen F. Beall. *A Spectrum of Innovation—Color in American Printmaking 1890–1960* (Worcester: Worcester Art Museum, 1990).

Acton, David, with David Amram and David Lehman. *The Stamp of Impulse—Abstract Expressionist Prints* (Worcester: Worcester Art Museum, 2001).

Adams, Clinton. *American Lithographers 1900-1960—The Artists and Their Printers* (Albuquerque: University of New Mexico Press, 1983).

Alone in a Crowd—Prints of the 1930s–1940s by African-American Artists from the Collection of Reba and Dave Williams [New York: 1992?].

American Identities—Twentieth-Century Prints from the Nancy Gray Sherrill, Class of 1954, Collection [exh. cat.] (Wellesley, [Mass.] Davis Museum and Cultural Center, Wellesley College, 2004).

American Women of the Etching Revival, exh. cat. by Phyllis Peet (Atlanta: High Museum of Art, 1988).

Field, Richard S., et al. *American Prints 1900–1950* [exh. cat.] (New Haven: Yale University Art Gallery, 1983).

Field, Richard S., and Ruth E. Fine. *A Graphic Muse—Prints by Contemporary American Women* [exh. cat.] (Holyoke [Mass.]: Mount Holyoke College Art Museum, and New York: Hudson Hills Press, 1987)

Fielding, Mantle. *American Engravers upon Copper and Steel, Biographical Sketches and Check Lists of Engravings, A Supplement to David McNeely Stauffer's American Engravers* ([Reprint] N. Y.: Burt Franklin, 1964, 1971).

Groce, George C., and David H. Wallace. *The New York Historical Society's Dictionary of Artists in America 1564–1860* (New Haven: Yale University Press, 1966).

Hansen, Trudy V., David Mickenberg, Joann Moser, and Barry Walker. *Printmaking in America—Collaborative Prints and Presses 1960–1990* (New York: Harry N. Abrams, 1995).

Kushner, Marilyn S. *Digital Printmaking Now* (New York: Brooklyn Museum of Art, 2001).

Marzio, Peter C. *The Democratic Art—Chromolithography 1840–1900: Pictures for a 19th-Century America* (Boston: David R. Godine, 1979).

Moser, Joann. *Atelier 17—A 50th Anniversary Retrospective Exhibition* [exh. cat.] (Madison: Elvehjem Art Center, University of Wisconsin, 1977).

Pierce, Sally, with Catharina Slautterback and Georgia Brady Barnhill. *Early American Lithography—Images to 1830* (Boston: Boston Athenaeum, 1997).

Watrous, James. *A Century of American Printmaking 1880-1980* (Madison: University of Wisconsin Press, 1984).

Printmaking—Maine

Gallant, Aprile, and David P. Becker. *In Print: Contemporary Artists at the Vinalhaven Press* (Portland: Portland Museum of Art, 1997).

Perspectives, The Art of the Book, exh. brochure by Aprile Gallant (Portland: Portland Museum of Art, 1997).

Podmanisczky, Christine B., and Earle G. Shettleworth, Jr. *Through a Bird's Eye: Nineteenth-Century Views of Maine* (Rockland: William A. Farnsworth Library and Art Museum, 1981) [Includes a census of "Lithographed Views of Cities and Towns in Maine 1835–1905"].

Shettleworth, Earle G., Jr. "Portland, Maine, Engravers of the 1820s," *Old-Time New England—Bulletin of the Society for the Preservation of New England Antiquities*, vol. 61, nos. 3–4 (Winter and Spring, 1971), pp. 59–65, 105–10.

Individual Printmakers

Included here are selected references specifically related to an artist's printmaking, unless there are none, in which case more general sources may be included.

Arms, John Taylor S. William Pelletier, "John Taylor Arms—His World and Work," *Georgia Museum of Art Bulletin*, vol. 17 (1993), *passim.*

Bacon, Peggy *Peggy Bacon—Personalities and Places*, exh. cat. by Roberta K. Tarbell, with catalogue of prints by Janet Flint (Washington: National Collection of Fine Arts, 1975); *Peggy Bacon's Prints, A Checklist of the Prints* (San Francisco: Alan Wofsy, 2001).

Barnet, Will Sylvan Cole, *Will Barnet: Etchings, Lithographs, Woodcuts, Serigraphs, 1932-1972—Catalogue Raisonné* (New York: AAA Gallery, 1972); David Acton, "The Prints of Will Barnet—A Supplemental Catalogue," *The Tamarind Papers*, vol. 16 (1996), pp. 83–96.

Baskin, Leonard Alan Fern and Judith O'Sullivan, *The Complete Prints of Leonard Baskin—A Catalogue Raisonné 1948-1983* (Boston: Little, Brown [New York Graphic Society], 1984); Robert Flynn Johnson, *Leonard Baskin—Monumental Woodcuts 1952–1963* [exh. cat.] (San Francisco: Fine Arts Museums, 2000).

Bellows, George Lauris Mason, assisted by Joan Ludman, *The Lithographs of George Bellows—A Catalogue Raisonné* [rev. ed.] (San Francisco: Alan Wofsy, 1992); D. Scott Atkinson and Charlene S. Engel, *An American Pulse: The Lithographs of George Wesley Bellows* [exh. cat.] (San Diego: San Diego Museum of Art, 1999).

Benson, Frank W. Adam E. M. Paff, Arthur W. Heintzelman, *Etchings and Drypoints of Frank W. Benson* (Boston: Houghton Mifflin, 1917–1959); John T. Ordeman, *Frank W. Benson's Etchings, Drypoints and Lithographs, an Illustrated and Descriptive Catalogue* (Summit [N.J.]: Hickok-Bockus, 1994).

Berry, Carroll Thayer Elwyn Dearborn, *The Down East Printmaker: Carroll Thayer Berry—A Catalogue Raisonné of His Wood Engravings, Woodcuts, and Linocuts* (Camden: Down East Books, 1983).

Bileck, Marvin *Marvin Bileck/Emily Nelligan—Cranberry Island: Drawings and Prints,* [exh. cat.] essay by Alison Ferris (New York: Alexandre Gallery, 2005).

Cook, Howard Betty and Douglas Duffy, with Janet A. Flint. *The Graphic Work of Howard Cook—A Catalogue Raisonné* (Bethesda [Md.]: Bethesda Art Gallery, 1984).

Cornell, Thomas *Thomas Cornell—Drawings and Prints* [exh. cat.] (Brunswick: Bowdoin College Museum of Art, 1971).

Dohanos, Stevan *Stevan Dohanos, Images of America* [exh. cat.] (New Britain [Conn.]: New Britain Museum of American Art, 1986).

Drewes, Werner Ingrid Rose, *Werner Drewes—A Catalogue Raisonné of His Prints/Das graphische Werk* (Munich and New York: Verlag Kunstgalerie Esslingen, 1984); Martina Roudaboush Norelli, *Werner Drewes—Sixty-five Years of Printmaking* (Washington, D.C.: Smithsonian Institution Press, 1984).

Driskell, David Julie L. McGee, *David C. Driskell—Artist and Scholar* (San Francisco: Pomegranate Press, 2006).

Eby, Kerr Bernadette Passi Giardina, *Kerr Eby—The Complete Prints* (Bronxville [N.Y.]: M. Hausberg, 1997).

Estes, Richard John Arthur, *Richard Estes Paintings and Prints* (San Francisco: Pomegranate Art Books, 1993).

Fisher, Jonathan *The Arts and Crafts of the Versatile Parson Fisher 1768–1847* [exh. cat.] (Rockland: William A. Farnsworth Library and Art Museum, 1967).

Goodale, Rebecca *Threatened and Endangered—Artist's Books Created by Rebecca Goodale*, essay by Linda J. Docherty (Brunswick: Bowdoin College Library, 2004).

Hartley, Marsden *Marsden Hartley—Lithographs and Related Works*, exh. cat. by Charles C. Eldredge (Lawrence [Kan.]: University of Kansas Museum of Art, 1972).

Haskell, Ernest *Ernest Haskell (1876–1925) A Retrospective Exhibition*, exh. cat. intro. by Ruth Fine Lehrer (Brunswick: Bowdoin College Museum of Art, 1976).

Herman, Adriane, and Brian Reeves www.slopart.com

Hewitt, Charlie Retrospective exhibition catalogue of prints with essay by David P. Becker (Lewiston: Bates College Museum of Art [forthcoming 2006])

Homer, Winslow Lloyd Goodrich, *The Graphic Art of Winslow Homer* [exh. cat.] (New York: Museum of Graphic Art, 1968); Philip C. Beam, *Winslow Homer's Magazine Engravings* (New York: Harper & Row, 1979).

Hopper, Edward Carl Zigrosser, "The Etchings of Edward Hopper," in *Prints* (New York: Holt, Rinehart and Winston, 1962), pp. 155–73; Gail Levin, *Edward Hopper—The Complete Prints* [exh. cat.] (New York: Whitney Museum of American Art, 1979).

Indiana, Robert Susan Sheehan, et al., *Robert Indiana Prints—A Catalogue Raisonné 1951-1991* (New York: Susan Sheehan Gallery, 1991).

Ipcar, Dahlov *Dahlov Ipcar—Seven Decades of Creativity* [exh. cat.] (Portland: Portland Museum of Art, 2001).

Jacquette, Yvonne Hilarie Faberman, et al., *Aerial Muse—The Art of Yvonne Jacquette, including a Catalogue Raisonné of Prints* [exh. cat.] (Stanford: Iris & B. Gerald Cantor Center for Visual Arts at Stanford University, 2001).

Jensen, Dorothy Hay *Maine Pioneers in Maine Art: 1900–1945* [see above, Art—Maine—General], p. 17; Dorothy Hay Jensen, "Art and the WPA," *Down East* (June 1987), pp. 78–81, 103.

Katz, Alex Nicholas P. Maravall, *Alex Katz—The Complete Prints* (New York and London: Alpine Fine Arts, 1983); Merlin James, *Alex Katz—The Woodcuts and Linocuts from 1951–2001* (New York: Peter Blum, 2001).

Kent, Rockwell Dan Burne Jones. *The Prints of Rockwell Kent—A Catalogue Raisonné* (Chicago and London: University of Chicago Press, 1975 [revised edition: San Francisco: Alan Wofsy, 2002]).

Kimball, Charles Frederick *Charles Frederick Kimball 1831–1903—Painting Portland's Legacy*, exh. brochure by Earle G. Shettleworth, Jr. (Portland: Portland Museum of Art, 2003)

Kuhn, Walt *Walt Kuhn as Printmaker, 1877–1949* (New York: Kennedy Galleries, 1967); *Walt Kuhn Paintings, Drawings, Prints—A Study of Related Works*, exh. cat. by Efram L. Burk (Orono: University of Maine Museum of Art, 1989).

Kuniyoshi, Yasuo Richard A. Davis, *Yasuo Kuniyoshi—The Complete Graphic Work* (San Francisco: Alan Wofsy, 1991).

Lankes, J. J. Welford Dunaway Taylor, *The Woodcut Art of J. J. Lankes* (Boston: David R. Godine, 1999).

Lasansky, Mauricio – Mauricio and Phillip Lasansky and John Thein. *Lasansky, Printmaker* (Iowa City: University of Iowa Press, 1975); see also Phillip Lasansky's Web site, www.lasanskyart.com.

Lozowick, Louis Janet Flint, *The Prints of Louis Lozowick—A Catalogue Raisonné* (New York: Hudson Hills, 1982).

Marin, John Carl Zigrosser, *The Complete Etchings of John Marin* (Philadelphia: Philadelphia Museum of Art, 1969).

Meissner, Leo Sarah Stiles, comp., *Leo Meissner Prints* (Boston: Childs Gallery [1980]).

Muench, John Judith Sobol and Martin Dibner, *John Muench—Paintings and Prints 1950–1990* (Freeport, Me: Maquoit Press, 1991),

Nevelson, Louise Una Johnson, *Louise Nevelson—Prints and Drawings* (Brooklyn: Brooklyn Museum, 1967); Gene Baro, *Nevelson—The Prints* (New York: Pace Editions, 1974).

Patterson, Margaret Jordan *Margaret Jordan Patterson 1867–1950—Retrospective Exhibition* [exh. cat.] (Cambridge [MA]: James R. Bakker Antiques, 1988)

Peregrine Press www.peregrinepress.com

Porter, Fairfield Joan Ludman, et al., *Fairfield Porter—A Catalogue Raisonné of His Prints* (Westbury [N.Y.]: Highland House, 1981).

Schrag, Karl Una E. Johnson, *Karl Schrag: A Catalogue Raisonné of the Graphic Works 1939-1970* (Syracuse [N.Y.]: School of Art, 1971); August L. Freundlich, *Karl Schrag: A Catalogue Raisonné of the Graphic Works 1971–1990* (Syracuse, N.Y.: Syracuse University Art Collection, 1980–1990).

Walker, John *John Walker: Prints 1976–1984*, exh. cat. with essay by Memory Holloway (London: Tate Gallery, 1985); *A Theater of Recollection: Paintings and Prints by John Walker*, exh. cat. with essay by John Stomberg (Boston: Boston University Art Gallery, 1997); *A Maine Tidal Cove: Paintings by John Walker*, exh. brochure by Katy Kline (Brunswick: Bowdoin College Museum of Art, 2001). *John Walker Works on Paper 1990–2004*, exh. cat. with essay by Ruth Fine (Portland: Portland Museum of Art, 2005).

Welliver, Neil *Neil Welliver Prints 1973–1995* (Camden: Down East Books, 1996).

Wengenroth, Stow Ronald and Joan Stuckey, *The Lithographs of Stow Wengenroth 1931–1972* (Boston: Boston Public Library, 1974).

Woodbury, Charles George M. Young, *Force through Delicacy—The Life and Art of Charles H. Woodbury* (Portsmouth [N.H.]: Peter E. Randall, 1998).

Zorach, Marguerite Efram L. Burk, "The Graphic Art of Marguerite Thompson Zorach," *Woman's Art Journal*, vol. 25, no. 1 (Spring–Summer 2004), pp. 12–17.

Zorach, William Efram L. Burk. "The Prints of William Zorach," *Print Quarterly*, vol. 19, no. 4 (Dec. 2002), pp. 353–73.

PHOTO CREDITS

Black and White, Inc.: Plate 31

Steve Briggs: Plate 41

Dennis Griggs, Tannery Hill Studios: Plates 14, 15, 16, 18, 22, 23, 24, 29, 35, 38, 43, 47, 51, 52, 55, 56, 60, 61, 63, 64, 65, 67, 68, 69, 70

Greg Hart: Plate 5

Katya Kallsen: Plates 20, 42

Alan LaVallee: Plates 45, 48

Melville McLean: Plate 66

Meyersphoto.com: Plates 17, 30, 39, 40, 44, 46, 49

Steve Morrison: Plates 7, 13, 21, 33, 34, 37

Kim Murphy: Plate 59

Adam Reich: Plate 54

GLOSSARY OF PRINTMAKING TERMS

Print—an image that has been impressed on a support, usually paper, by a process capable of being repeated. Most printmaking techniques (a major exception being digital prints) require the previous design and manufacture of a printing surface.[1] The five primary types of print techniques are **relief**, **intaglio**, **planographic**, **screenprint**, and **digital**.

Aquatint—An **intaglio** process by which tones may be achieved in an **etching**. Traditionally, a rosin powder is sprinkled on a metal printing plate, which is then heated to affix the particles to the surface. When the plate is placed in an acid or other corrosive bath, the agent will eat away the areas in between the rosin particles, leaving (depending on the particle size) a fine or coarse network of lines and crevices that when inked and printed creates areas of tone. "Spit bite" is a variant in which acid, often mixed with saliva, is brushed over an aquatint ground to bite selected areas of an image. [As examples, see Welliver, Plate #62, and Hepler, #63.]

Collagraph—A hybrid technique in which various elements (cardboard, metal plates, natural materials, etc.) are adhered to a printing plate, which may be inked and printed in a **relief** or **intaglio** method, or even printed without being inked for a purely embossed impression. [As an example, see Driskell, #43.]

Digital print, inkjet print—An image created or manipulated on a computer and printed by a linked printer, using inkjet or laser technology. "Iris prints" and "giclée prints" are among other terms for digital prints.

Drypoint—A type of **intaglio** print in which lines or tones are scratched into the surface of a bare metal plate with a sharp metal point, sometimes tipped with diamond. The action of drawing the tool through the plate raises a ridge of metal, called a burr, on one or both sides of the furrow. The upturned burr will retain ink when it is applied to the plate, and when printed will reveal a soft, more or less broad area of ink in certain areas on the print. Drypoint is often used in combination with other intaglio techniques. Some artists have used other tools such as files, wire brushes, or Dremel™ drills to create varying types of drypoint marks. The upturned drypoint burr wears down quickly in the great pressure of printing, and very few rich impressions are possible, unless the plate is reinforced by steel-facing. [As examples, see Washburn, #13, Bacon, #39, and Harris, #61.]

Edition—A number of printed images, or **impressions**, from the same master plate or block using the same ink colors and printing methods, as established by the artist and/or publisher. The practice of numbering individual impressions from an edition only became widespread in the twentieth century. The impressions in such a "limited" edition are usually signed and numbered progressively, for instance 1/50, 2/50, etc., for a total edition of fifty impressions; after the total is reached, the plate or stone is "cancelled" or destroyed. Often a few impressions will be printed outside the regular edition for the collaborators (artist, printer, publisher). Impressions printed during the development process to test the printing or try out color variations are called "proofs" or "progressive proofs."

NOTE

1. This specific definition adapted in part from Antony Griffiths, *Prints and Printmaking—An Introduction to the History and Techniques* (Berkeley and Los Angeles: University of California Press, 1996), p. 9. For more detailed technical descriptions, see the general printmaking references on p. 128.

Engraving—A type of **intaglio** print in which lines are cut into a metal plate with a sharp tool called a burin, which is formed from a square steel rod, the end of which is cut on an angle, forming a very sharp diamond-shaped point. The burin actually removes most of the metal as it moves along, creating a very clear, smooth v-shaped furrow. An engraved plate is inked and printed in the same manner as other intaglio prints, in which the engraved lines are filled with ink and the surface is usually wiped clean. When put through a roller press under great pressure, the paper is forced into the engraved lines, transferring the ink and creating a slightly raised line in the printed impression, along with an embossed platemark, caused by the pressure of the edge of the metal printing plate. [As an example, see Hinshelwood, #9.]

Etching—A type of **intaglio** print in which the lines and/or tonal areas of an image have been corroded, or "bitten," into the surface of a metal plate by the action of a corrosive agent, called a mordant. Traditionally nitric acid has been used, but increasingly less toxic materials are being introduced, such as ferric chloride. A metal plate is first covered with an acid-resistant substance (ground) through which the image is drawn with a needle or other tool, exposing the bare metal. When immersed in the mordant, only those exposed areas are subject to its action. Recently, photopolymer etching has been developed, whereby a drawing, photograph, or digital image is transferred to a photosensitive polymer plate and processed into a relief or intaglio printing plate. [As examples, see Moran, #10, Haskell, #15, and Marin, #26.]

Impression—A single printed image (usually on paper) from a printing surface. Multiple impressions may be printed from the same etching plate, woodblock, lithographic stone, or other surface.

Intaglio—(from the Italian word *intagliare*, to carve or incise) A category of printmaking in which the surface of a printing plate has been incised with a design by one or a mixture of techniques. In order to print the image, ink is applied and wiped across the surface of the plate, filling the recessed areas. Usually the excess ink is then cleaned off the unworked surface of the plate. When printed under great pressure, the paper is forced into those incised marks, thus picking up the ink and often creating ridges and raised areas in the final printed impression. Types of intaglio prints are **engraving**, **etching**, **aquatint**, and **mezzotint**.

Linocut—A **relief** printmaking process, similar to **woodcut**, in which a sheet of linoleum (oxidized linseed oil) is used, often mounted to a wooden block. Linoleum has no grain or texture, so it produces an uninflected, smooth surface when printed. [As an example, see Zorach, #23.]

Lithography—A planographic (i.e., planar, flat) printmaking process, in which an image is drawn or transferred to a stone or metal plate using a greasy medium, such as ink (often called "tusche") or crayon. Artists are able to draw directly on the printing surface or on specially treated paper, which can then be transferred to the stone or plate. The printing surface is then treated with a solution of acid and gum arabic, setting the image and sealing the undrawn areas of the surface against further greasy touches. The printing process depends on the chemical resistance of oil and water: when rolled onto the stone (which has been expressly dampened), the printing ink adheres only to the areas previously drawn by the artist and is repelled by the wet areas. Paper is placed on the stone or plate and run through a press to make the impression. It is considered the most draftsmanlike of printmaking processes for its ability to preserve the artist's gestures so accurately. [As examples, see Minot, #2, Wengenroth, #31, and Hodsdon, #66.]

Mezzotint — Literally "half-tint," an **intaglio** process in which the surface of a metal plate is completely and evenly roughened by a curved metal tool with many small points, called a "rocker." If the plate is inked at this point, it would print an evenly black tone. Working literally from dark to light, the artist creates the image by scraping or burnishing the textured surface in areas to be lightened. The more an area is burnished smooth (in order to carry less ink), the brighter the highlight. This process creates very soft, velvety gradations of tone.

Monotype — A type of print in which a drawing or painting executed on a flat, unworked printing plate or other surface is transferred through pressure to a sheet of paper. As most of the image is transferred in the printing process, only one strong impression can be taken, hence the term monotype (unique, single impression). A monotype is distinct from a **monoprint**, which is a uniquely inked and printed impression from a traditional print matrix, such as an etching plate or woodblock. [As examples, see Dougherty, #20, and Jacquette, #68.]

Planography — see **Lithography.**

Relief — A category of printmaking in which a design on a flat surface is carved with a knife or chisel, removing the areas that the printmaker does not want to be printed. When the surface is then rolled with ink and printed, the resulting impression will only show the lines and shapes of the design left on the unworked surface by the artist. The most common types of relief prints are **woodcut**, **wood engraving**, and **linocut**.

Screenprint / Silkscreen — A stencil printmaking process, in which ink is pushed through a fine mesh screen onto a sheet of paper. The artist cuts the image out of a sheet of protective film that is then affixed to the screen. Using a squeegee, the printer pushes ink through the screen in only the areas in which the artist has removed the film. Several different screens may be used to print an image in several colors. The stencil may also be drawn or transferred using a light-sensitive resist that is then developed photographically, opening the areas of the screen through which the image may then be printed. Unusually for printmaking, the image is not reversed through the silkscreen printing process.

State — Any intermediate change made by the artist while creating an image fixed on a plate, stone, or block, as reflected in **impressions** or proofs printed during the development process of a printed image.

Woodcut — A **relief** process, using the side grain of a plank of wood, in which the printmaker cuts away the areas around the desired image. In order to print impressions, ink is rolled onto the surface of the cut block, printing only the areas left on the surface; the cut-away areas do not print. A printing press may be used, or impressions may be printed by hand, using a wooden spoon or other tool. [As examples, see Patterson, #21, Drewes, #42, and Hewitt, #50.]

Wood Engraving — A process similar to woodcut, but a much more finely-grained type of wood is used, and the block is carved from the end of a plank, rather than its side. As a result, much more detailed engraving tools may be used to create the image. Often, wood engravers have worked from dark to light, i.e., creating highlights from a dark (unworked) background, rather than cutting away larger areas around lines to be printed against a lighter background. [As examples, see Fisher, #4, Meissner, #34, and Beckman, #55.]